"Greg Goswell's book is an extremely fasci[...] issues that interpreters simply take for granted but shouldn't. He clearly shows that the company that books keep matters, and that the titles of books—as well as chapter divisions and verses—are not just decorations but provide hermeneutical guidance. Widely read and well-versed in biblical scholarship, Goswell writes in clear and direct prose. While I demur about some of his conclusions, I highly recommend this book for biblical students to add to their exegetical toolbox."

STEPHEN G. DEMPSTER, emeritus professor
of religious studies, Crandall University

"Goswell has collated years of research and writing into this helpful and accessible volume that clearly demonstrates the importance of the Bible's paratextual features and their significance for interpretation. *Text and Paratext* is the perfect starting point for further study in this important area of biblical studies."

MILES V. VAN PELT, Alan Hayes Belcher, Jr. Professor of Old
Testament and Biblical Languages and director of Summer Institute
for Biblical Languages, Reformed Theological Seminary, Jackson

"For years Goswell has been reflecting on the Christian canon and its significance for interpretation, and in this helpful primer, he shares a storehouse of canonical insights that aid our understanding of the Bible's meaning. In *Text and Paratext*, he focuses on the shape of the canon (rather than the process by which it developed), and in each chapter, he offers hermeneutical implications arising from the collection, ordering, titles, and divisions within books found in the final form of the text. These textual characteristics, Goswell argues, are paratextual features which assist in interpretation because they function as a kind of implicit commentary upon the text of Scripture. Goswell's work offers expert guidance for and generous invitation to appreciating the hermeneutical difference canon makes in hearing the Bible as the church's book."

DARIAN LOCKETT, professor of New Testament,
Talbot School of Theology, Biola University

"Greg Goswell has provided us with an excellent introduction to a paratextual approach of the two-testament Bible's final form—an interpretive approach that he has helped pioneer in biblical studies. This is a clearly written and engaging book with pedagogical aids that are exceptionally student (and teacher) friendly. I am confident that his work will introduce readers to a fresh way of understanding the rhetorical design of the entire biblical canon by more carefully considering what is typically overlooked: the text's paratextual elements—book titles, chapter divisions, the sequence of books within their canonical collections, and the intracanonical relations between them. This new learning will surely excite and inspire a deeper understanding of the Bible for use in the church's worship and the academy's instruction. I strongly encourage its use by clergy and faculty alike."

ROBERT W. WALL, Paul T. Walls Professor Emeritus of Scripture and Wesleyan Studies, Seattle Pacific University and Seminary

"Most biblical readers value resources that help them understand the Scriptures but often take for granted the various interpretive aids that are already embedded in the Bibles they are reading. In this volume, Goswell explains the meaning and function of paratextual features such as the ordering of books in canonical collections, the titles given to individual works, and the subtle ways manuscripts and print editions mark and divide sections within biblical texts. Far from being beside the point, these features that are physically 'beside the text' have the potential to influence the way a reader approaches and navigates a passage of Scripture or a biblical book. Drawing on Goswell's extensive scholarly work on these features, this volume is rich with analysis of ancient evidence, synthesis of contemporary scholarship, and reflective connections to biblical theology. Because of these factors, this volume itself would be an excellent paratextual resource to come alongside your study of God's word."

CHED SPELLMAN, associate professor of biblical and theological studies, Cedarville University; author, *Toward a Canon-Conscious Reading of the Bible*

"What Goswell has done for biblical studies here amounts to the little child pointing out that the emperor is not wearing any clothes. For all the centuries of careful scholarship on the text of the Bible, the obvious but easily overlooked fact is that there are factors not in the text per se that pre-shape how we read and interpret the text before us. Kudos to Goswell for not only drawing our attention to these shaping factors but also how and why these influence our interpretations of the Bible: unnoticed but ubiquitous, unrecognized but crucially important."

RAY LUBECK, professor of Old Testament, Multnomah University

"When we read the Bible we are generally not conscious of how we are influenced by features other than the text itself. Greg Goswell over many years has researched with much detail matters such as the order of the books of the Bible, the titles they are given, and the divisions into verses, paragraphs, and chapters—the paratextual elements. The breadth and depth of his careful research covering centuries of the Bible and its readership, both Jewish and Christian, makes him the right person to write this most helpful work. At last there is one book that brings the details together so clearly, respecting diverse understandings, along with questions encouraging further exploration."

JOHN OLLEY, research fellow, Morling College

TEXT AND PARATEXT

Book Order, Title,
and Division as Keys
to Biblical Interpretation

TEXT AND PARATEXT

Book Order, Title, and Division as Keys to Biblical Interpretation

GREGORY GOSWELL

LEXHAM
ACADEMIC

Text and Paratext: Book Order, Title, and Division as Keys to Biblical Interpretation

Copyright 2023 Gregory Goswell

Lexham Academic, an imprint of Lexham Press
1313 Commercial St., Bellingham, WA 98225
LexhamPress.com

Print ISBN 9781683596110
Digital ISBN 9781683596127
Library of Congress Control Number 2022933932

Lexham Editorial: Derek Brown, Claire Brubaker, Katherine Joyce, Jessi Strong
Cover Design: Joshua Hunt, Brittany Schrock
Typesetting: Mandi Newell

CONTENTS

Abbreviations...ix

Introduction..1

PART I CANONICAL STRUCTURE

1   The Structure of the Hebrew Canon 11

2   The Structure of the Greek Canon 32

3   The Structure of the New Testament 54

PART II BOOK TITLES

4   Titles of Old Testament Books 79

5   Titles of New Testament Books 104

PART III TEXTUAL DIVISIONS

6   Textual Divisions within Old Testament Books 125

7   Textual Divisions within New Testament Books............................. 149

Conclusions...173

Glossary of Key Words 185

Appendix..189

Study Questions for Further Exploration 197

Bibliography...205

Subject Index 231

Scripture Index 239

ABBREVIATIONS

1 Esd	1 Esdras
2 Bar	2 Baruch
2 Macc	2 Maccabees
4Q112	Daniel[a]
4Q174	Florilegium
4QMMT	4Q394–399
4Q51	Samuel[a]
A	*kephalaia* in Alexandrinus
AB	Anchor Bible
ABR	*Australian Biblical Review*
ABS	Archaeology and Biblical Studies
AG	Analecta Gorgiana
Ag. Ap.	Josephus, *Against Apion*
AJFS	*Australian Journal of French Studies*
Ant.	Josephus, *Jewish Antiquities*
ArBib	The Aramaic Bible
AUSS	*Andrews University Seminary Studies*
AV	Authorized Version
b.	Babylonian Talmud
B. Bat.	Baba Batra
BBB	Bonner biblische Beiträge
BBR	*Bulletin for Biblical Research*
BECNT	Baker Exegetical Commentary on the New Testament
Ber.	Berakhot
BETL	Bibliotheca Ephemeridum Theologicarum Lovaniensium
BHS	*Biblia Hebraica Stuttgartensia*. Edited by Karl Elliger and Wilhelm Rudolph. Stuttgart: Deutsche Bibelgesellschaft, 1983
Bib	*Biblica*
BJS	Brown Judaic Studies

BJSUCSD	Biblical and Judaic Studies from the University of California, San Diego
BLS	Bible and Literature Series
BNTC	Black's New Testament Commentaries
BO	Berit Olam
BSac	*Bibliotheca Sacra*
BT	*The Bible Translator*
BTB	*Biblical Theology Bulletin*
BTNT	Biblical Theology of the New Testament
BZAW	Beihefte zur Zeitschrift für die alttestamentliche Wissenschaft
c.	circa
CBET	Contributions to Biblical Exegesis and Theology
CBQ	*Catholic Biblical Quarterly*
CBQMS	Catholic Biblical Quarterly Monograph Series
CGTC	Cambridge Greek Testament Commentary
ch(s).	chapter(s)
CI	*Critical Inquiry*
Colloq	*Colloquium*
ConBOT	Coniectanea Biblica: Old Testament Series
Cons.	Augustine, *De consensu evangelistarum*
Contempl.	Philo, *On the Contemplative Life*
COT	Commentary on the Old Testament
CSHB	Corpus Scriptorum Historiae Byzantinae
CTJ	*Calvin Theological Journal*
DJD	Discoveries in the Judaean Desert
EBC	Expositor's Bible Commentary
EC	*Early Christianity*
ESEC	Emory Studies in Early Christianity
EvQ	*Evangelical Quarterly*
ExpTim	*Expository Times*
FAT	Forschungen zum Alten Testament
fig(s).	figure(s)
FOTL	Forms of the Old Testament Literature
FRLANT	Forschungen zur Religion und Literatur des Alten und Neuen Testaments

Gk.	Greek
GNB	Good News Bible
GNC	Good News Commentary
GNS	*Good News Studies*
GNT⁴	*The Greek New Testament (Fourth Revised Edition)*
Haer.	Irenaeus, *Adversus haereses*
HAR	*Hebrew Annual Review*
HBT	*Horizons in Biblical Theology*
Heb.	Hebrew
Hen	*Henoch*
Hist. eccl.	Eusebius, *Historia ecclesiastica*
HS	*Hebrew Studies*
HTR	*Harvard Theological Review*
HUCA	*Hebrew Union College Annual*
ICC	International Critical Commentary
IEJ	*Israel Exploration Journal*
Int	*Interpretation*
ITS	Invitation to Theological Studies
JBL	*Journal of Biblical Literature*
JESOT	*Journal for the Evangelical Study of the Old Testament*
JETS	*Journal of the Evangelical Theological Society*
JGRChJ	*Journal of Greco-Roman Christianity and Judaism*
JQR	*Jewish Quarterly Review*
JSNT	*Journal for the Study of the New Testament*
JSNTSup	Journal for the Study of the New Testament Supplement Series
JSOT	*Journal for the Study of the Old Testament*
JSOTSup	Journal for the Study of the Old Testament Supplement Series
JSS	*Journal of Semitic Studies*
JTI	*Journal for Theological Interpretation*
JTS	*Journal of Theological Studies*
K	*kephalaia* in Sinaiticus
KJV	King James Version
LHBOTS	The Library of Hebrew Bible/Old Testament Studies
LNTS	The Library of New Testament Studies
LXX	Septuagint

MasS	Masoretic Studies
MB	Manuscripta Biblica
Meg.	Megillah
MT	Masoretic Text
NA[27]	Aland, Barbara, et al., eds. *Novum Testamentum Graece.* 27th ed. Stuttgart: Deutsche Bibelgesellschaft, 1993
NASB	New American Standard Bible
NEB	New English Bible
NIB	*The New Interpreter's Bible.* Edited by Leander E. Keck. 12 vols. Nashville: Abingdon, 1994–2004
NICNT	New International Commentary on the New Testament
NICOT	New International Commentary on the Old Testament
NIGTC	New International Greek Testament Commentary
NIV	New International Version
NLH	*New Literary History*
NovT	*Novum Testamentum*
NovTSup	Supplements to Novum Testamentum
NSBT	New Studies in Biblical Theology
NT	New Testament
NTM	New Testament Monographs
NTOA	Novum Testamentum et Orbis Antiquus
NTR	New Testament Readings
NTS	*New Testament Studies*
NTTSD	New Testament Tools, Studies, and Documents
OBO	Orbis Biblicus et Orientalis
OT	Old Testament
OTL	Old Testament Library
par(r).	parallel(s)
PAST	Pauline Studies
PL	Patrologia Latina [= *Patrologiae Cursus Completus*: Series Latina]. Edited by Jacques-Paul Migne. 217 vols. Paris, 1844–1864
PNTC	Pillar New Testament Commentary
RB	*Revue biblique*
ResQ	*Restoration Quarterly*
RSV	Revised Standard Version
RTL	*Revue théologique de Louvain*
RTR	*Reformed Theological Review*

S	numbered chapters in Sinaiticus
Sanh.	Sanhedrin
SANT	Studien zum Alten und Neuen Testaments
SBLDS	Society of Biblical Literature Dissertation Series
SBLMS	Society of Biblical Literature Monograph Series
SBS	Stuttgarter Bibelstudien
SemeiaSt	Semeia Studies
sg.	singular
SHS	Scripture and Hermeneutics Series
Sir	Sirach or Ecclesiasticus
SJOT	*Scandinavian Journal of the Old Testament*
SNTSMS	Society for New Testament Studies Monograph Series
SR	*Studies in Religion*
ST	*Studia Theologica*
STI	Studies in Theological Interpretation
SymS	Symposium Series
TBS	Tools for Biblical Study
TDNT	*Theological Dictionary of the New Testament.* Edited by Gerhard Kittel and Gerhard Friedrich. Translated by Geoffrey W. Bromiley. 10 vols. Grand Rapids: Eerdmans, 1964–1976
TENTS	Texts and Editions for New Testament Study
TNTC	Tyndale New Testament Commentaries
Tob	Tobit
TOTC	Tyndale Old Testament Commentaries
TJ	*Trinity Journal*
TynBul	*Tyndale Bulletin*
V	numbered chapters in Vaticanus
VT	*Vetus Testamentum*
VTSup	Supplements to Vetus Testamentum
WBC	Word Biblical Commentary
WTJ	*Westminster Theological Journal*
WUNT	Wissenschaftliche Untersuchungen zum Neuen Testament
y.	Jerusalem Talmud
ZAW	*Zeitschrift für die alttestamentliche Wissenschaft*
ZNW	*Zeitschrift für die neutestamentliche Wissenschaft und die Kunde der älteren Kirche*

INTRODUCTION

THIS THING CALLED PARATEXT

A common experience of students of the Bible is that they continue to make discoveries even in well-known passages. The cry is: "Why have I never noticed that before?" Something may not be noticed—even if it is staring us in the face—until it is pointed out. There are features in every Bible that many readers have never noticed, or if they have noticed them, they have not seen their relevance for interpretation. Some of these neglected features come under the heading of "paratext."[1] Paratext may be defined as everything in a text *other than the words*, that is to say, those elements that are adjoined to the text but are not part of the text itself if "text" is limited strictly to the words.[2] The paratext of Scripture embraces features such as the order of the biblical books, the names assigned to the different books, and the differing schemes of textual division within the books. Since these elements are adjoined to the text and frame the text, whether a reader notices or not, they have an influence on reading and may assist (or sometimes hinder) the interpretation of the text of Scripture.

THERE IS MORE IN THE BIBLE THAN JUST THE WORDS!

The biblical paratext is not part of the text as such. Since the paratext does not derive from the work of the original prophetic or apostolic authors, we are allowed to agree or disagree with the prompts provided. For example, the presumption is that titles of the biblical books were not supplied by their

---

1. The term was coined by Gérard Genette. See Genette, *Paratexts: Thresholds of Interpretation*, trans. Jane E. Lewin (Cambridge: Cambridge University Press, 1997).

2. See Martin Wallraff and Patrick Andrist, "Paratexts of the Bible: A New Research Project on Greek Textual Transmission," *EC* 6 (2015): 239: "All contents in biblical manuscripts except the biblical text itself are *a priori* paratexts."

authors. Evidence for this, for instance, is the similarity of the names given to the Gospels ("The Gospel according to [name of the reputed author]"), which suggests that these titles were not affixed by their authors at the point of composition but were added by those who brought the four Gospels together as a collection. Accepting this, it is at least possible to suspect that in some cases the title affixed to a text may be at variance with its content and message.

Of course, it is impossible in a study such as this to ignore the text itself, and it is not my plan to do so, for text and paratext, though conceptually differentiated, are for all practical purposes inseparable and have an important interrelationship that influences reading. It is not my intention, however, to downgrade the status of the revered text of Scripture by placing it on a par with the paratext of Scripture. It must be asserted that there is a fundamental distinction between text and paratext, the first derived from the authors of the Bible and the second placed as a frame around the text by later readers.[3] The ordering of the books is a paratextual phenomenon that should not be put on the same level of authority as the text itself, for it is readers rather than authors who are responsible for it.[4] The biblical authors generated the text and are the *makers* of meaning,[5] whereas readers, by putting the books in a particular canonical order, or affixing a title to a book, or dividing it into paragraphs, provide a paratextual frame for the text, reflecting their *understanding* of the meaning of the text.[6] The placing of the books in a certain order is a postauthorial imposition on the text of Scripture—albeit an inescapable one when texts of diverse origin are assembled in a literary corpus— as is the layout of the text (e.g., how much text is on each page). That being

---

3. See the address to readers by Virginia Woolf, *The Common Reader: Second Series*, ed. Andrew McNeille (London: Hogarth, 1986), 269: "Thus, with our taste to guide us, we shall venture beyond the particular book in search of qualities that group books together; we shall give them names and thus frame a rule that brings order into our perceptions."

4. See Graham A. Cole, "Why a Book? Why This Book? Why the Particular Order within This Book? Some Theological Reflections on the Canon," in *The Enduring Authority of the Christian Scriptures*, ed. D. A. Carson (Grand Rapids: Eerdmans, 2016), 473, 475–76.

5. This is the case irrespective of the precise compositional history of a work (e.g., the possibility of multiple authors, editions, and stages of redaction).

6. See Ched Spellman, *Toward a Canon-Conscious Reading of the Bible: Exploring the History and Hermeneutics of the Canon*, NTM 34 (Sheffield: Sheffield Phoenix, 2014), 109–10: "Where an individual writing is positioned in relation to other writings in a collection (either materially or conceptually) has significant hermeneutical ramifications."

the case, a text cannot be without a paratext,[7] but their inseparability does not mean that they are not distinct in origin and function.

Not all scholars accept that the distinction between text and paratext is as absolute as I am indicating.[8] However, there is a clear demarcation between the two, both in concept and practice. For example, Hendrik Koorevaar wants to blur the distinction in the interest of arguing in favor of "an original and authoritative order in the Hebrew canon,"[9] and he has in mind the order found in the Talmud (b. B. Bat. 14b). Particularly significant for Koorevaar is the final placement of Chronicles in the Talmudic listing of books in the Writings, which he sees as a canon-conscious move by the biblical author. Koorevaar claims that the Chronicler specifically wrote his book to close the whole canon and so it would be a retrograde step to place it in any other position.[10] It cannot be denied that Chronicles in final position makes a great deal of sense, especially when the book is viewed as a summary of the period from creation to the decree of Cyrus.[11] However, its position at the *start* of the Writings in early Hebrew Bibles (Aleppo and Leningrad) also makes sense but has a *different* sense. With its glowing portraits of David and Solomon, Chronicles in premier position helps to draw attention to the fact (presumably noted by early readers) that many of the books in this third canonical section have either a liturgical or wisdom orientation. As well, given its similarities with the book of Kings, on which it draws, Chronicles at the start of the Writings also helps to bridge the canonical sections Prophets and Writings. In sum, there is no evidence that the Chronicler when composing

---

7. There are, however, paratexts without texts. See Gregory Goswell, "Titles without Texts: What the Lost Books of the Bible Tell Us about the Books We Have," *Colloq* 41 (2009): 73-93.

8. Hendrik J. Koorevaar specifically critiques my viewpoint in "The Torah Model as Original Macrostructure of the Hebrew Canon: A Critical Evaluation," *ZAW* 122 (2010): 64-66.

9. Koorevaar, "Torah Model," 66.

10. Koorevaar, "Torah Model," 79: "The book of Chronicles can be considered to be just such a paratextual passage." For his detailed argument, see Koorevaar, "Chronicles as the Intended Conclusion to the Old Testament Canon," in *The Shape of the Writings*, ed. Julius Steinberg and Timothy J. Stone, Siphrut 16 (Winona Lake, IN: Eisenbrauns, 2015), 207-36.

11. This was noticed as early as Jerome in his introduction to Chronicles in the Vulgate. He speaks of the summative character of the book: "All the teaching of Scripture is contained in this book" (*quod omnis eruditio Scripturarum in hoc libro continetur*). See *Praefationes Sancti Hieronymi in Liber Paralipomenon*, in *Biblia Sacra, Iuxta Latinam Vulgatam Versionem*, vol. 7, *Verba Dierum* (Rome: Typis Polyglottis Vaticanis, 1948), 9.

his work had any particular canonical position in view, and the distinction between text and paratext remains intact.[12]

EVERY BIBLE IS A STUDY BIBLE

In this book, I make no pretense to look at every alternative order for the biblical books, or to collate all the names ever used for the different biblical books, or to comment on every alternative division of the text. Instead, this book is put forward as a contribution to what I hope will be an ongoing examination of the effect of paratextual elements on the reading of the biblical text. Too often a vast array of information is assembled,[13] but there is little or no discussion of possible hermeneutical implications. A standard feature of Old Testament and New Testament commentaries is an introductory section on the title and canonicity of the book under discussion, but it is seldom that the information gleaned is thought to throw light on the meaning of the text. Commentaries routinely present a suggested outline of the biblical book's contents, but this is almost always done without mentioning historical schemes of divisions (e.g., the chapters or paragraphs in ancient manuscripts). Nor do commentators usually explain and justify the textual divisions they suggest. The paratext of Scripture may reveal or hide, make plain or obscure, clarify or make opaque the meaning of the text, as *commentary* always has the potential of doing, and for this reason it deserves and demands critical evaluation.

The approach I take is in the context of a general movement in biblical studies in recent years away from a focus on genetics, that is, critical theories of the origin and composition of books (e.g., source criticism or redaction criticism), and toward *final form*, that is to say, a study of the Bible in the form in which we have it in our hands. There is as well a new interest in and respect for the insights of ancient readers, whether Jewish (e.g., Rashi) or Christian (e.g., Augustine). Some of the earliest stages of the long history of biblical interpretation are preserved in the paratextual features studied in this volume, and my focus is on how the three elements of the paratext

---

12. For an extensive defense of the distinction between text and paratext, see Gregory Goswell, "Should the Church Be Committed to a Particular Order of the Old Testament Canon?," *HBT* 40 (2018): 17–40.

13. E.g., the work on the names of the NT books by H. F. von Soden, *Die Schriften des Neuen Testaments I. Teil Untersuchungen I. Abteilung die Textzeugen* (Berlin: Arthur Glaue, 1902).

of Scripture—book order, book titles, and internal divisions within books—may assist the reader in interpreting the sacred text. Giving attention to these paratextual elements is an example of properly valuing the rich tradition of biblical interpretation of which contemporary readers are the heirs. Exegetical humility demands that modern readers give consideration to how earlier generations of believers read the Scriptures.[14] Such an approach recognizes that we are not the first generation of believers to make an effort to interpret and apply the Bible.[15]

THE FOCUS OF THE PRESENT STUDY

The focus is not the *process* by which the canon developed, but the present *shape* of the canon, irrespective of the stages of its formation and the complexities of how the canon as we know it came to be.[16] Though it is right and proper to attempt to trace the history of the canon, many aspects of that process are hidden from view and will remain a matter of conjecture.[17] On the other hand, my approach of taking the biblical canon as an empirical datum will not be an uncritical exercise, for the biblical canon has in fact assumed more than one shape, and one can compare and contrast these diverse canonical traditions. Likewise, more than one title has been given to the same Bible book, and individual books have been internally partitioned according to various schemes, and I will examine and evaluate examples of such variations in the chapters that follow.

This book is not an effort to justify the limits of the canon, nor does it seek to explain why some unusual books were included in the canon (e.g., Esther, Ecclesiastes) or some popular books excluded (e.g., Shepherd of Hermas, Epistle of Barnabas). Nor is it an explanation of the historical process by which canonical arrangements of the books came into being (e.g., the role of the codex in the production of the four-Gospel collection). Instead, I will

---

14. David P. Parris, *Reading the Bible with Giants: How 2000 Years of Biblical Interpretation Can Shed Light on Old Texts* (Milton Keynes: Paternoster, 2006).

15. For an attempt to provide a theological basis for such an approach, see Stephen R. Holmes, *Listening to the Past: The Place of Tradition in Theology* (Grand Rapids: Baker Academic, 2002), 1–36.

16. For the distinction, see, e.g., Walter Brueggemann, *The Creative Word: Canon as a Model for Biblical Education*, 2nd ed., rev. Amy Erickson (Minneapolis: Fortress, 2015), 1–10. Brueggemann, however, favors process over final shape.

17. See, e.g., Lee Martin McDonald, *The Formation of the Biblical Canon*, vol. 1, The Old Testament: Its Authority and Canonicity (London: Bloomsbury T&T Clark, 2017).

seek to tease out the hermeneutical implications of the different canonical orders settled on by different communities of faith.

My aim is not to justify and promote a particular order of books as the exclusive basis for study and thinking on the meaning of the biblical text. It is not necessary to decide on any particular order of books, favoring it over other contending orders, for differing orders highlight different features of the books thus categorized, so that each order of books in its own way may be valid and useful to the reader. Likewise, though at times I will express a judgment as to the felicity of a particular name assigned to a biblical book, I do not argue that there is an exclusively *right* name for any one book. No title will say all that could be said about the contents of the book to which it is attached. Nor is there only one acceptable way of dividing up the text of a book, though some schemes of division (e.g., where a chapter break is placed) may be better than others in elucidating the structure of particular biblical books. Alternative schemes of internal division may each have a logic and justification and therefore throw light on the text, though that is not to suggest that the reader is allowed to divide a text into sections according to whim.

I make no claim to be able to get into the heads of those responsible for the alternative orders of the canonical books, the names of the books, and the divisions within the books, or to infallibly know what they intended and what motivated their particular choices. Robert Darnton warns against assuming that texts have "always worked on the sensibilities of readers in the same way."[18] We cannot recapture the inner experience of ancient readers and know what they thought about what they read and why they thought that way. However, on the assumption that books that are juxtaposed are connected in some way (e.g., a similar genre or featuring related themes), a study of book order preserved in canon lists and early Bibles,[19] or of the titles affixed to the books, or of the ways in which the books were subdivided provides clues as to how early readers responded to sacred texts.

The paratext of Scripture is to be viewed as implicit commentary on the text. The different orders, book names, and divisions within books provide suggestions to the reader regarding the meaning of the text. There is no

---

18. Robert Darnton, *The Case for Books: Past, Present, and Future* (New York: PublicAffairs, 2009), 201; Darnton, "First Steps towards a History of Reading," *AJFS* 23 (1986): 5–30.

19. See Edmon L. Gallagher and John D. Meade, *The Biblical Canon Lists from Early Christianity: Texts and Analysis* (Oxford: Oxford University Press, 2017).

suggestion that meaning is reader-dependent; rather, those who read scriptural texts *seek* meaning, and the paratext of Scripture can provide valuable clues, suggesting as it does ways of seeing the text. It does so by fossilizing and preserving for posterity alternative ways in which previous generations of readers have understood the text, and so it can also help to generate new and improved ways of reading.

With regard to the status that is to be given to paratextual elements, it is best to view them as ways of construing the text. An element of accident, tradition, and even prejudice may well have gone into the process that produced the paratext of Scripture, yet it still has an influence on the modern reader, who can scarcely conceive of the text without such features. We would be surprised to find a modern book without a title, or a book without chapters or paragraphs. The order of the biblical books, their titles, and their internal divisions provide a built-in commentary on the text. These paratextual elements have the heuristic value of starting points for interpretation. By means of a consideration of paratextual elements, the reader will be helped to see new insights into the meaning of the sacred text.

PART I

CANONICAL STRUCTURE

1

THE STRUCTURE OF
THE HEBREW CANON

INTRODUCTION

The order of the books of the Old Testament in the Hebrew and Greek canons is different, and this chapter will explore the implications of the two ways of ordering. Where a biblical book is placed relative to other books influences the reading of a book on the assumption that material that is juxtaposed is related in meaning in some way. Consciously or unconsciously, the reader's evaluation of a book is affected by the company it keeps in the library of Scripture. More than one organizing principle may lie behind the ordering of books in the Hebrew Bible.

THE TRIPARTITE STRUCTURE OF THE HEBREW CANON

Where a biblical book is placed relative to other books in the canon influences a reader's view of the book: what to expect and what the book may be about.[1] In this chapter I seek to tease out some of the implications of the canonical orders settled on by different communities of faith and discern how book order feeds into interpretation.[2] The aim is not to justify and promote a particular order of books, for the Hebrew and Greek orders may both contain valuable insights. The ordering of books can be classified according to

---

1. John H. Sailhamer, *The Meaning of the Pentateuch: Revelation, Composition and Interpretation* (Downers Grove, IL: InterVarsity, 2009), 216: "A book's order within a canonical list no doubt played a role in determining its meaning. If nothing more, it was a reflection of the book's relationship to other books in the list."

2. For an earlier version of material in this chapter, see Gregory Goswell, "The Order of the Books in the Hebrew Bible," *JETS* 51 (2008): 673–88. Used with permission.

a number of principles (e.g., their size, story line, or similar themes). These principles need not be mutually exclusive, for there may be more than one possible principle reflected in a particular order. In the case of the Bible, it is left to the reader to surmise what rationale is at work in the ordering of the books and literary blocks that make up the larger whole.

The arrangement of the books that make up the Old Testament varies between the Jewish and Christian communities, who share it as Scripture. In this chapter, I will look at the Hebrew canon (adopted by the Jews), and in the next chapter I will examine the Greek canon (preserved by the Christian church). Both canons basically have the same books but not the same order in which books are placed. The typical order of books in the Hebrew Bible is as follows:

Torah
    Genesis

    Exodus

    Leviticus

    Numbers

    Deuteronomy

Prophets
    Former Prophets
- Joshua
- Judges
- Samuel
- Kings

    Latter Prophets
- Isaiah
- Jeremiah
- Ezekiel

    The Twelve (= Minor Prophets)

Writings
  Psalms

  Job

  Proverbs

  Megilloth
  - Ruth
  - Song of Songs
  - Ecclesiastes
  - Lamentations
  - Esther

  Daniel

  Ezra-Nehemiah

  Chronicles

Commonly rehearsed arguments that the New Testament itself bears witness to the existence of the tripartite configuration of Old Testament books (e.g., Luke 11:51; 24:44) do not carry conviction.[3] Even if, for argument's sake, these passages did provide evidence of its existence at this early stage, neither Jesus nor the apostles are on record mandating the use of this particular order of books in preference to other canonical orders. Some Christian scholars have accepted arguments for the temporal (and therefore theological) priority of the Hebrew order and have used this order as the basis for reading the Old Testament, viewing it as the *right* way of doing things.[4] Of course, this is not a *wrong* way of proceeding, unless it is thought to be the *only* way of approaching the interpretation of the Old Testament books. When this is done, it gives one particular way of ordering the books undue influence over interpretation and forecloses other possible and legitimate

---

3. For details, see Goswell, "Should the Church Be," 24–26.

4. E.g., Paul R. House, *Old Testament Theology* (Downers Grove, IL: InterVarsity, 1998), 55–56; Stephen G. Dempster, *Dominion and Dynasty: A Biblical Theology of the Hebrew Bible*, NSBT 15 (Leicester: Apollos, 2003); Rolf Rendtorff, *The Canonical Hebrew Bible: A Theology of the Old Testament*, trans. David E. Orton, TBS 7 (Leiden: Deo, 2005), 4–6.

interpretive options. In other words, we should give serious consideration to both the Hebrew and the Greek way of ordering the books of the Old Testament, for both may throw light on the meaning of the text of Scripture.

The Hebrew Bible was given a tripartite structure (Tanak). Tanak is an acronym for the Torah (= Law), Nevi'im (= Prophets), and Ketuvim (= Writings) with helping vowels, these being the three canonical sections of the Hebrew Scriptures.[5] The first part (Torah) describes the making of a covenant between God and Israel. The second part (Prophets) offers instructions and warnings regarding Israel's violation of provisions of the covenant. Putting books that Christians usually view as histories (e.g., Samuel and Kings) in the same section as prophetic anthologies (Isaiah, Jeremiah, etc.) tends to make all these books prophetic in orientation, that is, they offer a critique of the behavior of God's people according to divinely instituted standards (see 1 Sam 12; 2 Kgs 17). The placement of Joshua–Kings after the Torah suggests an understanding of these four books as illustrating and applying the teaching of the Pentateuch, and so too the prophets whose oracles are recorded in the Latter Prophets are viewed as preachers of the law. This understanding of the books is supported by a cluster of references to God's law at the beginning and end of the Former Prophets (e.g., Josh 1:8; 8:31-34; 2 Kgs 22:8, 11; 23:24-25). Likewise, the Latter Prophets (MT) start and close with references to the law (Isa 1:10; Mal 4:4).

The third part of the canon (Writings) provides prudential wisdom for typical situations of life. The Writings, however, do not simply include wisdom texts (e.g., Job, Proverbs) but also what look like historical works (Ezra-Nehemiah and Chronicles). The tone of Chronicles differs from Kings by virtue of its tendency to extract a moral lesson from historical events (e.g., 2 Chr 15:1-7; 16:7-9, 12).[6] It is perhaps possible, on that basis, to view Chronicles as a wisdom book of sorts.[7] There is, as well, the wisdom theme of

---

5. For what follows in this paragraph, I acknowledge my dependence on Charles Elliott Vernoff, "The Contemporary Study of Religion and the Academic Teaching of Judaism," in *Methodology in the Academic Teaching of Judaism*, ed. Zev Garber, Studies in Judaism (Lanham, MD: University Press of America, 1986), 30-32.

6. See Raymond B. Dillard, "Reward and Punishment in Chronicles: The Theology of Immediate Retribution," *WTJ* 46 (1984): 164-72.

7. See Joseph Blenkinsopp, "Wisdom in the Chronicler's Work," in *In Search of Wisdom: Essays in Memory of John G. Gammie*, ed. Leo G. Perdue, Bernard Brandon Scott, and William Johnston Wiseman (Louisville: Westminster John Knox, 1993), 19-30.

Daniel (e.g., Dan 1:4, 17, 20; 11:33, 35) and the exemplary behavior of the Jewish heroes in the "tales from the diaspora" in Daniel 1-6 and Esther.[8] Features such as these lead Brevard Childs to suggest that the whole of the Writings has been "sapientalized."[9] What Childs means is that the Writings as a whole provide a view on life that reflects wisdom ways of thinking, and its books are distinctly ethical in orientation.

THE TORAH

The placement of the Torah first does not need to imply that the Old Testament is turned into ethical instruction and no more, for the Pentateuch has the same primary position in the Christian Bible.[10] Indeed, the Pentateuch could hardly be put in any other position, for it recounts the origins of the world and of Israel, and by so doing provides the background for all that follows. Many key biblical themes receive an initial airing in the Pentateuch.

Moreover, the five books could not be put in any other order than the one they are in, given the story line that connects them, so that historical sequence explains the ordering of these five books.

Genesis can be conceived as the introduction to the story of Israel proper, which begins in Exodus. It is a family history of the forefathers (Abraham, Isaac, etc.), but the emphasis on progeny prepares the reader for the great nation that the family has become by the start of Exodus (Exod 1:7). The Sinai events are preceded and succeeded by an account of the wilderness wanderings, which lead the people from Egypt to Sinai and then from Sinai to the edge of the promised land (Exod 15-18; Num 10-21), and this places Leviticus and its theology of holiness at the heart of the Pentateuch. The books Leviticus and Numbers form a pair, for Numbers does *physically* what Leviticus does theologically; it forges a link between Sinai and the Holy Land, for in Numbers the people travel from the holy mountain to the border of the land. In Numbers the old generation, who experienced the exodus and

---

8. W. L. Humphreys, "A Life-Style for Diaspora: A Study of the Tales of Esther and Daniel," *JBL* 92 (1973): 211-23.

9. Brevard S. Childs, *Biblical Theology of the Old and New Testaments: Theological Reflection on the Christian Bible* (London: SCM, 1992), 116.

10. So, too, in the NT, "law" (*nomos*) can be used as a synecdoche to mean Scripture as a whole without any legalist nuance; see John 10:34; 12:34; 15:25; Rom 3:19; 1 Cor 14:21, wherein non-Pentateuchal texts are cited and dubbed "law."

Sinai encounter with God (chs. 1–25), is replaced by a new generation in the desert forty years later (chs. 26–36).

Deuteronomy picks up and makes substantial homiletical use of the idea of the linkages between successive generations. Deuteronomy is set off sharply from the preceding books by its style, which is that of a series of speeches or sermons by Moses to Israel (Deut 1:1). It homiletically recapitulates the divine instructions received at Sinai in preparation for entering the promised land. Deuteronomy's position at the close of the Torah gives a lively interpretation of the law. The law's continuing relevance is stressed (e.g., Deut 5:2–3: "[The Lord God made a covenant] with us, all of us, here, alive, this day" [a literal rendering of the original]), for Moses addresses the *second* generation of Israelites as if they saw what their fathers did at Horeb some forty years earlier. Another example of the Deuteronomic merging of the generations is 29:14–15, where future generations are thought of as participants in the covenant on an equal footing with the contemporary generation addressed by Moses ("Nor is it with you only that I make this sworn covenant, but with him who is not here with us this day as well as with him who stands here with us this day before the Lord our God" [RSV]). In effect, all future generations are addressed by Moses. On that basis, Deuteronomy is the link between the Torah and the rest of the Old Testament, not simply with Joshua–Kings, and so, for example, the prophecy of Malachi makes extensive use of Deuteronomy.[11]

THE PROPHETS

The four books of the Former Prophets (Joshua, Judges, Samuel, Kings) precede and match in number the four books of the Latter Prophets (Isaiah, Jeremiah, Ezekiel, and the Book of the Twelve [= Minor Prophets]).[12] The Masoretic Text (MT) follows a generally chronological scheme, the order of books being Isaiah, Jeremiah, and Ezekiel, with the catchall collection of Twelve Prophets at the end. Certainly, the ministries of Haggai, Zechariah, and Malachi in the Persian period are to be dated later than those of the other prophets. There are other orders attested for the Latter Prophets, notably

---

11. William J. Dumbrell, "Malachi and the Ezra-Nehemiah Reforms," *RTR* 35 (1976): 42–52.

12. Early references to the canon count the Twelve (so named) as one book, e.g., 4 Ezra 14.45; Josephus, *Ag. Ap.* 1.38–41 (because of the number of books they count); Sir 49:10; Melito (recorded in Eusebius, *Hist. eccl.* 4.26.13–14), and the Talmud (B. Bat. 14b).

that found in a tradition preserved in the Babylonian Talmud tractate Baba Batra (14b), which reads: "Our rabbis taught that the order of the prophets is Joshua and Judges, Samuel and Kings, Jeremiah and Ezekiel, Isaiah and the Twelve. ... The order of the Writings is Ruth and the Book of Psalms, and Job and Proverbs, Ecclesiastes, Song of Songs and Lamentations, Daniel and the Scroll of Esther, Ezra[-Nehemiah] and Chronicles" (my translation). It is a baraita, a quotation of earlier rabbinic sources in the Tannaitic period (pre-AD 200).[13]

The sequence of four books in the Latter Prophets in Baba Batra 14b may be ordered according to decreasing length, a common mode of ordering in the biblical canon.[14] Or it may reflect an alternate method of computing chronological order,[15] noting that the latter part of the scroll of Isaiah foresees certain postexilic developments (mentioning Cyrus) and Haggai-Zechariah-Malachi concern events that postdate Jeremiah and Ezekiel.[16] The placing of these mostly prophetic anthologies (Jonah being the exception) side by side does not ignore, therefore, the historic settings of the ministries of the prophets, yet it also brings to the fore the relation of the prophets with one another, suggesting that the message of each prophet should be read in the context of the Latter Prophets as a canonical corpus, such that their mutual interaction is vital for correct interpretation.

A noticeable feature of the Talmudic listing is the *pairing* of the prophetic books.[17] The Baba Batra pairing of books (e.g., Joshua and Judges) is attested in the earliest printed versions of the Talmud from the Soncino-Pesaro edition of the 1510s onward, but the conjunctive *waw* is absent in all the medieval manuscripts, which leads to the conclusion that this is an editorial (and interpretive) insertion into the Talmudic text, and thus it is not represented

---

13. I. Epstein, ed., *Baba Bathra*, Hebrew-English Edition of the Babylonian Talmud, new ed., vol. 1 (London: Soncino, 1976).

14. This is the view of Roger T. Beckwith, *The Old Testament Canon of the New Testament Church and Its Background in Early Judaism* (London: SPCK, 1985), 162.

15. Louis Jacobs, *Structure and Form in the Babylonian Talmud* (Cambridge: Cambridge University Press, 1991), 35.

16. Edgar W. Conrad, *Reading the Latter Prophets: Toward a New Canonical Criticism*, JSOTSup 376 (London: T&T Clark International, 2003), 77-78. The discussion in Baba Batra itself suggests yet another explanation of the order (see below).

17. As commented on by Beckwith, *Old Testament Canon*, 156-57.

in recent English editions.[18] However, this way of reading this order of books could be justified in the following terms.

Joshua and Judges concern the conquest and its aftermath, with repeated notice of the death of the hero Joshua (Josh 24:29-31; Judg 1:1; 2:6-10). The connection of Samuel and Kings needs hardly to be be argued, since their linkage in the Greek Bible as Kingdoms 1-4 shows that many ancient readers saw their obvious relation with each other as a history of kingship from its rise to its demise. The books Jeremiah and Ezekiel belong together as collections of oracles from contemporary prophets. The relation between Isaiah and the Twelve may be due to the similarity of their superscriptions (Isa 1:1; Hos 1:1), both of which have "in the days of Uzziah, Jotham, Ahaz, and Hezekiah, kings of Judah,"[19] and some of the earlier and the larger sections of the Twelve (Hosea, Amos, Micah) are other eighth-century prophets. Also relevant is that both books near their end depict the prospect of universal pilgrimage to Zion (Isa 66:23; Zech 14:16). A further link between Isaiah and the Twelve is the synoptic passages about "the mountain of the house of the LORD" in Isa 2:2-4 and Mic 4:1-3. In addition, like the Book of the Twelve, the scroll of Isaiah begins with prophecies set in the era of Assyrian ascendancy (Isa 1-39) and ends with material about a projected restoration of the nation in the Persian period (Isa 40-66, mentioning Cyrus).

THE FORMER PROPHETS

With regard to the paratextual phenomenon of the order of the four books as self-standing literary blocks, their arrangement according to story line does not mean that this way of sequencing the biblical material is *natural* or *neutral*, for their enjambment still affects the interpretation of the individual books. For example, with Judges following Joshua, the period of the judges is made to appear even darker than it might have otherwise (Judg 2:10), given the contrast with the obedient generation of Joshua's day. The refrain in the final chapters of Judges ("In those days there was no king ...") is often viewed as recommending kingship as a way of overcoming the inadequacies of the

---

18. See, e.g., Jacob Neusner, trans., *The Talmud of Babylonia: An American Translation, XXII.A: Tractate Baba Batra, Chapters 1-2*, BJS 239 (Atlanta: Scholars Press, 1992), 69.

19. Julio Trebolle-Barrera, "Qumran Evidence for a Biblical Standard Text and for Nonstandard and Parabiblical Texts," in *The Dead Sea Scrolls in Their Historical Context*, ed. Timothy H. Lim with Graeme Auld, Larry W. Hurtado, and Alison Jack (Edinburgh: T&T Clark, 2000), 95.

period (17:6; 18:1; 19:1; 21:25).[20] It is not, however, that simple, for the books that follow Judges show that most of the kings were unfaithful, such that Gideon's adverse reaction to the suggestion that he rule over Israel is shown to be justified (Judg 8:22–23).[21]

With the book of Samuel following Judges, an absolute rejection of human kingship in Israel is also not possible, though that is the first reaction of Samuel *the judge* (1 Sam 8). David is not idealized in Samuel (esp. 2 Sam 12–20) but becomes a pious model against which later Judean kings are measured in the book of Kings (e.g., 1 Kgs 3:3; 11:4; 2 Kgs 14:3; 18:3).[22] This has sometimes caused readers of Samuel to take insufficient notice of the nuanced portrait of Davidic kingship in the person of the founder of the dynasty. On the other hand, after the parading of David's failures in the second half of 2 Samuel, the reader is not surprised to find in Kings a largely negative view of monarchy in Judah and Israel.

What I am seeking to illustrate is that the evaluation of individual biblical books must take into account their canonical setting, especially the interaction of neighboring books.

THE LATTER PROPHETS

A number of prophetic books have superscriptions relating to kings who are mentioned by name in the book of Kings, helping to bind together and coordinate the Former and Latter Prophets (e.g., Hos 1:1; Amos 1:1). This in part compensates for the virtual nonmention of the writing prophets in the book of Kings. Isaiah (2 Kgs 18–20) and Jonah (2 Kgs 14:25) are the only writing prophets mentioned in Kings. The Former Prophets, and Kings in particular, supply a narrative framework for the compilations of oracles by prophets that follow (starting either with Isaiah [MT] or Jeremiah [Baba Batra]). The synoptic passages, 2 Kings 18–20 and Isaiah 36–39, justify the juxtapositioning of Kings and Isaiah in the MT, and the two books assist to

---

20. William J. Dumbrell calls into question the traditional interpretation of Judg 21:25; see Dumbrell, "'In Those Days There Was No King in Israel; Every Man Did What Was Right in His Own Eyes': The Purpose of the Book of Judges Reconsidered," *JSOT* 25 (1983): 23–33.

21. For more, see Gregory Goswell, "The Attitude to Kingship in the Book of Judges," *TJ* 40 (2019): 3–18.

22. See Gregory Goswell, "King and Cultus: The Image of David in the Book of Kings," *JESOT* 5.2 (2016–2017): 167–86.

unite the larger canonical structure dominated by prophecy.[23] These synoptic passages represent an important turning point in their respective books when the fate of the Davidic house is announced (2 Kgs 20:16–18; Isa 39:5–7), either leading to an account of the final years of that house (2 Kgs 21–25) or precipitating a major thematic shift to an exclusive focus on divine kingship (Isa 40–66). These perspectives can be viewed as complementary, the one providing the historical record of the end of the house of David (Kings) and the other the theocratic framework within which to understand it, the higher and permanent kingship of YHWH (Isaiah).

The sequence of Jeremiah, Ezekiel, Isaiah, and the Twelve in Baba Batra 14b may be in descending order according to length,[24] or in accordance with an alternate understanding of chronological order,[25] for the latter part of the prophecy of Isaiah (mentioning Cyrus) and Haggai-Zechariah-Malachi concern events that postdate Jeremiah and Ezekiel. That is not the explanation of the order supplied by the rabbinic discussion recorded in Baba Batra itself. Baba Batra explains that Kings ends with destruction (ḥorbanaʾ) and Jeremiah is all destruction, Ezekiel commences with destruction and ends with consolation (naḥmataʾ), and Isaiah is full of consolation, so that "destruction is next to destruction and consolation is next to consolation" (b. B. Bat. 14b). The suggestion is, then, that thematic considerations predominate, so that, for example, the placing of Kings and Jeremiah side by side is due to their common theme of judgment and the disaster of exile. The placement of Jeremiah after Kings provides a prophetic explanation of the demise of the nation as plotted in 2 Kings 23–25. Moreover, the position of Jeremiah immediately after Kings is appropriate seeing that Jeremiah 52 is drawn from (and adapts) 2 Kings 24–25, so that these are synoptic passages. In addition, the oracles of Jeremiah are set in the closing years of the kingdom of Judah, which is what the final chapters of Kings describe. The effect of the order in

---

23. See Christopher R. Seitz, *The Goodly Fellowship of the Prophets: The Achievement of Association in Canon Formation* (Grand Rapids: Baker Academic, 2009), 90–91, 106, for a brief survey of crosslinks between the books that make up the prophetic section of the Hebrew canon.

24. The view of Beckwith, *Old Testament Canon*, 162.

25. Trebolle-Barrera, "Qumran Evidence," 98.

Baba Batra is to give the prophetic books an increasingly hopeful prospect, due to the extensive promises of restoration in Isaiah 40–66.[26]

The four Hebrew book titles "Joshua," "Judges," "Samuel," and "Kings" give the Former Prophets a distinct focus on leadership. The focus on kings and prophets in the book of Kings is therefore in line with the thematic orientation of the canonical grouping of which it is the climax. Kings plots the failure of the institution of kingship, both in Israel and Judah, with most kings failing to reflect the prototype of a good king provided by David. Consistent with this focus on kings, the prophets are styled as the critics of kings, and the ruin of the nation is blamed on the kings. With Jeremiah as the head book of the Latter Prophets (b. B. Bat. 14b), the interest in kings and prophets is picked up, for the prophet Jeremiah himself is a severe critic of contemporary kings (esp. chs. 21–23).[27]

The MT order (Isaiah, Jeremiah, Ezekiel, Twelve Prophets) is chronological.[28] Ezekiel was the younger contemporary of Jeremiah, and therefore Ezekiel's prophetic book follows that of Jeremiah. There is a fuller discussion of the exile and the hope for the nation beyond it in the prophecy of Ezekiel (Ezek 36–48) relative to Jeremiah (largely limited to Jer 30–33). The historical progression is also indicated by the different schemes of dating used in the two books. In the book of Ezekiel, the prophecies are often dated according to the years of Jehoiachin's exile (Ezek 1:2; 8:1; 20:1; 24:1; etc.), whereas in the book of Jeremiah, a number of the prophecies are dated according to the year of a reigning Judean king, often Zedekiah (Jer 25:1; 26:1; 27:1; 32:1; etc.). The placing of these four prophetic books side by side gives the impression of a (divinely provided) succession of prophets generation by generation, matching the succession of monarchs described in the book of Kings.

The order of the books in the Twelve (= Minor Prophets) is set in the Masoretic tradition,[29] though the order of the books in the Major Prophets varies considerably in Jewish lists. The evidence of the Qumran fragments

---

26. The discussion in B. Bat. 14b views Isaiah as "full of consolation" rather than only ending with consolation (as Ezekiel does).

27. A. Graeme Auld, *Kings without Privilege: David and Moses in the Story of the Bible's Kings* (Edinburgh: T&T Clark, 1994), 168.

28. The account of famous men in Sir 48:22–26; 49:1–10 follows this sequence, as noted by Francis Watson, *Paul and the Hermeneutics of Faith* (London: T&T Clark International, 2004), 80–81.

29. The LXX order is Hosea, Amos, Micah, Joel, Obadiah, Jonah, Nahum, etc.

of the Minor Prophets indicates that these twelve prophetic booklets were copied together on one scroll in ancient times. The order within the Twelve may well be intended to be chronological,[30] though the dating of several of these books is strongly debated (esp. Joel and Obadiah). The order within the Twelve gives no more than a rough approximation to the order of their real dates, with a basic twofold division into Assyrian (Hosea to Zephaniah) and Persian periods (Haggai, Zechariah, and Malachi).[31] Part of the explanation of the order may be a desire to achieve an alternation of prophets who ministered in Israel and Judah: Hosea (Israel), Joel (Judah), Amos (Israel), Obadiah (Judah), Jonah (Israel), and Micah (Judah).[32] According to C. F. Keil, this oscillating north/south sequence may continue a little further in the Book of the Twelve if Nahum were shown to be a northerner and Habakkuk a southerner.[33] This geographical schema encourages a hermeneutic that reads the prophetic threats and promises in the various booklets that make up the Twelve as applying to *both* kingdoms and, even more widely, to God's people generally, irrespective of time and location. In other words, this schematic arrangement encourages a theological synthesizing of the messages of individual prophets such that they are shown to have universal implications and applications.

Amos should be dated before Hosea, for example, seeing that the superscription of Amos only mentions Uzziah, whereas Hosea 1:1 also lists the three subsequent Judean kings. Hosea may stand at the head because of its size and because it is theologically formative.[34] It lays down the dynamics of the

---

30. In B. Bat. 14b, the arrangement of the books with Hosea in premier position is explicitly said to be chronological, in that Hos 1:2 is understood to mean that God spoke *first* to Hosea ("When the LORD first spoke through Hosea"). See also Marvin A. Sweeney, *The Twelve Prophets*, vol. 1, *Hosea, Joel, Amos, Obadiah, Jonah*, BO (Collegeville, MN: Liturgical Press, 2000), xxvii–xxviii.

31. Edgar W. Conrad, "The End of Prophecy and the Appearance of Angels/Messengers in the Book of the Twelve," *JSOT* 73 (1997): 65–79.

32. Raymond C. Van Leeuwen, "Scribal Wisdom and Theodicy in the Book of the Twelve," in Perdue, Scott, and Wiseman, *In Search of Wisdom*, 34. The idea goes back to C. F. Keil, *The Minor Prophets*, trans. J. Martin, COT 10 (repr., Grand Rapids: Eerdmans, 1980), 3.

33. The gentilic adjective "the Elkoshite" attached to the name of Nahum presumably refers to his hometown of Elkosh (Nah 1:1), whose location is unknown, but is possibly a village in Galilee (= Capernaum, meaning "the city of Nahum"), and the anti-Nineveh orientation of his prophecy is consistent with a concern about the threat that Assyria posed to northern Israel (though Nah 1:15 addresses Judah). The prophet Habakkuk is occupied with the Chaldean threat to Judah (1:6) and so presumably is to be classified as a southern prophet.

34. The suggestion is that of Paul R. House, *The Unity of the Twelve*, JSOTSup 97 (Sheffield: Almond, 1990), 74–76. In this and the following paragraph, I acknowledge my dependence on House.

covenant relationship, such that Hosea 1–3 functions to introduce the leading themes of the Twelve as a unit. The story of Hosea 1–3 is one of covenant infidelity and punishment, followed by restoration, and it can be viewed as providing a summary of the message of the Twelve as a whole. There is no chronological data supplied by Joel to explain its placement between Hosea and Amos. It must, then, be considerations of *content* that dictated Joel's position before Amos.[35] Joel widens the indictment of sin found in Hosea to include a general denunciation of the nations (e.g., Joel 3:1–8), which helps to prepare for the critique of various foreign powers in Amos 1–2. On the other hand, Amos 9:11–15 eases the transition to Obadiah, with Obadiah's largely anti-Edom message expanding on the mention of Edom in Amos 9:12.[36]

Not all scholars would read the Book of the Twelve as a literary corpus and interpret its component parts on this basis (e.g., Ehud Ben Zvi), but taking into consideration the order of books in the Twelve is hermeneutically productive and theologically important.[37] It assists the interpretation of the individual books and also enriches our understanding of their theology. For example, an eschatological context is provided for the Jonah narrative by the preceding book of Obadiah (e.g., v. 15: "For the day of the LORD is near upon all the nations" [RSV]) and by the pervasive theme of the day of the Lord in the Twelve. The Jonah section continues the theme of the relation of Israel and the nations that begins in Joel 3:9–21 and is elaborated in Amos 1–2 and Obadiah. In the LXX, the order of Obadiah followed by Jonah is the same as the MT, suggesting this sequence is of special significance in reading. The description of the response of fasting and repentance by Ninevites (Jonah 3) is reminiscent of Joel 1:13–14 and 2:15–16, which call for fasting and the donning of sackcloth by Israelites. The response of the sailors and Ninevites is to be read within the wider "nations" theme in the Twelve, in which the end-time conversion of the nations is a leading feature (e.g., Zeph 2:11; 3:9; Mal 1:11).

---

35. The transition between Joel and Amos is assisted by the fact that Amos echoes Joel twice (Amos 1:2 sounds like Joel 3:16a; Amos 9:13b sounds like Joel 3:18a).

36. Note how similar Obad 19a is to Amos 9:12a, with the verb "possess" (*yāraš*) found in both cases.

37. Christopher R. Seitz, *Prophecy and Hermeneutics: Toward a New Introduction to the Prophets*, STI (Grand Rapids: Baker Academic, 2007), 219. See Ehud Ben Zvi, "Is the Twelve Hypothesis Likely from an Ancient Readers' Perspective?," in *Two Sides of a Coin: Juxtaposing Views on Interpreting the Book of the Twelve/the Twelve Prophetic Books*, ed. Ehud Ben Zvi and James D. Nogalski, AG 201 (Piscataway, NJ: Gorgias, 2009), 47–96. Ben Zvi rejects the sequential reading of the Twelve (53).

This helps to explain why nothing is said in Jonah about these gentile converts having to become Jews to be acceptable to God (e.g., circumcision, food laws, Sabbath), for they prefigure the treatment of the nations in the end time. The canonical placement of Jonah by ancient scribal readers is a prompt for the narrative to be interpreted in this setting.[38]

Alan Cooper goes as far as to say that Jonah was "never intended to be read apart from that canonical context. An intertextual reading of the book is, therefore, both valid and necessary."[39] The message of Jonah will continue to baffle interpreters until they are willing to consider its canonical context.[40] The book of Jonah stands between Obadiah and Micah, and the paratextual considerations discussed above should shape the reader's understanding of the text, not a hypothetical reconstruction of its situation and purpose (e.g., that it was written to combat the ethnic restrictiveness of the Ezra-Nehemiah reforms).[41]

Micah's place after Jonah is appropriate in that it explains how sinful Israel could be destroyed by Assyria, which itself had evaded judgment by repenting.[42] The prophecy of Micah, however, anticipates Assyria's subjugation by Judean shepherds (Mic 5:5-6), and Nahum in turn portrays the eventual punishment of Nineveh, which plainly deserves God's wrath (Nah 3:18-19). With the removal of Assyria, Habakkuk is set in the context of the looming Babylonian crisis (Hab 1:6). The cosmic breadth of the devastation described in Zephaniah (e.g., Zeph 1:2-3) makes it a fitting climax for the first nine prophecies of the Twelve that focus on the theme of judgment, but it also introduces the restoration focus of Haggai-Zechariah-Malachi, with

---

38. Gregory Goswell, "Jonah among the Twelve Prophets," *JBL* 135 (2016): 283-99.

39. Alan Cooper, "In Praise of Divine Caprice: The Significance of the Book of Jonah," in *Among the Prophets: Language, Image, and Structure in the Prophetic Writings*, ed. Philip R. Davies and David J. A. Clines, JSOTSup 144 (Sheffield: Sheffield Academic, 1993), 159. Cooper has in mind its setting within the Hosea-Nahum sequence, which he views as concerned with the Assyrian crisis.

40. A point also made by John F. A. Sawyer, "A Change of Emphasis in the Study of the Prophets," in *Israel's Prophetic Heritage: Essays in Honour of Peter R. Ackroyd*, ed. Richard Coggins (Cambridge: Cambridge University Press, 1982), 242.

41. See the rebuttal of the usual critical theory by R. E. Clements, "The Purpose of the Book of Jonah," in *Congress Volume: Edinburgh 1974*, ed. J. A. Emerton et al., VTSup 28 (Leiden: Brill, 1975), 16-28.

42. Elmer Dyck, "Jonah among the Prophets: A Study in Canonical Context," *JETS* 33 (1990): 72.

Zephaniah 3:9–20 containing God's promise to restore the fortunes of Zion (3:20: "At that time I will bring you home" [RSV]).[43]

THE WRITINGS

In placing the Writings after Prophets, Marvin A. Sweeney views the Tanak as portraying the rebuilt temple and restored Jewish community in the postexilic period as a fulfillment of the hope of the prophets.[44] If the arrangement of the books *were* doing this, it would be at variance with the *contents* of the books. In the eyes of the Jews, the Tanak is complete in and of itself, insofar as it does not constitute a component of a larger body of Scripture—it is not "Old Testament," for it has no New Testament. However, the story of God's purposes is far from complete, for the restoration described in Ezra-Nehemiah is disappointing. It is not true that the Tanak, ending with Chronicles, has no sense of incompleteness, for it ends on a note of expectation; we are waiting for God's people to return to Jerusalem (2 Chr 36:23: "Let him go up"). According to the final books of the Tanak, the nation is still oppressed; for example, Nehemiah 9:32 speaks of their continued hardship "until this day," and in Nehemiah 9:36 there is the complaint to God by those who have returned to Jerusalem ("we are slaves"). The sweeping historical review provided by the penitential prayer of Nehemiah 9 makes depressing reading. Likewise, Ezra-Nehemiah shows the failure of God's people to reform themselves, ending as it does with the depressing account of the recurrence of problems (the final placement of Neh 13:4–31 demonstrates the people's inability to keep their pledge in Neh 10:28–39).

Contrary to John H. Sailhamer,[45] I am not convinced that ending the Tanak with Ezra-Nehemiah rather than Chronicles, as in the Leningrad and Aleppo codices, makes a material difference, for both books show that the people

---

43. Byron G. Curtis, "The Zion-Daughter Oracles: Evidence on the Identity and Ideology of the Late Redactors of the Book of the Twelve," in *Reading and Hearing the Book of the Twelve*, ed. James D. Nogalski and Marvin A. Sweeney, SymS 15 (Atlanta: Society of Biblical Literature, 2000), 182. Zeph 3:14–20, bridges "the gap from the preexilic prophets to the restorationist prophets."

44. Marvin A. Sweeney, "Tanak versus Old Testament: Concerning the Foundation for a Jewish Theology of the Bible," in *Problems in Biblical Theology: Essays in Honor of Rolf Knierim*, ed. Henry T. C. Sun and Keith L. Eades with James M. Robinson and Garth I. Moller (Grand Rapids: Eerdmans, 1997), 359.

45. John H. Sailhamer, "Biblical Theology and the Composition of the Hebrew Bible," in *Biblical Theology: Retrospect and Prospect*, ed. Scott J. Hafemann (Downers Grove, IL: InterVarsity, 2002), 34–36.

of God are still in exile. Chronicles was written long after the temple was rebuilt (c. 400 BC).[46] It was authored later than the Ezra-Nehemiah period. Ezra-Nehemiah depicts a physical return from exile, whereas Chronicles grapples with the mystery that despite the return described in the book of Ezra-Nehemiah, Israel is still awaiting the definitive return of the people of God as predicted by the prophets.[47] The Chronicler looks for a more ultimate return, when all God's people will be gathered into God's final kingdom, with the result that the Hebrew canon closing with Chronicles ends on an eschatological note.[48] In addition, Daniel 9 reinterprets Jeremiah's prophecy of a return from exile after seventy years (Dan 9:2) in terms of the much more extended "seventy weeks" (9:24), so that the fulfillment of Jeremiah's prophecy is projected to an indefinite time period far beyond the return of some exiles to Palestine from Babylon in the years following 586 BC.

The order of the individual books within the Writings greatly fluctuates in the Jewish tradition.[49] According to the Babylonian Talmud (B. Bat. 14b), the book of Ruth comes at the beginning of the Writings, maybe because the events narrated belong to the time of the judges (Ruth 1:1).[50] In that baraita, the relevant listing is "Ruth and Psalms and Job and Proverbs" (coupled together in the way indicated), so that this is a four-book mini-collection, with Ruth (ending with the genealogy of David) positioned as a preface to Psalms, and Psalms-Job-Proverbs forming a tripartite wisdom collection. "Qoheleth" is next in line, unconnected by the copula to books either before or after it, though it is strategically placed between books also viewed as Solomonic compositions.[51] Then, we find three *pairs* of books, "Song of Songs and Lamentations" (a genre grouping of songs: romantic and mournful), "Daniel and Esther" (both court tales wherein the safety of Jews is under

---

46. For this dating, see Sara Japhet, *I and II Chronicles: A Commentary*, OTL (London: SCM, 1993), 3–28.

47. William Johnstone, "Guilt and Atonement: The Theme of 1 and 2 Chronicles," in *A Word in Season: Essays in Honour of William McKane*, ed. J. D. Martin and P. R. Davies, JSOTSup 42 (Sheffield: Sheffield Academic, 1986), 113–38.

48. William Johnstone, "Hope of Jubilee: The Last Word in the Hebrew Bible," *EvQ* 72 (2000): 307–14.

49. See the tabulation of eleven alternate orders provided by Christian D. Ginsburg, *Introduction to the Massoretico-Critical Edition of the Hebrew Bible* (New York: Ktav, 1966), 7.

50. Rolf Rendtorff, *The Old Testament: An Introduction*, trans. John Bowden (London: SCM, 1985), 245.

51. Marvin H. Pope, *Song of Songs*, AB 7C (Garden City, NY: Doubleday, 1977), 18.

threat), and last, "Ezra(-Nehemiah) and Chronicles" (with their obvious similarities).

In some medieval manuscripts Chronicles comes at the beginning of the Writings; however, the present sequence became established in printed editions of the Bible. In Hebrew Bibles, at the beginning of the Writings is the group of "three great writings" (b. Ber. 57b), Psalms, Job, and Proverbs, in order of decreasing length.[52] In all the varying sequences for Writings, Psalms, Job, and Proverbs are always found together, either in that order or as Psalms-Proverbs-Job. The little group of Megilloth (meaning "scrolls") is placed next, and finally Daniel, Ezra-Nehemiah, and Chronicles. The Writings as a disparate group of books is given a measure of cohesion by the clumping of books with perceived similarities into the three units as specified above. Either positioning of Chronicles—at the beginning or end of the Writings—could be justified,[53] for Chronicles as a world history (beginning, as it does, with Adam [1 Chr 1:1]) makes an appropriate closure for the canon, which begins with Genesis, while its obvious similarities to Kings (on which it draws) means that at the beginning of Writings it helps to bridge Prophets and Writings.

The order of the five books of the Megilloth in the Leningrad Codex (B 19[A]), which is the base of the *Biblia Hebraica Stuttgartensia*, and in Sephardic codices, appears to be based on traditional notions of chronology: Ruth, Song of Songs (written by a young Solomon?), Ecclesiastes (written by Solomon when he was old?), Lamentations, and Esther.[54] It is usually said that these five books are grouped together for liturgical reasons, due to their public reading at the five main annual festivals, but this rationale has been questioned by Timothy Stone, who argues that the process was the reverse: It

---

52. Beckwith sees considerations of size as the dominating factor in the order of books (excluding the Former Prophets) in the Baba Batra listing (*Old Testament Canon*, 160–62). The baraita implies that the order of the Writings is meant to be chronological (= when authored) with the exception of Job, so that Sweeney is mistaken in thinking that a chronological principle is only reflected in the ordering of the Greek OT.

53. Japhet, *I and II Chronicles*, 2.

54. There is, however, some minor variability in the codices. See the tables provided by Michèle Dukan, *La Bible hébraïque: Les codices copiés en Orient et dans la zone séfarade avant 1280*, Bibliologia 22 (Turnhout: Brepols, 2006), 67; Peter Brandt, *Endgestalten des Kanons: Das Arrangement der Schriften Israels in der jüdischen und christlichen Bibel*, BBB 131 (Berlin: Philo, 2001), 148–71. The Aleppo Codex appears to have the same order as the Leningrad Codex, but due to damage, leaves are missing after several words in Song 3:11a. On Ecclesiastes, see Louis Ginzberg, *The Legends of the Jews*, trans. Henrietta Szold (Philadelphia: Jewish Publication Society of America, 1911), 6:301–2.

was because of the existence of the five-book grouping that Ruth, Song of Songs, and Ecclesiastes, in particular, began to be read at feasts, following the example of the obvious fit of Esther with Purim (see Esth 9).[55] Certainly, the link of Ruth with the Feast of Weeks, Song of Songs with Passover, and Ecclesiastes with Booths (Tabernacles) is not strong and could be viewed as manufactured.[56]

In other Hebrew Bibles, especially those used by Ashkenazic Jews, the order of the Megilloth reflects the sequence of the annual cycle of the major Jewish festivals (assuming the year starts with the month of Nisan [= March-April]): Song of Songs (Passover), Ruth (Weeks), Lamentations (Ninth of Ab), Ecclesiastes (Booths), and Esther (Purim).[57] The reading of the Song of Songs at Passover suggests that the song is viewed as an expression of God's love for Israel.[58] Ruth, read at the Feast of Weeks, during the wheat harvest, picks up the mention of the barley and wheat harvests in the book. Lamentations can be viewed as a response to the destruction of Solomon's temple on the ninth of the month of Ab. Reading Ecclesiastes at Tabernacles (Booths) reminds the people of the difficulties of their forefathers in the wilderness and reflects on the futility of life in general, and, most obvious of all, Esther is the rescue story behind the feast of Purim.

In the order of books Proverbs, Ruth, and Song of Songs (*BHS*), both Ruth and Song of Songs develop the picture of the virtuous and assertive woman pictured in Proverbs 31, and the woman is the main speaker in the song.[59] When followed by Song of Songs, the romance aspect of the book of Ruth is highlighted. Then, Ecclesiastes, Lamentations, and Esther follow in that order. The liturgical use of the Megilloth is further supported by the fact that it is placed directly after the Pentateuch in the editions of the Hebrew Bible in

---

55. Timothy H. Stone, *The Compilational History of the Megilloth: Canon, Contoured Intertextuality and Meaning in the Writings*, FAT 2/59 (Tübingen: Mohr Siebeck, 2013), 105–11.

56. See Peter S. Knobel, *The Targum of Qohelet: Translated, with a Critical Introduction, Apparatus, and Notes*, ArBib 15 (Collegeville, MN: Liturgical Press, 1991), 4–5.

57. L. B. Wolfenson, "Implications of the Place of the Book of Ruth in Editions, Manuscripts, and Canon of the Old Testament," HUCA 1 (1924): 157.

58. There is a long and distinguished history of this interpretation both in Judaism and the church. More than merely human sexual love may be in view. See Mark W. Elliot, "Ethics and Aesthetics in the Song of Songs," TynBul 45 (1994): 137–52.

59. See Tremper Longman III, Song of Songs, NICOT (Grand Rapids: Eerdmans, 2001), 2; and see the statistics provided by Athalya Brenner, "Women Poets and Authors," in *A Feminist Companion to the Song of Songs*, ed. Athalya Brenner (Sheffield: JSOT, 1993), 88.

the fifteenth and sixteenth centuries,[60] for the Pentateuch and the Megilloth are the only portions read in their entirety in the lectionary of the synagogue.

The Cyrus decree brackets the books of Ezra-Nehemiah and Chronicles in that order (Ezra 1:1-4; 2 Chr 36:22-23). After the people focus of Ezra-Nehemiah, with its many lists of names (e.g., Ezra 2; 8; Neh 3; 7), the reader meets the genealogies of 1 Chronicles 1-9, though H. G. M. Williamson has successfully debunked the earlier scholarly consensus that subsumed both books under the common authorship of the Chronicler.[61] Whenever the two books are placed side by side in Hebrew orders, Ezra-Nehemiah is *followed* by Chronicles, which would discourage an understanding that interprets them in terms of chronological continuity and theological homogeneity. Ezra 1 is not to be read as just picking up the story line from 2 Chronicles 36. Nor does the presence of some common themes (e.g., temple, priests) mean that the author of Ezra-Nehemiah and the Chronicler have identical theologies. Instead of being at the end of the Writings as in the standard editions, Chronicles in the oldest medieval codices (Aleppo and Leningrad) is at the beginning of the whole unit, so that with Ezra-Nehemiah, Chronicles forms an envelope around the Writings, providing a unifying and ordering framework for them.

According to David Noel Freedman, the major themes and emphases in the Chronicler's work are exemplified in the other associated works.[62] David and Solomon are prominent in Chronicles, and so there is in the Writings a heavy concentration of works connected with or attributed to the house of David. The two books that follow Chronicles, Psalms and Proverbs, are directly connected with the founding dynasts, David and Solomon.[63] Chronicles followed by Psalms gives the poetic pieces of the Psalter a liturgical setting in the musical cultus organized by David (see 1 Chr 23-27; 2 Chr 7:6; 8:14; 23:18; 29:25-30; 35:15), and a number of psalmic titles help to cement such a connection (e.g., the titles of Pss 42-50; 62).[64] The book of Ruth may be treated as part

---

60. For details, see Ginsburg, *Introduction to the Massoretico-Critical Edition*, 3-4; Wolfenson, "Implications of the Place," 155 n. 13.

61. H. G. M. Williamson, *Israel in the Books of Chronicles* (Cambridge: Cambridge University Press, 1977), 1-70.

62. David Noel Freedman, "The Symmetry of the Hebrew Bible," *ST* 46 (1992): 96.

63. There is psalmic material in Chronicles, most notably 1 Chr 16:7-36, which shows close relation to Pss 96; 105-6.

64. David L. Petersen, "Portraits of David: Canonical and Otherwise," *Int* 40 (1986): 130-42.

of the prehistory of David, since Ruth and Boaz are the great-grandparents of David (Ruth 4:18–22). The Song of Songs (e.g., 3:11) and Qoheleth (read as royal autobiography; e.g., 1:1, 12) both have connections with Solomon. The rescue story in Esther provides a happy ending to the Megilloth, especially when read after Lamentations. Daniel is in this position because of the court tales (Dan 1–6) that connect with tales of a similar character in Esther and Ezra-Nehemiah. Daniel following Esther (in the Talmud the order is reversed) provides a theological explanation for the confidence expressed in the book of Esther concerning the survival of the Jewish race in the genocidal crisis depicted in the book (Esth 6:13).

CHAPTER 1 IN SUMMARY

With regard to the orders of the books that make up the Hebrew Bible, the following may be said by way of summary. The ordering of books according to story line would seem to explain the sequence of books in the Pentateuch and the Former Prophets. The books of the Latter Prophets also are ordered according to chronology, whether the sequence is Isaiah, Jeremiah, Ezekiel, and the Twelve (MT), or Jeremiah, Ezekiel, Isaiah, and the Twelve (b. B. Bat. 14b). In these prophetic books the highs and lows of the covenant relationship between YHWH and Israel are plotted through time. The order in the Writings may in part reflect the presumed order of composition, with Davidic and Solomonic works at the beginning and Persian-period compositions at the end (Esther onward). It is not true, therefore, that only the Greek Old Testament is shaped by a historical principle.[65] In almost every case, the location of a book relative to other books in the Hebrew canon, whether in terms of the grouping in which it is placed or the books that follow or precede it, has hermeneutical significance. Therefore, a consideration of book order can assist in the process of interpretation and an appreciation of the contents of Scripture.

---

65. See the next chapter.

GUIDELINES FOR INTERPRETING
THE ORDER OF THE HEBREW CANON

1. Alternative canonical orders remind the reader that book order is a paratextual feature, and different orders suggest alternative (but often compatible) ways of reading the same book.

2. One of the features to notice when studying any biblical book is its position in the canon of the Old Testament. In which canonical section is it placed? What are its canonical neighbors?

3. When a book has more than one location in the Hebrew and Greek canonical traditions (e.g., Ruth, Daniel), explore what possible light this may shed on its contents, for more than one significant theme or genre may be present in the book, explaining its different locations.

4. Explore how neighboring books in the canon interact and behave as *conversation partners*, leading to a richer understanding of the meaning of the individual books (e.g., when Esther is put beside Daniel).

5. An Old Testament canon ending with either Ezra-Nehemiah or Chronicles shows that God's purposes await completion, for both arrangements prepare for the culmination of salvation history plotted in the New Testament.

2

THE STRUCTURE OF
THE GREEK CANON

INTRODUCTION

In the previous chapter, I surveyed and analyzed the order of the books in the Hebrew Bible, viewing the ordering of the books as an element of the paratext of Scripture. I now turn to the structure of the Old Testament in the Greek tradition, which will allow comparison between the Hebrew and Greek orders.[1] The Greek canon presents salvation history as a progressive movement through temporal stages toward an eschatological goal.[2] According to Sweeney, this gives the Greek canon a primarily historical orientation, providing a linear account of the divine purpose, moving from the creation to the consummation as promised by the prophets. By placing the prophets at the end of the canon, the Greek Old Testament points beyond itself to a future fulfillment, and the reader is led to consider eschatology as the guiding thread through the multifarious books of which Scripture is composed.[3] Despite the appropriateness of this configuration of books for a Christian reading of the Old Testament, the evidence is that the Greek arrangement of the books is a *pre-Christian* order and not shaped by Christian preconceptions. Contrary to Sweeney, *both* Tanak and Greek canon can be viewed as leading to the New Testament.[4]

---

1. For an earlier version of material in this chapter, see Gregory Goswell, "The Order of the Books in the Greek Old Testament," *JETS* 52 (2009): 449–66. Used with permission.

2. Sweeney, "Tanak versus Old Testament," 359.

3. John Barton, *Oracles of God: Perceptions of Ancient Prophecy in Israel after the Exile* (London: Darton, Longman & Todd, 1986), 21–23.

4. See Gregory Goswell, "Having the Last Say: The End of the OT," *JETS* 58 (2015): 15–30.

It is commonly asserted that the Greek canon basically transposes the second and third sections in the Hebrew ordering of the books. In this way the prophetic books (= Latter Prophets) close the Old Testament canon and, from a Christian perspective, provide a transition to the New Testament, signaling that the main connection of the New Testament is with the Old Testament prophetic word pointing forward to the consummation of God's purposes in Jesus Christ. Actually, it is only Vaticanus (B) of the three famous fourth- and fifth-century codices that places the prophetic books at the end of the canon, the Minor Prophets preceding the Major Prophets, with Daniel the last book listed. In Sinaiticus (א) and Alexandrinus (A) the poetic books are placed last, so that the final section in these two codices is somewhat similar to Writings of the Hebrew canon.[5] This is an indicator that we should not overplay the difference between the (relatively settled) Hebrew order and the by no means uniform Greek orders of the canonical books.[6] Despite all the variety in the Greek (and Latin) lists, what we can say is that the books Genesis-Ruth are a set grouping (Octateuch) and are always in premier position; Ruth is always placed after (or joined to) Judges; Chronicles almost always follows Kings; Lamentations, when separately listed, is placed after or near Jeremiah; and Daniel is almost invariably put with prophetic books.

These are clear trends and distinct differences from the Hebrew ordering, but we should not overplay the difference in ordering or view them as Jewish versus Christian canons.

Isaac Kalimi thinks otherwise and contrasts what he calls the Zionist motivation for the tripartite Hebrew canon closed by Chronicles and its call to return to Jerusalem (2 Chr 36:22-23) with what is found in the Christian Bible. He claims that Christianity adopted the order ending with Malachi because it suited its theology to have the Old Testament finish with a prophecy of the messianic era as a *bridge* to the New Testament (see Mal 3:1; 4:5-6). In other words, Kalimi reads the alternate canonical endings in terms of an ideological clash

---

5. See the appendix to this chapter. There is no uniform Greek order. See B. Botte and Pierre-Maurice Bogaert, "Septante et versions grecques," in *Supplément au Dictionnaire de la Bible*, ed. L. Pirot and A. Roberts (Paris: Letouzey & Ané, 1996), 12:541-43.

6. See the tables of lists of early Greek (Eastern) and Latin (Western) orders up to the fifth century provided in Lee Martin McDonald, *The Biblical Canon: Its Origin, Transmission, and Authority* (Peabody, MA: Hendrickson, 2007), 439-42.

between Jews and Christians.[7] Jack Miles is right in saying that the Hebrew Bible and the Old Testament are not the same thing—he is thinking of the different organization of their basically identical contents—but, like Kalimi, he goes too far when he claims that, since Christianity believed that the life of Christ fulfilled Old Testament prophecy, "the Christian editor edited the Hebrew Bible to reflect this Christian belief."[8] According to Miles, it was those responsible for ordering the Christian Old Testament who *shifted* the prophetic books from the middle of the Jewish canon to the end. These kinds of assertions have been endlessly repeated, but that does not make them correct.

In the case of Malachi, though readers of the English Bible are accustomed to finding this prophecy as the last book of the Old Testament, this arrangement is of comparatively recent origin and is not found in any Hebrew, Greek, or Latin canonical order.[9] Its late origin is due to the modification of the Vulgate tradition made in the Protestant Bible of the sixteenth century. In other words, only since the Reformation has Malachi closed the Old Testament. The Reformers rejected the canonical status of the Apocrypha, and this led to the removal of 1-2 Maccabees from after Malachi.[10] This adjustment of biblical book order *within* the Christian tradition had the unpremeditated consequence of making Malachi the last book of the Old Testament. This outcome had nothing to do with controversy with Jews but was due to disputes among Christians about the extent of the canon. Until that time the

---

7. Isaac Kalimi, *The Retelling of Chronicles in Jewish Tradition and Literature: A Historical Journey* (Winona Lake, IN: Eisenbrauns, 2009), 30-31. Nahum Sarna makes a similar contrast; see "The Authority and Interpretation of Scripture in Jewish Tradition," in *Understanding Scripture: Explorations of Jewish and Christian Traditions of Interpretation*, ed. Clemens Thoma and Michael Wyschogrod (New York: Paulist, 1987), 12; cf. Northrop Frye, *The Great Code: The Bible and Literature* (London: Routledge & Kegan Paul, 1983), 206-7.

8. Jack Miles, *God: A Biography* (New York: Knopf, 1995), 16, 18.

9. For a detailed listing of the various Latin orders (212 are provided), see Samuel Berger, *Histoire de la Vulgate: pendant les premiers siècles du moyen âge* (Hildesheim: Olms, 1976), 331-39. The only exception is the Mommsen Catalogue, an early canon of biblical books, known also as "the Cheltenham List," a tenth-century Latin manuscript which was discovered by the classical scholar Theodor Mommsen in 1885 at Cheltenham in England. A few years later he found another copy of the list in an eighth- or ninth-century manuscript at St. Gall in Switzerland. The list probably originated in North Africa in the fourth century. See William Sanday, "The Cheltenham List of the Canonical Books of the New Testament and of the Writings of Cyprian," S. R. Driver, T. K. Cheyne, and W. Sanday, Studia Biblica et Ecclesiastica: Essays Chiefly in Biblical and Patristic Criticism, Volume 3 (Oxford: Clarendon, 1891), 217-325, esp. 222-23.

10. For early Protestant editions of the Bible, see Roland Deines, "The Term and Concept of Scripture," in *What Is Bible?*, ed. Karin Finsterbusch and Armin Lange, CBET 67 (Leuven: Peeters, 2012), 240-48; cf. Thomas Hieke, "Jedem Ende wohnt ein Zauber inne ... Schlussverse jüdischer und christlicher Kanonausprägungen," in *Formen des Kanons: Studien zu Ausprägungen des biblischen*

main contenders for the book in final position in the various Old Testament canons were Ezra-Nehemiah, Chronicles, Daniel, and (only rarely) Esther.[11]

The early church used the Septuagint, and, for that reason, the influence of this tradition is reflected in the various sequences of the Greek Bible now preserved in ancient Christian codices. The early church did not adopt this canonical order because it supposedly reflected Christian values, but because the predominantly Greek-speaking church found the Septuagint convenient and of practical use both for teaching its converts and in apologetic argument with Jews, until Christian appropriation of the Septuagint caused most Jews to abandon it and replace it with other Greek renderings of the proto-Masoretic Hebrew text (e.g., Theodotion). What I am arguing is that the reason behind the Christian adoption of the Greek Old Testament was simply language. Many Christians in the early centuries spoke Greek, but did not understand Hebrew, and so used the Septuagint.

The four-part structure—Pentateuch, historical books, poetic books, and prophetic books—reflects the *generic* character of the books that comprise the Greek Old Testament, and, in contrast to the Tanak, there is no disparate literary category of Writings. The four sections together represent, according to Sweeney, a progressive movement of history: the remote past, the recent past, the present, and the future. The Pentateuch depicts the distant past, for it describes the origins of the world and of Israel.[12] The historical books recount the more recent past, up to and including the Persian period. The poetic books reflect perennial (and therefore present) concerns. Finally, the prophetic books describe the future envisaged by the prophets. Given their position in the Christian canon, they naturally point to the New Testament as the fulfillment of prophetic visions. Such historical periodization is also evident in the larger two-part canonical structure of Old Testament succeeded by New Testament.

The order of books in the Greek Old Testament in most Greek Bibles and canon lists (exemplified by Vaticanus) is as follows:[13]

Kanons von der Antike bis zum 19. Jahrhundert, ed. Thomas Hieke, SBS 228 (Stuttgart: Katholisches Bibelwerk, 2013), 245–46.

11. For the last alternative, see Gregory Goswell, "The Place of the Book of Esther in the Canon," *TJ* 37 (2016): 169–70.

12. Sweeney, "Tanak versus Old Testament," 360–61.

13. Asterisks indicate noncanonical works. The order of the Book of the Twelve is Hosea, Amos, Micah, Joel, Obadiah, Jonah, Nahum, etc.

Pentateuch

    Genesis

    Exodus

    Leviticus

    Numbers

    Deuteronomy

Historical Books

    Joshua

    Judges

    Ruth

    1–2 Kingdoms (= 1–2 Samuel)

    3–4 Kingdoms (= 1–2 Kings)

    1–2 Paraleipomena (= 1–2 Chronicles)

    Esdras A*

    Ezra-Nehemiah

Poetic Books

    Psalms (+ Psalm 151*)

    Proverbs

    Ecclesiastes

    Song of Solomon

    Job (+ Wisdom*, Sirach*)

    Esther (+ Judith*, Tobit*)

Prophetic Books

> The Book of the Twelve[#]
>
> Isaiah
>
> Jeremiah (+ Baruch*)
>
> Lamentations (+ Epistle of Jeremiah*) Ezekiel
>
> Daniel (+ Susanna*, Bel and the Dragon*)

THE PENTATEUCH

The Pentateuch has the same premier position in the Greek Bible as in the Hebrew canon, and one would not expect its canonical placement to change in any listing of Old Testament books, given that it describes the origin of the world and of Israel. The large area of commonality between the alternative canons should not be overlooked. Although the five books of the Pentateuch are followed by Joshua–Kings, classified as Former Prophets in the Hebrew canon, the fact that the Greek canon, as represented by the three great codices,[14] is consistent in the ordering of the books from Genesis to 2 Chronicles could be taken as suggesting that the Pentateuch is being viewed through the same *historical* lens as the historical books—that is, the story line is the important thing. On the other hand, the Chronicler cites a number of works authored by prophetic figures, if that is what the titles do indicate (e.g., "the records of the seer Samuel" [1 Chr 29:29]), which suggests that Chronicles itself embodies a prophetic representation and interpretation of historical events.[15] It is possible, then, that Sweeney and others overstress the differences between the two canons, for Joshua to 2 Chronicles may well be viewed as prophetic works even in the Greek tradition (see the portrait of prophets as historians in Josephus [*Ag. Ap.* 1.38–41]) and read as drawing lessons from history.

The creation backdrop (Gen 1) to subsequent events in the Pentateuch gives them a universal context and testifies of God's interest in humanity as a whole. The disastrous consequences of the fall and the spread of sin affect all humanity and disrupt the unity of the race (11:1–9). The divine call and

---

14. Vaticanus (B 03), Sinaiticus (א 01) and Alexandrinus (A 02).
15. Goswell, "Titles without Texts," 89–92.

commission of Abram is with the aim that the peoples of the world will find blessing through the descendants of Abram (12:1–3). For the most part, the patriarchs' relationship with other people groups is portrayed positively. The patriarchs strive to maintain peaceful relations with the Canaanites (e.g., 34:30), and the family of Jacob finally finds a safe refuge in a foreign land (Egypt). Balaam's fourth and final oracle speaks of Israel's dominion over various named nations and says, "A scepter shall rise out of Israel" (Num 24:17). At the end of the Pentateuch, though Israel is the focus of attention in the sermons of Moses, the issue of the nations is not ignored, if nothing else, due to the presence of the Canaanites in the land to be conquered. God's dealings with Israel take place on an international stage (e.g., Deut 4:5–8; 9:26–28; 15:6). Underlying such passages is the idea that Israel is divinely chosen to be an example for other nations to emulate.[16]

There is nothing in the Pentateuch, therefore, that is incompatible with the world mission that takes place in the New Testament; however, there is also no reason to see the theme of the nations as particularly highlighted in the Pentateuch.[17] The focus is rather on the unfaithfulness of God's people and, notwithstanding this, God's gracious dealings with them in the covenant relationship. The moral failings of the patriarchs—Abraham (Gen 12:10–20; 20:1–18), Isaac (26:6–16), Jacob (ch. 27), and Judah (ch. 38)—are not hidden or excused, and these revelations prepare the reader for the persistent unfaithfulness of Israel in the rest of the Pentateuch. The sin of the golden calf in Exodus 32–34 is a notable juncture, as is God's judgment of the rebellious wilderness generation for refusing to go up to the land (Num 13–14). Moses's preaching in Deuteronomy 9 makes clear that Israel is not receiving the land "because of [their] righteousness, for [they] are a stubborn people" (9:6). The future prospect provided by chapters 29 and 31–32 includes the expectation that Israel will fail to keep the law as required.[18] Moses anticipates the apostasy of God's covenant people and their expulsion from the land. The inverse of this theme is the revelation of the grace of God in being willing to forgive

---

16. T. Desmond Alexander, *From Paradise to the Promised Land: An Introduction to the Main Themes of the Pentateuch* (Carlisle: Paternoster, 1995), 178.

17. For the previous paragraph I depend on Sweeney. In surveying the Septuagint, he emphasizes the theme of Israel's interaction with the nations. Before we follow him in this, we should acknowledge the danger of reading back into the Greek OT the special focus on the gentiles in the New Testament.

18. See Paul A. Barker, "The Theology of Deuteronomy 27," *TynBul* 49 (1998): 277–303.

his people, the explanation being his gracious character (Exod 34:6-7; cf. Num 14:18-19). The hope is God's promise to circumcise the heart of the nation and bring them back to the land (Deut 30:1-10).[19] The interpretation of the Pentateuch is little affected by whether it is in the Hebrew or Greek canon.

THE HISTORICAL BOOKS

The bringing together of various books into one section (Joshua–Esther) suggests that these books are being read according to a historical perspective,[20] which is a feature of the Greek canon generally. The disadvantage in calling these books "histories" is that it may obscure for the reader that historical writings are not limited to this second section; indeed, the Bible as a whole has a narrative framework. The Pentateuch sketches the history of the world from creation to the death of Moses. The historical books (Joshua–Esther) present the history of Israel as one of failure, but then, so do the Former Prophets in the Hebrew Bible (Joshua–Kings), which move from land entrance to expulsion from the land. Israel gains the land in the book of Joshua and loses it in Kings.

According to Sweeney, the relations between Israel and the nations are traced through Joshua–Kings mainly in terms of antagonism, and this is again the theme he chooses to highlight.[21] For example, these history books narrate the conquest of Canaan (Joshua), the oppression of Israel by foreign kings (Judges), the Philistine threat (1 Samuel), the victories of David over surrounding nations (2 Sam 8), and the final defeat and deportation of God's people at the hands of the Assyrians (2 Kgs 17) and the Babylonians (2 Kgs 25).

This is not the only theme in these books, but it is one that shows their ready compatibility with the New Testament, which is the reason Sweeney selects it for special mention. The narrower scope of Chronicles, only tracing the southern line of kings, does not significantly change the picture, with the book closing with the Persian king Cyrus as the undisputed master of the world (2 Chr 36:22-23). In Ezra–Nehemiah, steps are taken to break up exogamous marriages. The antiforeigner attitude is reinforced by the inclusion of Esther at the conclusion of this canonical section, for in that book

---

19. J. Gary Millar, *Now Choose Life: Theology and Ethics in Deuteronomy*, NSBT 6 (Leicester: Apollos, 1998), 161–80.

20. The sequence is found in the English Bible (and in Sinaiticus).

21. For this paragraph, I depend on Sweeney, "Tanak versus Old Testament," 363.

the Jews slaughter their gentile adversaries (Esth 9). On this reading, the books Joshua-Esther show that God's intention that the world be blessed through Israel appears to be frustrated and remains unrealized. There is no reason, however, to see the theme of Jew-gentile relations as the leading theme of Joshua-Esther in the Greek canon. When history is reviewed in the Old Testament and a lesson drawn from God's dealings with his people in successive periods of history, the persistent focus of the presentation is the unfaithfulness of God's people and yet the graciousness of God's dealings with them. This is the case whether the review takes the form of historical psalms (e.g., Pss 78; 105-7),[22] speeches and summaries (e.g., 1 Sam 12; 2 Kgs 17), prophetic surveys (Hos 2; Ezek 16; 20; 23), or postexilic penitential prayers (Dan 9; Neh 9).

If a historical principle is reflected in Genesis-Esther in the Greek tradition, the periodization is in terms of the ups and downs of God's dealings with his wayward people. The book of Joshua ends with sober warnings (Josh 23-24). This is followed by the cycle of unfaithfulness plotted in Judges 2-3 and illustrated in the rest of the book. The people reject God in asking for a king (1 Sam 8). David is shown to have feet of clay (2 Sam 11-20). With only a few exceptions, the kings of Judah and Israel are reprobates (Kings), and the final paragraph of 2 Kings (25:27-30) gives no prospect of a revival of the house of David (agreeing with Martin Noth's minimalist reading of these final verses).[23] The presentation of Chronicles is little different in this regard and closes with Cyrus as world ruler (2 Chr 36:22-23).[24] Ezra-Nehemiah ends with the failure of God's people to do what they pledged (Neh 13:4-31). Whatever the reason for the nonmention of God in the book of Esther, the book is hardly a glowing endorsement of the character of Jews in the diaspora.

The placement of Chronicles after Kings in the Greek order makes it look like an addendum and supplement, and the Greek title assigned to it—"[The books] of the things left out" (*Paraleipomenōn*)—also has the effect of downgrading its importance. Chronicles has had to live in the shadow of Kings until the recent flowering of Chronicles scholarship. After a recapitulation of preceding events provided by the genealogies of 1 Chronicles 1-9, the

22. Erik Haglund, *Historical Motifs in the Psalms*, ConBOT 23 (Uppsala: Gleerup, 1984).

23. Martin Noth, *The Deuteronomistic History*, JSOTSup 15 (Sheffield: JSOT, 1981), 98.

24. William Riley, *King and Cultus in Chronicles: Worship and the Reinterpretation of History*, JSOTSup 160 (Sheffield: Sheffield Academic, 1993), esp. ch. 3.

detailed story is picked up at the death of Saul (1 Chr 10 [= 1 Sam 31]), so that Chronicles could be understood as supplementing the information given in 2 Samuel and 1–2 Kings. Only the brief final paragraph of 2 Chronicles (36:22–23) takes the reader beyond the point at which the account closes in 2 Kings. What is more, that only the Judean line of kings is traced might confirm the reader in the impression of Chronicles as an appendix to the story given a broader scope in Kings, but Chronicles is better viewed as world history, seeing that it begins with Adam (1 Chr 1:1). The effect of placing Chronicles, Ezra-Nehemiah, and Esther after Kings (rather than in the Writings) is that the history plotted in Joshua to Kings is extended into the postexilic period. In the Greek Bible, these three books are viewed as histories rather than as moral tales, as they might be construed in their alternate setting in the Hebrew canon. However, the distinction I have drawn is not absolute, for in both canons the story recounted has moral applications.

The Greek order of Chronicles *followed* by Ezra-Nehemiah gives an impression of continuity and may obscure for the reader the theological distinctives of each work.[25] The "overlap" (as it is often called) in 2 Chronicles 36:22–23 and Ezra 1:1–3a seems to confirm their continuity, but that description prejudges the issue. With regard to the Greek codices, an ellipsis in Sinaiticus makes it unclear whether 2 Esdras (= Ezra-Nehemiah) directly follows Chronicles. In Alexandrinus, 1 and 2 Esdras are nowhere near Chronicles. In Vaticanus, the deuterocanonical book of 1 Esdras (= Esdras A) intrudes between Chronicles and Ezra-Nehemiah, which is an appropriate setting for it, in that it reproduces (and rewrites) the substance of 2 Chronicles 35–36, the whole of Ezra (partly rearranged), and then jumps to Nehemiah 8 (which also features the figure of Ezra), so that it spans Chronicles and Ezra-Nehemiah. First Esdras is a *rewriting* of the biblical text to emphasize the contribution of Josiah, Zerubbabel, and Ezra in the reform of Israel's worship, so that it has a different orientation to the people focus of Ezra-Nehemiah.[26] In 1 Esdras, Zerubbabel is viewed as in the line of wise Solomon who built the temple, and his Davidic lineage is mentioned (1 Esd 5:5), whereas it is not in Ezra-Nehemiah. Tamara Eskenazi argues that 1 Esdras was in fact written

---

25. Gregory Goswell, "Putting the Book of Chronicles in Its Place," *JETS* 60 (2017): 283–99.

26. Tamara Cohn Eskenazi, *In an Age of Prose: A Literary Approach to Ezra-Nehemiah*, SBLMS 36 (Atlanta: Scholars Press, 1988).

by the Chronicler,[27] so that its placement after Chronicles in Vaticanus is fitting. The upshot of all this is that putting Ezra-Nehemiah straight after Chronicles, as in the English Bible, runs the danger of blurring the individual teaching of each book.

Ezra-Nehemiah is followed by Esther (only in Sinaiticus) because it is set in the reign of Ahasuerus (Esth 1:1), and this king (mentioned in Ezra 4:6) preceded Artaxerxes, who was the royal master of Ezra and Nehemiah. The account of Esther's marriage to a Persian king, therefore, follows Ezra-Nehemiah and that book's negative reference to Solomon's marriages to foreign women (Neh 13:26). The book of Esther continues the negativity about foreigners that is present in Ezra-Nehemiah (e.g., Ezra 9:1-2). Mordecai's and Esther's disobedience to the king is based on their Jewish identities. Mordecai's refusal to bow before Haman is "because [Mordecai] told them he was a Jew" (Esth 3:4). In the three Greek codices, Esther is always placed with Judith and Tobit (though the order is Esther-Tobit-Judith in Sinaiticus and Alexandrinus). These three books teach diaspora ethics, an example being the model provided by the pious, law-abiding character of Tobit as shown in the description of his godly ways (Tob 1) and his instructions to his son, Tobias (Tob 4). In the same vein, Mordecai and especially Esther serve as models of energetic effort and risk-taking for the sake of the welfare of the Jewish people.[28] Judith's beauty and wisdom are emphasized in that she beguiles and cuts off the head of Holofernes, commander-in-chief of Nebuchadnezzar's army. With regard to the genre of these three books, they are placed in different positions in the codices. Sinaiticus treats them as histories (seeing that they are narratives), and they are followed by 1 and 4 Maccabees. In Vaticanus, they follow (and join) wisdom books, and both entertain and instruct readers on the need to sustain a Jewish ethos in the midst of a pagan world.

There is a preponderance of feminine imagery for wisdom in Proverbs. For example, in Proverbs 1-9, the adulterous and foolish woman stands over

---

27. Tamara Cohn Eskenazi, "The Chronicler and the Composition of 1 Esdras," *CBQ* 48 (1986): 39-61.

28. Sandra Beth Berg, *The Book of Esther: Motifs, Themes and Structure*, SBLDS 44 (Missoula, MT: Scholars Press, 1979).

and against Lady Wisdom, and they are the two potential lovers of the son,[29] and the final embodiment and epitome of wisdom in Proverbs is the "woman of worth" of Proverbs 31. This makes it appropriate to have female moral exemplars in the books of Esther and Judith (and let us not forget Sarah in the book of Tobit). In Alexandrinus, Esther-Tobit-Judith follow Daniel (with its narrative additions of Susanna and Bel and the Dragon), so that like Daniel, they are classed as paradigmatic diaspora tales. In Alexandrinus, the grouping of Esther-Tobit-Judith is followed by 1 Esdras, Ezra-Nehemiah, and 1-4 Maccabees, indicating that all belong together as postexilic histories.

THE POETIC BOOKS

The Psalter, by its placement between Job and Proverbs in the English Bible (conforming to the order in the Latin Vulgate),[30] is designated as a wisdom book, and this classification is supported by the wisdom psalms sprinkled through it (e.g., Pss 1; 32; 34; 37; 49; 112; 128) and by the various other psalms that show a wisdom influence (e.g., Pss 25; 31; 39-40; 62; 78; 92; 94; 111; 119; 127).[31] This setting makes Psalms a wisdom book rather than a hymn book for temple praise, despite the musical notation found in some psalm titles (e.g., "To the choirmaster"), such that this canonical position adds support to the thesis of Gerald H. Wilson, who reads the Psalter along these lines.[32] The religious connections of the Psalter, however, do not have to be denied entirely and are reflected in some of the titles assigned to this book (e.g., *Psaltērion*).

In the Greek codices, the Psalter commences a section usually classified as poetic, but seeing that most of the other books in this section are obviously wisdom in character (i.e., Proverbs, Ecclesiastes, Job, Wisdom, and Sirach), it seems best to view the section in toto as consisting of wisdom books. Psalms is followed by either Proverbs (Vaticanus and Sinaiticus) or

---

29. Gale A. Yee, "I Have Perfumed My Bed with Myrrh: The Foreign Woman in Proverbs 1-9," *JSOT* 43 (1989): 53-68.

30. Also in the *Prologus Galeatus* of Jerome.

31. While scholars do not agree on which psalms are to be classified as wisdom poems, the four psalms on which there is widest agreement are Pss 1; 37; 49; 112. See Roland E. Murphy, "The Classification 'Wisdom Psalms,' " in *Congress Volume Bonn 1962*, ed. G. W. Anderson et al., VTSup 9 (Leiden: Brill, 1963), 156-67.

32. See Gerald H. Wilson, "Shaping the Psalter: A Consideration of Editorial Linkage in the Book of Psalms," in *The Shape and Shaping of the Psalter*, ed. J. Clinton McCann Jr., JSOTSup 159 (Sheffield: JSOT, 1993), esp. 78-81, where he focuses on the apparent clustering of wisdom psalms in book 1 (Pss 1-41) and in book 5 (Pss 107-50), giving a "wisdom frame" around the whole Psalter.

Job (Alexandrinus). The placement of the Song of Solomon in this section makes it *another* wisdom book, with the Solomon connection in the Greek title adding weight to this classification. The Song is more than an effusive outpouring of amorous sentiment but is a means of instruction; see, for example, the warnings in the refrain-like verses at 2:7; 3:5; and 8:4 about the power of love. The position of Job at the beginning of this section in the English Bible is presumably due to chronological priority, given the setting of the story in the patriarchal age.[33]

The juxtapositioning of Proverbs and Ecclesiastes (with Job not far away) is a sign that Job and Ecclesiastes are not to be viewed as "wisdom in revolt" or "protest wisdom,"[34] with these two books, according to this theory, aiming to correct or counter Proverbs. Instead, the propinquity of the three books assumes and asserts their ready compatibility, as does the "epilogue" of Ecclesiastes (12:9–14), which closes with the exhortation, "Fear God and keep his commandments" (RSV).[35] Like the other two books, Proverbs insists that no degree of mastery of the rules of wisdom can confer absolute certainty on human actions and their consequences (e.g., 16:1–2, 9; 19:14, 21; 20:24; 21:30–31). A failure to notice this strain of teaching in the book of Proverbs has led many to perceive a tension, if not an irreconcilable conflict, between Job-Ecclesiastes and Proverbs. The truth of the matter is that the three books are aligned in their teaching.

THE PROPHETIC BOOKS

If the prophetic books are placed at the end of the Old Testament (as in Vaticanus), it is implied that prophecy is mainly foretelling, pointing forward to the eschaton, in which God's plan of salvation for Israel and the nations will come to completion. That a number of prophetic books are capped by oracles of hope shows that this is not a tendentious reading of the prophets

---

33. E.g., Job's wealth is in livestock and servants (Job 1:3; cf. Gen 12:16; 13:2–13); he offers sacrifices without priestly mediation and intercedes for others (Job 1:5; 42:7–9; cf. Gen 12:7; 18:22–33); and he lives to a great age (Job 42:16; cf. Gen 25:7).

34. "Wisdom in revolt": *Pace* R. B. Y. Scott, *The Way of Wisdom in the Old Testament* (New York: Macmillan, 1971). "Protest wisdom": as in, e.g., Bruce C. Birch et al., *A Theological Introduction to the Old Testament*, 2nd ed. (Nashville: Abingdon, 2005), 401–23.

35. See Gerald H. Wilson, "'The Words of the Wise': The Intent and Significance of Qohelet 12:9–14," *JBL* 103 (1984): 178–79, who suggests that the phraseology resonates with the content of Qohelet but is sufficiently general to connect to the broader wisdom tradition, particularly Proverbs.

(e.g., Isa 40-66; Ezek 40-48; Amos 9:11-15; Mic 7:8-20). In Vaticanus (B), Alexandrinus (A), and Greek orders generally, the Minor Prophets *precede* the Major Prophets, perhaps because the ministries of Hosea and Amos must have preceded in time that of Isaiah. The accustomed English ordering of these two prophetic blocks is found in Sinaiticus (א). The usual Hebrew order follows a general chronological scheme, beginning with Isaiah, followed by Jeremiah and Ezekiel (his younger contemporary), with the catchall Book of the Twelve at the end.

There is a slight difference in the order of the sequence within the Twelve in the Greek Bible (Hosea, Amos, Micah, Joel, Obadiah, Jonah, Nahum, etc.) compared to the MT.[36] The last six books are in identical sequence in both versions.[37] Significant for interpretation is the fact that oracles with a northern provenance (Hosea, Amos, Jonah), those originating from the Southern Kingdom (Joel, Obadiah, Micah, Nahum, Habakkuk, Zephaniah), and those addressed to postexilic returnees (Haggai, Zechariah, Malachi) are placed together and even mixed together, so that they become in this larger canonical conglomerate the word of God for God's people *irrespective* of time and location. The reference to both northern and southern kings in the superscription in Hosea 1:1 and Amos 1:1 has the same effect. In the Greek canon, the order of Obadiah followed by Jonah is the same as the MT. The juxtapositioning of Jonah and Nahum is supported by the Nineveh orientation of both books (Nah 1:1a: "An oracle concerning Nineveh"). The bringing together of Hosea, Amos, and Micah places these three larger books at the head of the Book of the Twelve, with Micah 1:1 indicating a later dating than either Hosea or Amos, and the smaller books follow in their train, so that size appears to be a contributing factor to the Greek arrangement.

---

36. See Emanuel Tov, *The Greek Minor Prophets Scroll from Naḥal Ḥever (8ḤevXIIgr) (The Seiyâl Collection I)*, DJD 8 (Oxford: Clarendon, 1990). This scroll supports the MT order (the scroll preserving parts of columns containing Jonah–Zechariah).

37. See the comparison and analysis by Marvin. A. Sweeney, "Sequence and Interpretation in the Book of the Twelve," in Nogalski and Sweeney, *Reading and Hearing*, 49–64. In the thirty-four-page codex Washington-Freer 5 (LDAB 3124) the order is Hosea, Amos, Joel, Obadiah, Jonah, Nahum.

THE ALTERNATIVE POSITIONING
OF PARTICULAR OLD TESTAMENT BOOKS

That the books such as Ruth, Lamentations, and Daniel can be placed in quite different positions in the Hebrew Bible and the Greek Old Testament shows that book order reflects evaluation of what a book is about. The positioning of a book due to thematic considerations means that alternative placements are possible, for any book is likely to have more than one theme.

The Book of Ruth

The position of Ruth varies among canons, and the purpose of the present discussion is not to discover the *original* position of Ruth. Are we to read the book of Ruth as a lead-up to David, as a festal scroll (Megilloth), or as an historical book following Judges? There may be no right or wrong answer; rather, the point is that the differing canonical positions make a difference to how one views and reads the book. Different sorts of questions arise out of distinct literary contexts. The popular critical view has been that Ruth is a late work, written against the extreme antiforeigner theology of Ezra and Nehemiah that protested exogamous marriages. Though the MT places Ruth in the third section of the canon, it does not read like a postexilic political tract written against the Ezra-Nehemiah reforms. What is undeniable is that Ruth does not contain any open polemic.

In the listing of books in Baba Batra, Ruth precedes the Psalter and can be read as a prehistory of David the chief psalmist, who is shown in Psalms to be one who "takes refuge" (root ḥsd) in God (Pss 2:11; 7:1; 11:1; 16:1, etc.) just as did his ancestress (Ruth 2:12: "under whose wings you have come to take refuge" [RSV]).[38] This suggests that the heroine, Ruth, is being viewed by the ancient readers as responsible for this canonical order as an embodiment of the implied ethic of the Psalter, in which David turns to God in times of distress.[39] The conjoining of Ruth and the Psalter helps to bring to light the thematic links between the two books, which include the key terms "refuge," "wings," and "kindness." This way of ordering the books highlights the connection of Ruth with David the psalmist, and Ruth personifies the

---

38. Jerome F. D. Creach, *Yahweh as Refuge and the Editing of the Hebrew Psalter*, JSOTSup 217 (Sheffield: Sheffield Academic, 1996).

39. Peter H. W. Lau and Gregory Goswell, *Unceasing Kindness: A Biblical Theology of Ruth*, NSBT 41 (London: Apollos, 2016), 53–70.

implied ethic of total reliance on God as taught in the Psalter. Just as Ruth embodies and experiences God's "kindness" (ḥesed),[40] so also in the Psalter David praises God as the one who "shows kindness to his anointed, to David and his seed for ever" (Ps 18:50 my translation). In Ruth 2:12, Boaz evokes the image of the protecting "wings" (kānāp) of YHWH, the God of Israel, a metaphor that apparently is in no need of explanation or elaboration, with its meaning immediately understood. Indeed, this motif is found a number of times in the Psalter (17:8; 36:7; 57:1; 61:4; etc.).[41] The ancestress of the chief psalmist anticipates the piety of David, who calls on God to defend and help him in his troubles.[42]

Ruth as the first of the Megilloth follows immediately on Proverbs (in the Leningrad Codex) because of a link in their subject matter. Proverbs closes with a poem celebrating the "worthy woman" (31:10, ʾēšet ḥayil), and the book of Ruth goes on to describe just such a woman. In Ruth 3:11, Boaz actually calls Ruth a "worthy woman" (ESV; ʾēšet ḥayil). The description in Proverbs 31:31 fits Ruth ("her deeds will praise her in the gates" [my translation]), about whom Boaz says something very similar (Ruth 3:13), and Proverbs 31:23 applies to Boaz ("Her husband is known in the gates when he sits among the elders of the land" [ESV]), for this sounds like an allusion to the scene in Ruth 4. This placement suggests a reading of Ruth as a wisdom piece, with Ruth the Moabitess as a real life example of the piety taught in Proverbs and embodied in the exemplary woman of Proverbs 31.[43] Ruth followed by Song of Songs in the Megilloth (or preceded by it, according to the order of the annual festivals) emphasizes the love story aspect of Ruth, and Ruth, for its part, gives an agrarian setting for the pastoral images of Song of Songs.[44]

---

40. The English translation supplied reflects the fact that the Hebrew term denotes *non-obligatory* generous action on God's part, as demonstrated by Francis I. Andersen, "Yahweh, the Kind and Sensitive God," in *God Who Is Rich in Mercy: Essays Presented to Dr. D. B. Knox*, ed. Peter T. O'Brien and David G. Peterson (Homebush West, NSW: Lancer Books, 1986), 41–88.

41. Alec Basson, *Divine Metaphors in Selected Hebrew Psalms of Lamentation*, FAT 2/15 (Tübingen: Mohr Siebeck, 2006), 99–100.

42. Gert Kwakkel, "Under Yahweh's Wings," in *Metaphors in the Psalms*, ed. Antje Labahn and Pierre Van Hecke, BETL 231 (Leuven: Peeters, 2010), 143.

43. Carlos Bovell wants to relate Orpah to the "strange woman" of Proverbs. See "Symmetry, Ruth and Canon," *JSOT* 28 (2003): 183–86.

44. Wolfenson, "Implications of the Place," 157. For more, see Gregory Goswell, "Is Ruth Also among the Wise?," in *Exploring Old Testament Wisdom: Literature and Themes*, ed. David G. Firth and Lindsay Wilson (London: Apollos, 2016), 115–33.

On the other hand, Ruth 1:1 locates the action in the period of the judges, and Ruth forms a sharp contrast with the story of the Levite from Bethlehem (Judg 17:8–9) and that of the Levite's concubine, who comes from Bethlehem (19:1–2), and with the drastic method used to provide wives for the surviving Benjaminites (Judg 21).[45] The LXX places it after the book of Judges, and the intention may be to magnify the royal house of David, in effect picking up the refrain in the last portion of Judges (17:6; 18:1; 19:1; 21:25).[46] In the other direction, there are connections between the figures of Ruth and Hannah, who through her son Samuel (the anointer of the first two kings) is also related to the coming monarchy. It must be said, then, that the book of Ruth works well in all these canonical positions. The different canonical orders each have their own logic, and no one order of books can be proved to be of superior worth to the other two.[47]

Lamentations

With regard to Lamentations, one frequent suggestion for its origin is that the songs come from ceremonies of lamentation such as those mentioned in Zechariah 7:3, 5; 8:19. This is, however, pure speculation. In the Hebrew Bible, the book is placed in the third division of the canon, in the Megilloth. Lamentations is read on the annual festal memorial of the fall of Jerusalem in 587 BC, so that in Jewish liturgy it is associated with the ninth day of Ab, the anniversary of that event. Specific clues to dating are difficult to discern in Lamentations itself (e.g., it makes no reference to the Babylonians).[48] That Lamentations gives little away as to the specific crisis to which it is the response shows that the author is not interested in wedding the book to any one historical event. As with Psalms 74 and 79, where those who sacked the

---

45. E. F. Campbell, *Ruth*, AB 7 (Garden City, NY: Doubleday, 1975), 35–36. Jerome states that Ruth's location in the action in the period of the judges is the reason for this placement (*Prologus Galeatus*); for a translation, see Beckwith, *Old Testament Canon*, 119–20. In Josephus, *Ant.* 5.318–337, the story of Ruth follows that of the judges. So too, in the list of Melito (Eusebius, *Hist. eccl.* 4.26.13–14), Ruth follows Judges, and in Origen (Eusebius, *Hist. eccl.* 6.25.2), Ruth is joined to Judges as one book.

46. For details, see Gregory Goswell, "The Book of Ruth and the House of David," *EvQ* 86 (2014): 116–29.

47. For more, see Gregory Goswell, "The Ordering of the Books of the Canon and the Theological Interpretation of the Old Testament," *JTI* 13 (2019): 1–20.

48. Iain W. Provan, "Reading Texts against a Historical Background: The Case of Lamentations 1," *SJOT* 1 (1990): 130–43.

temple are not identified, the lack of specificity within Lamentations fits it for reuse in new contexts. Its liturgical use is a recognition and affirmation of this ongoing role in the religious life of God's people. It alludes to destroyed Jerusalem's widow status (Lam 1:1; see also 5:3), and this forms a parallel to Naomi's situation as featured in the book of Ruth (e.g., 1:1, 5, 20-21). Ruth and Lamentations each in their own way wrestle with the problem of theodicy.[49] Ecclesiastes shares the somber mood of Lamentations and generalizes its negative experience of life.

Lamentations is traditionally assigned to Jeremiah, and its placement in the LXX (Sinaiticus)[50] directly after the prophecy of Jeremiah is an authorship attribution. Lamentations acts as a vindication of the preaching of the much-maligned prophet. The poems can be read as the personal reaction by Jeremiah to the fall of Jerusalem, the account of which immediately precedes in Jeremiah 52, though the suffering community is also given a voice in chapter 5. The pain of Daughter Zion is acknowledged (e.g., 1:17; 2:1-2),[51] so that what is found in Lamentations could be viewed as an adjustment of the Jeremianic tradition. The male figure who laments in chapter 3 (esp. 3:1-20) can be viewed as a modification of the persona of Jeremiah (see Jer 20:14-18). He acts in effect as a representative of the suffering Daughter Zion, who does not speak for herself in that chapter, but whose grievous suffering is acknowledged and felt (e.g., 3:48, 51). In other words, placing the book of Jeremiah and Lamentations side by side underlines the sympathy that the prophet has for his afflicted people and results in a rapprochement between the prophet and the people whom he roundly condemned in his prophecy.[52]

The Book of Daniel

The quite different character of the two halves of Daniel seems to be what caused the different positioning of the book in Hebrew and Greek canons. In the latter canon, which became the Bible of the primitive church, Daniel

---

49. Noted by Marjo C. A. Korpel, *The Structure of the Book of Ruth*, Pericope 2 (Assen: Van Gorcum, 2001), 230-31.

50. In Vaticanus and Alexandrinus the order is Jeremiah, Baruch, Lamentations, Epistle of Jeremiah.

51. Carleen R. Mandolfo, *Daughter Zion Talks Back to the Prophets: A Dialogic Theology of the Book of Lamentations*, SemeiaSt 58 (Atlanta: Society of Biblical Literature, 2007), 74-76.

52. For more, see Gregory Goswell, "Assigning the Book of Lamentations a Place in the Canon," *JESOT* 4 (2015): 1-19.

is regarded as a prophet (the subscription of Alexandrinus names the book *Daniēl prophētou* [Daniel the prophet]), and his book follows that of Ezekiel as the last of the great prophets.[53] This tradition shows itself in a florilegium of biblical passages from Qumran, in the New Testament, in Josephus, in Melito, and in Origen,[54] all of which refer to Daniel as a prophet. The inclusion of Daniel among the prophets was perhaps suggested by the visionary character of chapters 7-12, and as the last of the large prophetic books it suggests that the expectation of the dawning of God's kingdom is fundamental to the message of the prophets.

Rabbinic thought rejected the designation of Daniel as a prophet, declaring, "They [Haggai, Zechariah, and Malachi] are prophets, while he [Daniel] is not a prophet" (b. Sanh. 93b), which need not be understood as downgrading the book so much as a *post eventum* recognition of the book's position among the Writings. Accordingly, in the Hebrew canon, Daniel comes after Esther and before Ezra-Nehemiah, that is, between books that are considered histories. Maimonides confirms that Daniel was among the Writings in *The Guide for the Perplexed* 2.45.[55] He justifies the placement of Daniel in the Writings by the fact that Daniel received his revelation through the medium of dreams, which is one degree below that of full prophecy as defined by Maimonides. More likely, it was the narrative character of the court tales of chapters 1-6 that caused the book to be placed among the postexilic histories. As well, Daniel's characterization as a wise man (1:3-5; 2:48-49) and the book's wisdom theme generally (e.g., 11:33, 35; 12:3) suits its position in the third section of the Hebrew canon, whose nucleus is made up of wisdom

---

53. This is the order in Vaticanus and Alexandrinus (Sinaiticus is defective): Ezekiel, Susanna-Daniel-Bel and the Dragon, all viewed as one book in Alexandrinus (the subscription ["the end of Daniel the prophet"] only coming after Bel and the Dragon). 𝔓 967 is a Greek manuscript dated c. AD 200 (the earliest witness to the Old Greek version) and has the order Ezekiel, Daniel, Susanna, Bel and the Dragon, Esther. For the subscription of Alexandrinus, see H. J. M. Milne and T. C. Skeat, *Scribes and Correctors of the Codex Sinaiticus* (London: British Museum, 1938), plate 24; F. G. Kenyon, ed., *The Codex Alexandrinus (Royal MS. 1 D V-VIII) in Reduced Photographic Facsimile: Old Testament Part III Hosea-Judith*, British Museum (London: Longmans, 1936), plate 417.

54. John M. Allegro, *Qumrân Cave 4.1 (4Q158-4Q186)*, DJD 5 (Oxford: Clarendon, 1968), 54, 70. 4QFlor 2:3 ("[whi]ch is written in the book of Daniel the prophet"); Matt 24:15; Mark 13:14; Josephus (*Ag. Ap.* 1.8; *Ant.* 10.11.7; 10.26.7-8; 11.8.5); the order of the prophets (so designated) in Melito is Isaiah, Jeremiah, the Twelve in one book, Daniel, Ezekiel (Eusebius, *Hist. eccl.* 4.26.13-14); Origen in his exposition of Ps 1 includes the catalogue Isaiah, Jeremiah-Lamentations-Letter, Daniel, Ezekiel (Eusebius, *Hist. eccl.* 6.25-26).

55. M. Friedländer, ed. and trans., *The Guide for the Perplexed*, 2nd rev. ed. (New York: Dover, 1956), 241-45.

books.[56] It is not necessary to decide which is the correct positioning of the book of Daniel, given that both canonical locations throw light on its contents (albeit on different aspects).[57]

CHAPTER 2 CONCLUSIONS

The following comments may be made about the order of the books that make up the Greek Old Testament. The reader naturally assumes that the placement of books in close physical proximity implies that they are related in some way. An historical principle is reflected in the arrangement of the Greek Bible into four sections reflecting a chronological sequence (Vaticanus), though the fact that Sinaiticus and Alexandrinus end with poetry, not prophecy, is one of a number of factors that show that we are not to exaggerate the contrast between the Greek and Hebrew traditions. These *rival* orders are not to be seen as sectarian in origin or polemical in purpose.

GUIDELINES FOR INTERPRETING
THE ORDER OF THE GREEK CANON

1. Proximity indicates that there is a significant connection between books so conjoined. The reader should look for links of various kinds between neighboring books in the Greek Old Testament canon. This Greek arrangement has shaped the order of the books in the Bibles we use today.

2. Historical sequence or story line is the guiding principle of the Greek arrangement of books in the Pentateuch and the historical books. This is not to be seen as a natural or neutral principle that has no influence on interpretation. For example, the position of the book of Ruth following Judges and preceding Samuel suggests that Ruth, ending with a genealogy that culminates in David (4:18-22), provides a theological undergirding for the house of David in the good purposes of God for his

---

56. Max L. Margolis, *The Hebrew Scriptures in the Making* (Philadelphia: Jewish Publication Society of America, 1922), 80.

57. For more, see Gregory Goswell, "The Canonical Position(s) of the Book of Daniel," *ResQ* 59 (2017): 129-40.

people. In other words, this canonical position highlights the David connection that becomes explicit at the end of the book.

3. The placement of Psalms alongside *other* wisdom books shows that some ancient readers viewed the Psalter in that light.

4. The Greek placement of Chronicles after Kings has contributed to its comparative neglect.

5. The placement of Proverbs next to Ecclesiastes and Job indicates that the three books are readily compatible in outlook. In each case, the reader's approach to each book should be influenced by the other books close at hand.

6. That books such as Ruth, Lamentations, and Daniel can be placed in quite different positions in the Hebrew Bible and Greek Old Testament shows that book order reflects readerly perception of what a book is about. The positioning of a book due to thematic considerations means that alternative placements are possible on this basis, for any book is likely to have more than one theme. What this means for readers is that they should be open to looking at a Bible book from more than one perspective, for example, noticing the ethics of Daniel (prompted by its placement in the Writings) but also seeking to understand its kingdom of God eschatology (prompted by its placement among the prophetic books).

7. Lamentations is found after Jeremiah in the Greek Bible, due to the attribution of common authorship, but in the Hebrew Bible it is put among the Megilloth, as one of five festal scrolls, showing that the message of Lamentations is not tied to any one historical crisis. Both positions throw light on its contents.

8. Probably it is the different generic character of the two halves of Daniel (chs. 1-6; 7-12) that explains its placement alongside other court tales with moral lessons (Hebrew Bible) and its alternate classification as prophecy (LXX).

9. When a book is placed in alternative positions in different canonical arrangements, this fact may assist the reader to notice features of the book that are normally obscured or underplayed, and so assist in refining interpretation.

3

THE STRUCTURE OF
THE NEW TESTAMENT

INTRODUCTION

This chapter deals with the location of the books of the New Testament, with "location" defined as physical proximity in the anthology of Scripture.[1] The habits of readers mean that the act of putting biblical books next to each other is a clue that significant relations are to be discerned between a book and its neighbors in the library of canonical books. The assumption is that a book is more closely related to books next to it or nearby, and less closely related to books placed far from it. This chapter explores the implications of the order of the books of the New Testament for understanding.[2]

THE FOURFOLD GOSPEL

The premier position of the Gospels in the New Testament underscores the foundational importance of the life, death, and resurrection of Jesus Christ for all the writings of the New Testament (see 1 Cor 2:2; 3:11). Robert Wall makes this point in the following terms: "[The Gospels are] the subtext for all the writings that follow in the New Testament."[3] There is the danger of overestimating the church's conscious intention in the ordering of the

---

1. Pierre Bayard uses the term "location" to indicate that "what counts in a book is the books alongside it," with meaning indicated by how a book is situated relative to other books. He also makes use of the analogy of a library; see *How to Talk about Books You Haven't Read*, trans. Jeffrey Mehlman (London: Granta Books, 2007), 11.

2. For an earlier version of material in this chapter, see Gregory Goswell, "The Order of the Books in the New Testament," *JETS* 53 (2010): 225-41. Used with permission.

3. Robert W. Wall, "The Significance of a Canonical Perspective of the Church's Scripture," in *The Canon Debate*, ed. L. M. McDonald and J. A. Sanders (Peabody, MA: Hendrickson, 2002), 536.

four-Gospel canon, though, as stated by D. Moody Smith, the final order "projects a kind of intention that can scarcely be ignored."[4] As to their order, John is treated as the climax of the four, although it is quite different from the preceding three (the Synoptics). There is no set order in patristic lists or discussions,[5] but the order that is now standard in printed Bibles predominated in Greek manuscripts. Irenaeus (died c. AD 200) treated the common order of Matthew-Mark-Luke-John as the chronological order of composition (*Haer.* 3.1.1), but this may be no more than a supposition on his part. His repeated treatment of the Gospels also made use of other orders (notably Matthew-Luke-Mark-John; *Haer.* 3.9-11; 3.11.7; 4.6.1).

The priority of Matthew may be due to its popularity in the early centuries, especially in the West.[6] The commission at the end of Matthew (28:20) is in part fulfilled by the subsequent Gospels (and letters), through which the nations will be taught "to observe all that [Jesus has] commanded." The positioning of Mark after Matthew gives Mark the appearance of being a digest of Matthew.[7] Until majority scholarship decided on the chronological priority of Mark, that Gospel lived in the shadow of the larger Gospel that preceded it.[8]

The preface to Luke (1:1-4) is a possible explanation for its canonical placement after Matthew and Mark. Its nonpejorative reference to previous "attempts" (*epecheirēsan*) at writing an account of what Jesus said and did can be understood in canonical context as referring to the Gospels of Matthew and Mark. We could even go as far as to suggest that Luke's reference to "eyewitnesses and ministers of the word" (Luke 1:2 ESV) has in mind

---

4. D. Moody Smith, "John, the Synoptics, and the Canonical Approach to Exegesis," in *Tradition and Interpretation in the New Testament: Essays in Honor of E. Earle Ellis*, ed. Gerald F. Hawthorne with Otto Betz (Grand Rapids: Eerdmans, 1987), 171. See Brevard S. Childs, *The New Testament as Canon: An Introduction* (London: SCM, 1984), 143-56.

5. Bruce M. Metzger, *The Canon of the New Testament: Its Origin, Development, and Significance* (Oxford: Clarendon, 1987), 296-97, and the inventory of twelve different sequences provided in Pierre-Maurice Bogaert, "Ordres anciens des évangiles et tétraévangile en un seul codex," *RTL* 30 (1999): 297-314.

6. Graham N. Stanton, "The Early Reception of Matthew's Gospel: New Evidence from Papyri?," in *The Gospel of Matthew in Current Study: Studies in Memory of William G. Thompson S.J.*, ed. David E. Aune (Grand Rapids: Eerdmans, 2011), 42-61.

7. Augustine notes the same thing (*Cons.* 1.2.4; 4.10.11); see C. Clifton Black, *Mark: Images of an Apostolic Interpreter* (Columbia: University of South Carolina Press, 1994), 127-31.

8. For a discussion of the preeminence of Matthew, see R. T. France, *Matthew: Evangelist and Teacher* (Exeter: Paternoster, 1989), 15-20.

Matthew and Mark in turn.[9] The association of the first Gospel with Matthew, one of the Twelve, assumes that the writer was an eyewitness to many of the events narrated. While unrelated to authorship, the designation "minister/ servant" (*hypēretēs*) is applied to (John) Mark in Acts 13:5 in his assistant role on an early mission trip.

John is placed last, and its self-reference to "this book" (20:30) can be taken as an implicit acknowledgment of *other* books, the three preceding Gospels. John 21:25 makes an appropriate ending not only to this one Gospel with its selective focus on a few, larger cameos ("I suppose that the world itself could not contain the books that would be written" [ESV]) but to the four-Gospel collection as a whole.[10] This is not to claim that any other order of the four Gospels is impossible but to show the effect of the common order on the reader's perception of the larger narrative.[11]

In a sequential reading of the four Gospels in their usual order, Matthew provides an account of the infancy of Jesus (chs. 1–2).[12] He gives special prominence to the teaching of Jesus, especially in what are often identified as five great discourses, Matthew 5–7; 10; 13; 18; and 24–25. At the end of this Gospel, the risen Jesus commands his followers to disciple all the nations by "teaching them to observe all that I have commanded you" (28:20 ESV). Mark has the appearance of abbreviating Matthew, with a strong concentration on the cross of Jesus.[13] The rejection and suffering of Jesus are anticipated as early as Mark 2:20 (see also 3:6). Mark does not feel the need to provide any information about the early years of Jesus and so begins at the equivalent of Matthew 3, the preparatory ministry of John, while omitting the teaching of Jesus. In effect, this brings the miracles of Jesus into greater focus.

The Gospel of Luke looks like a recombination and adjustment of the preceding two Gospels with a more even balance of miracles and teaching.

---

9. The suggestion is Trobisch's.

10. See David Trobisch, *The First Edition of the New Testament* (Oxford: Oxford University Press, 2000), 78, 97–101.

11. There was the so-called Western order (codices Bezae and Washington, the Chester Beatty codex known as 𝔓45): Matthew, John, Luke, Mark, whose rationale may be to give pride of place to the two Gospels attributed to apostles.

12. For comments on reading Matthew first, see Robert W. Wall, "The Canonical View," in *Biblical Hermeneutics: Five Views*, ed. Stanley E. Porter and Beth M. Stovell (Downers Grove, IL: InterVarsity, 2012), 122–26.

13. See J. D. Kingsbury, "The Gospel in Four Editions," *Int* 33 (1979): 364–67.

To say that is not to propound a theory of Gospel origins—that Luke made use of Matthew and Mark in composing his story of Jesus—but to suggest that this is the impression created in the mind of the reader. Luke gives his own version of the infancy narratives (Luke 1–2). The story of Jesus as told by Luke begins and ends in the temple in Jerusalem (1:5–23; 22:53), and Jesus's final journey to Jerusalem dominates the center of the Gospel (9:51–21:38), not unlike Mark's account of Jesus's way to the cross that follows Peter's confession. The appearances of the risen Christ occur in and around Jerusalem (ch. 24).

In John's Gospel, Jesus makes a series of trips to Jerusalem (chs. 2; 5; 7; 12). There are instances where John can be understood as presupposing his readers' familiarity with the Synoptic tradition, if not with one or several of the written Gospels.[14] However, rather than following them, he probes the deeper theological implications of various synoptic motifs in addition to drawing on his eyewitness recollection.[15] This suits John's fourth position in the lineup of Gospels,[16] for it is treated as the climax of the four portraits of Jesus. What is more, the strategic placement of John's Gospel makes it the interface between the Gospel corpus and the books that follow and helps to connect the evangelists' portrait of Christ and Paul's teaching about Jesus as the "Son of God." Standing at this canonical seam, John's Gospel also paves the way for mission developments in Acts. The positioning of the three letters of John in the Catholic Epistles implies the harmony of the teaching of the apostles Peter and John, as well as their compatibility with the witness of James and Jude, the half-brothers of Jesus.

John 2–11 is organized around a select series of signs and teaching related (more or less directly) to them. There is a closer coordination of miracle and teaching ("sign" and discourse) than in the preceding Gospels; for example, in

---

14. E.g., such allusive comments as John 1:40; 3:24; 4:44; 6:67, 71; 11:2; 18:24, 28. See Craig L. Blomberg, *The Historical Reliability of John's Gospel* (Leicester: Apollos, 2001), 46–49. John A. T. Robinson, however, argues for the priority of the Gospel of John, by which he means that we must approach this Gospel on its own terms rather than trying to slot it into the Synoptic picture of Jesus. See Robinson, *The Priority of John*, ed. J. F. Coakley (London: SCM, 1985).

15. Andreas J. Köstenberger, "John's Transposition Theology: Retelling the Story of Jesus in a Different Key," in *Earliest Christian History: History, Literature, and Theology: Essays from the Tyndale Fellowship in Honor of Martin Hengel*, ed. Michael F. Bird and Jason Maston, WUNT 2/320 (Tübingen: Mohr Siebeck, 2012), 191–26.

16. For more details, see Gregory Goswell, "The Johannine Corpus and the Unity of the New Testament Canon," *JETS* 61 (2018): 721.

John 6 the feeding of the five thousand leads to Jesus's claim to be "the bread of life."[17] The Johannine signs have a clear christological symbolism, establishing a closer connection between miracle (or prophetic sign-act) and dominical teaching.[18] The focus on fewer miracles compared to the preceding Gospels makes it look as if the Fourth Evangelist is giving a highly selective sampling of the revelatory actions of Jesus (John 20:31). John's longer discourses give a profound recasting of dominical teaching such as is appropriate for those who have read and digested the preceding three Gospels. Before this is attributed to imaginative creativity on John's part, it would be well to note the suggestion of J. A. T. Robinson that "the process may be one of deepening truth rather than falsification or fiction."[19] Robinson lodges the claim that the Johannine presentation of the teaching material of Jesus "could be *both* the most mature *and* the most faithful to the original truth about Jesus."[20] The idiolect of the Johannine portrait of Jesus is not without connection with the way Jesus speaks in the Synoptics, with the so-called Johannine thunderbolt in Matthew 11:27 (and the parallel in Luke 10:22) being the famous example (see also Mark 13:32; John 3:35; 10:15).[21] The significance of reading the four Gospels in the usual order is that the Christian reader is in a position to appreciate what is said by and about Jesus in John's Gospel after having learned about Jesus's story through reading the first three Gospels.

In John's Gospel, there are seven positive references to Jesus as the "Son of God" (1:49; 3:18; 5:25; 10:36; 11:4, 27; 20:31) and one that is disparaging (19:7). Likewise, there are seven uses of the title in 1 John (3:8; 4:15; 5:5, 10, 12, 13, 20), clustered toward the end of the letter. The tally of seven instances in each case is hardly accidental and suggests the presence of numerical symbolism

---

17. See the schema of Leon L. Morris, in which he strives to connect the seven Johannine signs (according to Morris's tabulation) with seven discourses (*Jesus Is the Christ: Studies in the Theology of John* [Grand Rapids: Eerdmans, 1989], 23).

18. See Dorothy A. Lee, *The Symbolic Narratives of the Fourth Gospel: The Interplay of Form and Meaning*, JSNTSup 95 (Sheffield: Sheffield Academic, 1994). For a case for the temple clearing in John 2 as a Johannine sign, see Andreas J. Köstenberger, "The Seventh Johannine Sign: A Study in John's Christology," *BBR* 5 (1995): 87–103.

19. Robinson, *Priority of John*, 299.

20. Robinson, *Priority of John*, 342 (emphasis original). For the issue of Johannine diction, see Craig L. Blomberg, *The Historical Reliability of the Gospels*, 2nd ed. (Downers Grove, IL: IVP Academic, 2007), 231–36.

21. See the discussion provided in Adelbert Denaux, "The Q-Logion Mt 11,27 / Luke 10,22 and the Gospel of John," in *John and the Synoptics*, ed. Adelbert Denaux, BETL 101 (Leuven: Peeters, 1992), 163–99.

as a way of underlining its thematic significance.[22] Of course, the Synoptics also portray Jesus as the Son of God, but there it is others rather than Jesus himself who designate him as such.[23] The significance of this listing is that recognition of his divine sonship is not a natural human accomplishment but comes only by special revelatory insight.[24] On the other hand, in John's Gospel Jesus regularly refers to himself as the Son. Even more often, he speaks of the Father in an absolute sense that implies his own unique sonship (e.g., John 5:17; 11:41; 16:32).

The effect of placing the Gospels *side by side*, with the three Synoptic Gospels next to each other, is that each must now be read in the light of the other three. We should allow for a measure of historical contingency in the process that gave us such canonical aggregations,[25] but that does not mean that the four-Gospel collection is without hermeneutical significance. One obvious alternative that was not taken up was to conjoin Luke and Acts "as one unit in a mutually interpretive two-part treatise."[26] There are some Gospel orders in which Luke is placed fourth;[27] however, Luke is not placed next to Acts in any extant old manuscript. Their lack of proximity in any known canonical arrangement is a statement about the *differing* contexts in which each volume should be read.

Given the retention of the fourfold form, the four Gospels have been placed side by side in the canon, inviting comparison, but not harmonization.

---

22. For the use of heptads in John's Gospel (the seven "I am" sayings, etc.), see Michael A. Daise, *Feasts in John: Jewish Festivals and Jesus' "Hour" in the Fourth Gospel*, WUNT 2/229 (Tübingen: Mohr Siebeck, 2007), 32-34.

23. The angel Gabriel (Luke 1:35), Satan (Matt 4:3, 6 [// Luke 4:3, 9]), demons (Mark 3:11; Luke 4:41; Mark 5:7 [// Matt 8:29]; Luke 8:28), the Twelve (Matt 14:33); Peter (Matt 16:16), the high priest (Matt 26:63 [// Luke 22:70]), his mockers (Matt 27:40, 43), and the centurion (Mark 15:39 [// Matt 27:54]). See Andreas J. Köstenberger, *A Theology of John's Gospel and Letters: The Word, the Christ, the Son of God*, BTNT (Grand Rapids: Zondervan, 2009), 383 n. 166. In addition, Mark designates him "the Son of God" (Mark 1:1), and God (the Father) announces that Jesus is his "beloved Son" (Mark 1:11 [par. Matt 3:17; Luke 3:22]; 9:7 [par. Matt 17:5; Luke 9:35]).

24. Or else the people using the title "Son of God" are depicted as saying more than they realize to be true (expressing incredulity or speaking in jest).

25. See Robert W. Wall and Eugene E. Lemcio, *The New Testament as Canon: A Reader in Canonical Criticism*, JSNTSup 76 (Sheffield: JSOT, 1992), ch. 1. I acknowledge my substantial dependence on Wall and Lemcio in this paragraph.

26. Michael F. Bird, "The Unity of Luke–Acts in Recent Discussion," *JSNT* 29 (2007): 440. See Graham N. Stanton's discussion of the early separation of Luke and Acts in "The Fourfold Gospel," *NTS* 43 (1997): 334-35.

27. Bogaert, "Ordres anciens," 299-301, 304-305.

Their variety is to be seen as a resource, and the unique message of each must be proclaimed rather than a homogenized blend.

The multiple accounts of the same person, Jesus Christ, and even the same events, such as the feeding of the five thousand (Matt 14:13-21; Mark 6:30-44; Luke 9:10-17; John 6:1-14), invite the reader to compare and contrast them. Moreover, the Gospels have a united theological orientation, with their focus on the words and deeds of the *earthly* Christ. We can easily overstress their circumstantial character and should recall that Matthew preserves 90 percent of Mark's material. Moreover, the passion narrative represents a significant amount of common ground between the four Gospels. The early church recognized that the four belonged together and neither gave preferential treatment to one nor harmonized the four into a single blended story.[28] The diversity of the four is an asset for the church.[29]

ACTS

The Pauline corpus, as we now have it in the English Bible, is prefaced by the book of Acts. In such a position, Acts forms a bridge between the Gospels and the Letters.[30] David E. Smith favors the wider thesis that Acts is the "glue" that holds all the pieces of the New Testament together.[31] Indeed, Acts plays a key canonical role in displaying the unity of the early Christian leaders and affirms the compatibility of the teachings attributed to them.[32] Being the second volume of Luke's two-part work, Acts bears a resemblance to the

---

28. See Andreas J. Köstenberger, *The Jesus of the Gospels: An Introduction* (Grand Rapids: Kregel, 2020), 23-25. Marcion (c. AD 140) had (and maybe only knew of) one Gospel, Luke, and Tatian (c. AD 170) produced a Gospel harmony, the Diatessaron, but neither option was followed by the wider church.

29. For the argument that the four Gospels balance each other, preventing a one-sided Christology, see Robert Morgan, "Which Was the Fourth Gospel? The Order of the Gospels and the Unity of Scripture," *JSNT* 54 (1994): 24.

30. Childs, *New Testament as Canon*, 219-25; cf. Robert W. Wall, "The Acts of the Apostles in Canonical Context," *BTB* 18 (1988): 16-24. Wall takes the work of Childs further. I acknowledge my substantial dependence on Wall for this paragraph.

31. David E. Smith, *The Canonical Function of Acts: A Comparative Analysis* (Collegeville, MN: Liturgical Press, 2002), 39-40, for criticisms of Childs and Wall.

32. See Gregory Goswell, "Authorship and Anonymity in the New Testament Writings," *JETS* 60 (2017): 733-49

Gospel genre,[33] and Acts 1:1 briefly resumes the prologue of Luke's Gospel (Luke 1:1-4) that thereby applies to both parts. Yet, instead of focusing on one main character (Jesus), Acts broadens its scope to present key episodes in the lives of several early church figures, especially Peter and Paul, though it could be argued that the main character of Acts is the Holy Spirit.[34] Frequently, in Acts the disciples mimic some facet of Jesus's life as described in Luke. For example, they teach in the temple courts (Acts 3; cf. Luke 19:47-48; 22:23-38) and perform healings (Acts 9:32-35; cf. Luke 5:17-26). Jesus's journey to Jerusalem finds a parallel in Paul's journeys to Jerusalem and Rome.[35] All this gives Acts somewhat the character of a "fifth Gospel." What is more, the mission ending of three of the four Gospels (Matt 28:16-20; Luke 24:44-49; John 21) helps to prepare for the spread of the gospel, which occurs in Acts.[36]

In the other direction, churches planted by Paul in Acts receive letters from the same apostle: Thessalonica, Corinth, Philippi, and so on. Acts provides the background to help situate individual Pauline letters in their time and location.[37] Canonically, the Paul of Acts is the same Paul who wrote the letters.[38] Though Acts makes no allusion to Paul writing letters, scholars have recently argued that his letters were used by the author of Acts as one of the unacknowledged sources on which he drew for his own composition, and according to Richard Pervo, "The cumulative evidence that Luke made use of Pauline letters is rather persuasive."[39]

What is more, there are obvious parallels between the activities of Peter and Paul recorded in Acts (e.g., the healing of a lame man, 3:1-10; 14:8-10).

---

33. Richard A. Burridge, *What Are the Gospels? A Comparison with Graeco-Roman Biography*, 2nd ed. (Grand Rapids: Eerdmans, 2004), 236-39, 275-79.

34. Peter is already prominent in the four Gospels, with Luke being no exception (e.g., 5:1-11; 8:45; 9:20, 32; 12:41).

35. See Susan Marie Praeder, "Jesus-Paul, Peter-Paul, and Jesus-Peter Parallelisms in Luke-Acts: A History of Reader Response," in *SBL 1982 Seminar Papers*, ed. Kent Harold Richards (Chico, CA: Scholars Press, 1984), 23-39.

36. Mark's longer ending (16:9-20) likely represents a later addition. For the possible theological significance of the John-Acts collation, see Goswell, "Johannine Corpus," 724-26.

37. Colossians is an exception, for the church in Colossae was not founded by Paul (see Col 2:1).

38. Stanley E. Porter, *The Paul of Acts: Essays in Literary Criticism, Rhetoric, and Theology*, WUNT 115 (Tübingen: Mohr Siebeck, 1999), 187-206.

39. Richard I. Pervo, *Dating Acts: Between the Evangelists and the Apologists* (Santa Rosa, CA: Polebridge, 2006), 145.

The harmony between Paul's gentile mission and the Jewish mission of James, Peter, and John prefaces the apostolic witness of the letters that follow (see Gal 2:9, where the "pillars" are listed in the same order as the Catholic Epistles). At the heart of Acts is the Jerusalem Council (Acts 15:1–21) where potential discord between the Pauline mission and the Jerusalem apostles is resolved.[40] There, Peter and James are portrayed as supporting Paul. In its canonical setting, Acts is a consensus document that provides the context for interpreting the Pauline and non-Pauline corpora not as competing traditions within the early church, but as compatible and complementary.[41] David Trobisch, likewise, sees the names of the Gospel authors Mark and Luke as cross-references to passages in Acts, 1 Peter, and the letters of Paul, indicating the essential harmony between the Jerusalem authorities and Paul.[42]

In my view, Paul's correction of Peter in Galatians 2 assumes without stating it that Peter accepted the rebuke and the two men were reconciled later. Peter's commendation of the teaching of Paul in 2 Peter 3:15–16, accepted as genuinely Petrine, adds weight to this assumption by the reader.[43] Acts asserts the normative status of the different perspectives enshrined in the Pauline and non-Pauline letter collections. The Catholic Epistles document the teaching of other primitive apostolic figures, especially the "pillar apostles" (Gal 2:9), and give a broader sampling of the apostolic witness than simply that of the Pauline Epistles. The coordinating function of Acts implies that the Pauline Epistles are not just for the gentiles, nor are the non-Pauline epistles only for Jewish believers.

In Vaticanus and Alexandrinus, Acts stands between the four Gospels and the Catholic Epistles, with the Pauline Epistles following. Yet, in Sinaiticus the order is Gospels–Pauline Epistles–Acts–Catholic Epistles. The positioning of the non-Pauline epistles after Acts, where they are in all Greek witnesses,[44] means that Acts and the Catholic Epistles are a single collection (*Praxapostolos*), with the result that Acts can be viewed as presenting key

---

40. See the discussion of Trobisch, *First Edition*, 82–83.

41. See Dieter Lührmann, "Gal 2 9 und die katholischen Briefe: Bemerkungen zum Kanon und zur regula fidei," *ZNW* 72 (1981): 72: "Gal 2 1–10 ist mit Act 15 1–35 in der Alten Kirche der locus classicus für die Einheit der apostolischen Lehre."

42. Trobisch, *First Edition*, 45–46.

43. Michael J. Kruger, "The Authenticity of 2 Peter," *JETS* 42 (1999): 645–71.

44. See the listing provided in GNT⁴, 6*–18*.

proponents of early Christianity in addition to Paul. This appears to reverse Luke's implicit intention of defending Paul against his detractors, given the series of apologetic speeches by Paul in the latter portion of Acts.[45] In the Vulgate—which determined the order in the Western Bible, Protestant and Catholic—Acts is placed between the Gospels and the Pauline Epistles.[46] This has the potential effect of relegating the non-Pauline epistles to the category of a mere appendix and of confirming the theological dominance of Paul in modern New Testament scholarship. However, as Bauckham contends, "Nothing about the canon requires us first to learn what Christianity is from Paul and then to see what James and others have to add."[47]

The order Acts-Catholic Epistles-Pauline Epistles reflects the presentation within Acts itself, in which Peter largely dominates chapters 1-12, and chapters 13-28 center on Paul. The Orthodox churches arrange the books of the New Testament in this order. Again, it is not a question of right and wrong positionings, for the alternative placement of books throws a different light on their contents so that exegetical choices are placed before the reader. The logic of the placement of Paul's letters immediately after Acts is that Paul's story dominates the second half of that book. The (alternative) logic of having non-Pauline letters follow Acts is that this order draws attention to how Acts features apostles other than Paul (especially Peter, who is the leading figure in the first half of the book). The existence of two different canonical orders warns the reader against prescribing one or the other order as determinative for interpretation. To give exclusive rights to any one order of books would be to fail to see the character of paratext as commentary on the text.

Nevertheless, it may be possible to argue that the Greek order precedes the Latin (and English) order and has therefore a certain claim to preeminence,

---

45. For more details, see Gregory Goswell, "The Place of the Book of Acts in Reading the NT," *JETS* 59 (2016): 67-82.

46. See Berger, *Histoire de la Vulgate*, 339 (order no. 1). In the Muratorian Fragment, "the acts of all the apostles" is discussed after Luke and John and before the Pauline Epistles. So too in Eusebius (*Hist. eccl.* 3.25.1-2), the order of discussion of the *homologoumena* (accepted or recognized writings) is Gospels, Acts, Pauline Epistles (and Revelation).

47. Richard Bauckham, *James: Wisdom of James, Disciple of Jesus the Sage*, NTR (London: Routledge, 1999), 116 (emphasis original).

which may serve as a corrective to the Protestant penchant to give priority to Paul.[48]

THE LETTERS OF PAUL

As for the Pauline corpus, the manuscript evidence before printing indicates fluidity in the order of the letters.[49] In the present sequence, the letters are roughly ranked according to their (decreasing) length and audience, with letters to the same church/individual placed together.[50] Though the position of Romans at the head of the Pauline corpus is due to the mechanical principle of length, it is also the most treatise-like of Paul's letters and so appropriately functions as a theological introduction to the Pauline corpus.[51] As Acts ends with Paul in Rome, it is fitting that Romans should immediately follow it in modern printed Bibles, with Romans 1:8–15 and 15:22–29 discussing a possible visit to Rome. Moreover, Romans naturally follows after Acts 28, for Romans explains the Jewish hardening predicted in the Isaiah 6 quotation of Acts 28:26–27 (see Rom 9–11). Romans also gives content to Paul's preaching of "the kingdom of God" (Acts 28:31; see Rom 1:3) and is an answer to the false charge made against Paul in Acts 21:28, with Romans being an authentic summary of his teaching.[52]

His letter is written to enlist the help of the church in Rome, so that these believers might speed him on his way to Spain (Rom 15:22–29). The teaching of this letter, which is the most theologically comprehensive of the Pauline Letters, is designed to lay a platform for Roman support of his mission, and so

---

48. See, e.g., Dirk Jongkind et al., eds., *The Greek New Testament, Produced at Tyndale House, Cambridge* (Wheaton, IL: Crossway, 2017), which features the NT books in the order Gospels–Acts–Catholic Epistles–Pauline Epistles (including Hebrews)–Revelation.

49. Jack Finegan, "The Original Form of the Pauline Collection," *HTR* 49 (1956): 88–90; David Trobisch, *Die Entstehung der Paulusbriefsammlung: Studien zu den Anfängen christlicher Publizistik*, NTOA 10 (Freiburg: Universitätsverlag, 1989), 14–61.

50. The order Ephesians-Galatians in 𝔓[46] is perhaps due to the differing systems of stichometry in use in antiquity, for the two letters are closely similar in length. See Jerome Murphy-O'Connor, *Paul the Letter-Writer: His World, His Options, His Skills*, GNS 41 (Collegeville, MN: Liturgical Press, 1995), 123–24.

51. Lemcio and Wall, *New Testament as Canon*, 144. In his final book, Brevard Childs explores the significance of the premier position of Romans. See *The Church's Guide for Reading Paul: The Canonical Shaping of the Pauline Corpus* (Grand Rapids: Eerdmans, 2008), 7, 66–67, 104, 117. He suggests that the rest of the corpus is to be read through the lens of the mature and comprehensive survey of Pauline teaching found in Romans.

52. Gregory Goswell, "Reading Romans after the Book of Acts," *JETS* 62 (2019): 353–71.

it comes in the form of a "theological resume."[53] It does appear that this letter, in contrast to the ones that follow, is less influenced by the contingent factors and local problems that need to be addressed to assist the church to which it was sent.[54] The letter to the Romans is a *Missionsbreif*, serving to introduce the message of Paul the missionary and, given the completion of his mission from Jerusalem to Illyricum (Rom 15:19), to promote a mission to Spain in the west (15:24, 28),[55] which suggests that its contents should be put under the heading of missional theology. The missional theology of Romans is the canonical context of the Pauline Letters that follow, which are to be understood as providing applications of that theology in the different churches founded by Paul and his coworkers. Instructed by Romans, the reader of the epistles that follow in canonical order is helped to notice when Paul sets his doctrinal and ethical instructions in a missional frame.

The canonical presentation of the letters of Paul as a collection invites readers to compare the individual letters, such that the primary context of Philippians, for example, is not the original situation at Philippi (insofar as it can be recovered) but that it now comes within a collection of thirteen letters by Paul.[56] Though the contents of Paul's letters were originally evoked by contemporary and contingent factors in the lives of particular churches— for example, the problem of disunity in the church at Philippi, including the dispute between Euodia and Syntyche (Phil 4:2-3)[57]—their gathering into an

---

53. See Sam K. Williams, "The 'Righteousness of God' in Romans," *JBL* 99 (1980): 245-55, with the quoted expression found on 254.

54. This is an important aspect of Childs's argument (see *Church's Guide for Reading Paul*, 139, 145, 147, 179).

55. Robert W. Wall, "The Problem of the Multiple Letter Canon of the New Testament," *HBT* 8 (1986): 31 n. 41; cf. Childs, *Church's Guide for Reading Paul*, 75: "The Letter to the Romans with its prominent position as the introduction to the Pauline corpus sets forth the most comprehensive formulation of Paul's missionary message."

56. See Michael Prior, *Paul the Letter-Writer and the Second Letter to Timothy*, JSNTSup 23 (Sheffield: JSOT, 1989), 130-35, esp. 131: "Paul is not presuming to address himself to the particular situation of the Church in Rome, but is, rather, dealing with the more general theological and missiological question of the world-wide significance of salvation in Jesus Christ, and the consequential ecclesiological question of the place of Jews and Gentiles within that mystery." In the case of Philippi, several features of Acts 16 emphasize the Romanness of the Roman colony (e.g., Acts 16:12, 21, 38) and the obsession in Philippi with rank and social status. See Joseph H. Hellerman, *Reconstructing Honor in Roman Philippi: Carmen Christi as Cursus Pudorum*, SNTSMS 132 (Cambridge: Cambridge University Press, 2005), 110-28.

57. E.g., Davorin Peterlin, *Paul's Letter to the Philippians in the Light of Disunity in the Church*, NovTSup 79 (Leiden: Brill, 1995).

epistolary corpus means that they are no longer being viewed as *occasional* letters. Rather, the positioning of the individual letters in the canonical collection (*Sitz im Kanon*) is an important index of their meaning, and the canon provides a fixed context and thus stability of meaning. In this regard, canon differs from intertextuality, which is the free association of *all* other texts without deference to any canonical concept.

The Pauline order is set out in two major categories: letters to churches, then letters to individuals (and the churches behind them).[58] Because of this, Colossians is separated from Philemon (compare the names of persons mentioned near the end of each of these letters). The order of Paul's letters to churches, Romans to Thessalonians, appears to be according to a stichometric principle (from longest to shortest). Similarly, in the next series of four letters addressed to individuals, 1 Timothy appears first as the longest letter, and Philemon, the shortest, is placed at the end, while 1 and 2 Timothy are kept together because they are addressed to the same recipient, even though the letter to Titus likely precedes 2 Timothy in time of writing. Features such as the general ecclesial instructions given in 1 Timothy and Titus for Timothy and Titus as apostolic delegates to pass on to others (e.g., 1 Tim 3:14–15; 4:11; Titus 2:1), the character of 2 Timothy as a "testament" of Paul (anticipating his death), and the fact that others besides Philemon are addressed (Phlm 1–2) make the wider application of the four letters obvious, so that the differentiation made between letters to churches and to individuals is at least to some extent schematic.[59]

Paul wrote letters to seven churches (Romans, Corinthians, Galatians, Ephesians, Philippians, Colossians, Thessalonians), just as there are letters

---

58. See Jerome D. Quinn, "𝔓⁴⁶: The Pauline Canon?," CBQ 36 (1974): 379–85, with this codex containing Pauline documents that were read as letters to the churches, as the title each of the letters bears indicates: "To Hebrews," "To Corinthians," etc. This is the oldest known copy of the Pauline Epistles, and it places Hebrews after Romans, possibly due to considerations of length (seeing that Hebrews is longer than 2 Corinthians). The Muratorian Fragment differentiates between Paul's letters to seven churches and the letters he wrote "out of affection and love one to Philemon, one to Titus and two to Timothy" (lines 59–60). A translation is provided in Metzger, *Canon of the New Testament*, 305–7.

59. The suggestion is that of N. A. Dahl, "The Particularity of the Pauline Epistles as a Problem in the Ancient Church," in *Neotestamentica et Patristica: Eine Freundesgabe, Herrn Professor Dr. Oscar Cullmann zu seinem 60. Geburtstag überreicht*, ed. W. C. van Unnik, VTSup 6 (Leiden: Brill, 1962), 266.

to seven churches in Revelation 2-3.[60] The Muratorian Fragment explicitly relates Paul's seven letters to the seven letters in Revelation, saying, "The blessed apostle Paul himself, following the example of his predecessor John, writes by name to only seven churches. ... It is clearly recognized that there is one church spread throughout the whole extent of the earth, for John also in the Apocalypse, though he writes to seven churches, nevertheless speaks to all."[61] The early church fathers argued that Paul's letters were intended from the beginning for the *ecclesia catholica*,[62] an argument that needed to ignore the inclusion of Hebrews in the Pauline corpus. If Hebrews were to be included, the point can perhaps be salvaged by noting that there are fourteen (7 × 2) Pauline letters in total.[63] What can be gleaned about Marcion's Pauline collection indicates that it consisted of ten letters, with letters to the same destination (seven destinations in total) clumped together in the following order: Galatians, 1-2 Corinthians, Romans, 1-2 Thessalonians, Laodiceans (= Ephesians), Colossians-Philemon, and Philippians.[64] Bringing together Paul's letters to form a *Corpus Paulinum* encourages a hermeneutic in which Paul's instructions and advice on local issues (whether to church or individual) are departicularized so as to be applicable in all times and places.

HEBREWS

Greek manuscripts commonly situate Hebrews after Philemon (D, L, Y, other majuscules, most minuscules) or between 2 Thessalonians and the letters to Timothy and Titus. In other words, Hebrews is treated as the last of Paul's letters to churches and before his letters to individuals (ℵ, A, B, C, H, I, K, P,

---

60. Comparison can also be made to the seven letters of Ignatius (*To the Ephesians*, *To the Magnesians*, *To the Trallians*, *To the Romans*, *To the Philadelphians*, *To the Smyrnaeans*, *To Polycarp*). The pattern is the same as the common ordering of the Pauline corpus, letters to churches (six) followed by a letter to an individual (Polycarp, bishop of Smyrna).

61. Muratorian Fragment, lines 48-50, 57-59 (translation provided by Metzger, *Canon of the New Testament*, 307).

62. Krister Stendahl, "The Apocalypse of John and the Epistles of Paul in the Muratorian Fragment," in *Current Issues in New Testament Interpretation: Essays in Honor of Otto A. Piper*, ed. William Klassen and Graydon F. Snyder (London: SCM, 1962), 239-45.

63. A point made by J. K. Elliott, "Manuscripts, the Codex and the Canon," *JSNT* 63 (1996): 109. *Festal Letter* 39 of Athanasius notes that the letters of Paul (placing Hebrews after the two letters to the Thessalonians) number fourteen. Eusebius's tally of fourteen Pauline epistles must include Hebrews (*Hist. eccl.* 3.3.4-5).

64. David C. Parker, *An Introduction to the New Testament Manuscripts and Their Texts* (Cambridge: Cambridge University Press, 2008), 251.

etc.).[65] Either placement is a clear assertion that Hebrews belongs within the *Corpus Paulinum*.[66] The latter sequence is found in the famous list in *Festal Letter* 39 of Athanasius (AD 367).[67] 𝔓46 is the oldest manuscript of Paul's letters (c. AD 200-250), but it breaks off after 1 Thessalonians 5:28. In 𝔓46 Hebrews is placed between Romans and 1-2 Corinthians on account of its size, being shorter than 1 Corinthians but longer than 2 Corinthians. Trobisch suggests that the stichometric principle was compromised due to a desire to keep the Corinthian correspondence together.[68] In Vaticanus, the chapters of the Pauline Epistles are continuously numbered as if one book (chs. 1-93). In that codex, though Hebrews is physically placed after 2 Thessalonians, the six section numbers assigned to Hebrews (which is defective after 9:14a; chs. 59-64) suggest that in the codex from which Vaticanus was copied, Hebrews followed Galatians. The Vulgate (and hence English Bibles) conforms to the majority of late Byzantine manuscripts and places Hebrews at the end of Paul's letters.[69]

With regard to its canonical positioning after Philemon in modern printed Bibles, Hebrews looks both backward and forward. The juxtaposition of the Pauline letters with non-Pauline letters, and with Paul's letters in what is now the common ordering *preceding* the non-Pauline letters, gives primacy to Paul's teaching and implies that the letters of James, Peter, and John play a subordinate role. This has, at times, distorted exegesis, for example, when James's discussion of faith and works (2:14-26) is viewed in a Pauline frame, James supposedly using terms borrowed from Paul, and so seen as anti-Pauline; or when James 2:14-26 is just given more prominence than is due

---

65. For more details, see Bruce M. Metzger, *A Textual Commentary on the Greek New Testament*, 2nd ed. (Stuttgart: Bibelgesellschaft, 1994), 591-92.

66. Frederic G. Kenyon, *The Chester Beatty Biblical Papyri Descriptions and Texts of Twelve Manuscripts on Papyrus of the Greek Bible: Fasciclus III Supplement Pauline Epistles* (London: Emery Walker, 1936), xi, xii.

67. See the Greek text and translation supplied by A. Souter, *The Text and Canon of the New Testament* (London: Duckworth, 1912), 214-15. In the Sahidic version of the festal letter, Hebrews is found between 2 Corinthians and Galatians. See T. C. Skeat, "The Codex Sinaiticus, the Codex Vaticanus and Constantine," *JTS* 50 (1999): 600.

68. David Trobisch, *Paul's Letter Collection: Tracing the Origins* (Minneapolis: Augsburg Fortress, 1994), 17.

69. See W. H. P. Hatch, "The Position of Hebrews in the Canon of the New Testament," *HTR* 29 (1936): 149-50. According to Hatch, Hebrews only found a settled place after the Pauline corpus in printed editions of the NT. For more, see Gregory Goswell, "Finding a Home for the Letter to the Hebrews," *JETS* 59 (2016): 747-60.

in the overall teaching of the letter. Sandwiched as it now is between the two collections, Hebrews helps to coordinate the Pauline and non-Pauline corpora, not least because it broadens the theology attributed to the Pauline circle, most notably serving to fill out the covenant theology implicit in Paul's letters.[70] In that way, too, Hebrews serves as a glue between the Pauline and the non-Pauline epistles similar to the way in which Acts serves as the glue between the Gospels and the letters.

There is a certain appropriateness in placing Hebrews immediately before the Catholic Epistles, for Hebrews is more sermon than letter (as are James, 1 John, and 1 Peter). In some early English Bible orders (e.g., Tyndale [1526], Coverdale [1550], and Matthews [1549]), Hebrews is even positioned *among* the Catholic Epistles (after the epistles of Peter and John, and before the epistles of James and Jude), despite the fact that it is still given the title "The Letter of St. Paul unto the Hebrews." This ordering of the books is probably due to the influence of Luther's *Das Neue Testament* (1522). This order also places the letters attributed to apostles together (1-2 Peter, 1-3 John) and letters attributed to the half-brothers of Jesus together (James, Jude).

On the other hand, Hebrews has connections to Paul. The closing verses of Hebrews do not claim a direct link with Paul by attributing authorship to him (13:22-24); rather, they make an indirect connection by their reference to "our brother Timothy," whom the anonymous author acknowledges as coworker and companion. This places the writer within the Pauline circle. The letter's stress on faith (e.g., the roll call of Heb 11) fits such a setting, though its definition of faith as enduring hope (10:39; 11:1-2) is a different concept of faith from that which is usual for Paul (yet see Acts 14:22).[71] Its affirmation of the heavenly session of Christ (Heb 1:3) is in accord with the high Christology of Ephesians (Eph 2:6) and Colossians (Col 3:1). Its extensive interaction with Old Testament texts suggests a relation to Romans, with its many citations of the Old Testament (esp. Rom 9-11).[72] If the author is not Paul, this marks the teaching as contemporary with Paul (or nearly so) and

---

70. See the discussion of Childs as to how the inclusion of Hebrews affected the subsequent reading of the Pauline corpus (*Church's Guide for Reading Paul*, 250-52).

71. See Goswell, "Finding a Home," 754-60. This, of course, presents Paul through a Lukan lens.

72. Childs, *Church's Guide to Reading Paul*, 251-52, 258.

compatible and complementary to the Pauline corpus. Because of its affinities with both collections, Hebrews brings Pauline and non-Pauline corpora into a mutually enriching canonical conversation.

THE CATHOLIC EPISTLES

The common order of the Catholic Letters shows letters attributed to James and Jude, the two half-brothers of Jesus, surrounding (inclusio) the apostolic letters of Peter and John. The placing of the letters of Peter and John side by side shows the compatibility of their witness to Christ. This becomes a final canonical comment on the implicit competition between Peter and "the beloved disciple" (= John) that is plotted in the final chapters of John's Gospel (John 13:21-30; 18:15-18; 20:1-10; 21:15-24). Second Peter follows 1 Peter due to their relative lengths, but 2 Peter 3:1 ("This is now the second letter that I have written to you" [RSV]) presumably refers to 1 Peter or was understood as so doing.

Jude's self-reference as the "brother of James" (Jude 1) is an intracanonical link with the Letter of James. The similarities between 2 Peter and Jude, whatever their explanation,[73] help to unify the Catholic Epistles. We might have expected Jude to follow straight after 2 Peter, but it was not allowed to intrude on the James-Peter-John sequence (the order of names in Gal 2:9). Jude, however, is well situated after the discussion about false teachers in the three letters of John. Moreover, Jude draws on intertestamental apocalypses (e.g., vv. 9, 14), and its theme of challenges to faith "in the last time" (e.g., v. 21) anticipates and helps to pave the way for the book of Revelation. The limitation of the Catholic Epistles to seven is another way in which their universal scope and intention is indicated.[74] Epistles by the same author are kept together and, as in the case of the Pauline Letters, they are ordered according to decreasing length.[75] So, canonical order is no indicator of chronological order of composition.

---

73. See Terrance Callan, "Use of the Letter of Jude by the Second Letter of Peter," *Bib* 85 (2004): 42- 64. Callan argues that 2 Pet 2:1-3:3 has thoroughly reworked and freely paraphrased material from Jude 4-18.

74. First commented on in Eusebius, *Hist. eccl.* 2.23.25.

75. This is the order found in Sinaiticus, Alexandrinus, and Vaticanus.

For all their individuality, the seven letters share a number of key themes.[76] In most cases, these themes can be found in the prefacing book of Acts: for example, the eyewitness testimony of the apostles to the glorified and resurrected Jesus, the joyful endurance of trials, the apostolic tradition that embodies the truth about Jesus, the danger posed by false prophets, the love command, the sharing of possessions, the practice of hospitality, the observance of the law, the prospect of the Lord's coming, and the rescue call for those who have wandered from the faith.[77] The overall impression gained from the letters is the harmony of the teaching of the half-brothers of Jesus (James and Jude) and the apostles (Peter and John), which is what one would expect to find after the presentation given in Acts. Like with the Pauline Epistles, the appropriate method of interpretation is to allow neighboring letters to inform the reading of the individual letters that make up the Catholic Epistles.[78]

REVELATION

Revelation, with its letters and vision addressed to actual churches, is probably to be seen as a circular letter to seven churches in the Roman province of Asia Minor, appropriating the letter form to transmit its vision. Revelation 1:4-5 and 22:21 provide the book with a formal epistolary framework (prescript and postscript). It is not clear that the letter form has materially influenced its contents,[79] but its positioning after *other* letters has the effect of making it another letter. This generic classification implies its circumstantial character, though writing to seven quite different churches (as evidenced by the contents of chs. 2-3) expands the scope of the remainder of the book, similar to Paul's letters to seven churches and the seven Catholic Epistles. Its epistolary genre needs to be taken into account in exegesis,[80] rendering

---

76. For what follows, see Robert W. Wall, "A Unifying Theology of the Catholic Epistles: A Canonical Approach," in *The Catholic Epistles and the Tradition*, ed. Jacques Schlosser, BETL 176 (Leuven: Peeters, 2004), 43-71.

77. Darian Lockett, *Letters from the Pillar Apostles: The Formation of the Catholic Epistles as a Canonical Collection* (Eugene, OR: Pickwick, 2017), 201-9.

78. For more, see Gregory Goswell, "The Early Readership of the Catholic Epistles," *JGRChJ* 13 (2018): 129-51.

79. M. Karrer attempted an analysis of Revelation as a letter. See his *Die Johannesoffenbarung als Brief: Studien zu ihrem literarischen, historischen und theologischen Ort*, FRLANT 140 (Göttingen: Vandenhoeck & Ruprecht, 1986).

80. Richard Bauckham, *The Theology of the Book of Revelation* (Cambridge: Cambridge University Press, 1993), 12-17.

unlikely the supposition that Revelation offers a detailed timetable for history. Its future orientation as "prophecy" (see 1:3; 22:7, 9, 10, 18, 19) does not need to be denied, and this has determined its final position in the New Testament.

Given its Johannine authorship (1:1, 4, 9), Revelation belongs among the other non-Pauline letters.[81] What is more, the theme of its final paragraph (22:18-21), the return of the Lord Jesus, and its warnings against adding or subtracting from the words "of this book" make these words appropriate concluding remarks not just for Revelation but for the whole New Testament and, indeed, for the entire Bible.[82] The threat uttered by the risen Christ against any who add to its words is that they will experience the plagues that accompany the opening of the seven seals or the trumpeting of the seven angels or the last seven plagues of Revelation 15–16. In addition, those who subtract from its words lose their share in "the tree of life and in the holy city" (22:1–22:5).

The book of Revelation stands in last position in the vast preponderance of ancient canonical lists and manuscripts, though it follows the Gospels in a few instances.[83] This less common position can be explained in that Revelation opens with an appearance of the risen Christ (ch. 1) and records the words of the resurrected Jesus (esp. chs. 2–3). When Revelation is found at the end of the New Testament, the book may have more than one function.[84] There is an obvious canonical logic to its position at the end of the New Testament, preoccupied as it is with the consummation of God's purposes in human history.[85] As such, it is the goal of the narrative trajectory of the canonical arrangement of the books of the New Testament: The Gospels present the foundational work of Jesus Christ; Acts depicts the spread of the message about Jesus Christ through the mission of the apostles and others; the epistles instruct those in the churches planted as a result of that mission; and finally, Revelation traces salvation history through to the eschaton.

---

81. For the implications of this, see William W. Klein, Craig L. Blomberg, and Robert L. Hubbard Jr., *Introduction to Biblical Interpretation*, 3rd ed. (Grand Rapids: Zondervan, 2017), 558–61.

82. See Sinaiticus, Alexandrinus, and Ephraemi Rescriptus (C). See Peter Balla, "Evidence for an Early Christian Canon (Second and Third Century)," in McDonald and Sanders, *Canon Debate*, 375; Michael J. Kruger, *The Question of Canon: Challenging the Status Quo in the New Testament Debate* (Nottingham: Apollos, 2013), 63; Külli Tõniste, *The Ending of the Canon: A Canonical and Intertextual Reading of Revelation 21–22*, LNTS 526 (London: Bloomsbury T&T Clark, 2016), 189–92.

83. Metzger, *Canon of the New Testament*, 295 n. 1; GNT[4], 10*–18*.

84. For the possible functions of an ending, see Tõniste, *Ending of the Canon*, 132–38.

85. See. e.g., Spellman, *Canon-Conscious Reading*, 84, 172–73.

Like the books that immediately precede (e.g., Jude), Revelation may be best classified as another letter. As such, it picks up and develops a number of themes from the letters of Paul and others (especially the need for endurance, the danger of false teaching, and the coming of Christ). Revelation has a kinship relation to earlier New Testament apocalyptic passages that display similar concerns (Matt 24 and parr.; 2 Thess 2; 2 Pet 3; Jude). In terms of its relation to other Johannine writings, it elaborates on, for example, the pneumatology of John's Gospel.[86] It also elaborates on the link between the Spirit and prophetic activity in 1 John.[87] We expect the book placed last in a connected series to draw together important thematic threads from the books that precede. Indeed, what is picked up (and what is not) can be taken as an indication of the things that matter most in the New Testament canon as a whole.

Early readers gave Revelation special prominence and importance by putting it in final position in the biblical canon,[88] where it forms an inclusio with the first book of the Bible.[89] Genesis describes the creation of the world and the entrance of evil to spoil it, and Revelation matches Genesis by forecasting the final defeat of evil and the renewal of the created order (esp. Rev 21–22).[90] The story of the Bible is not fully told until the book of Revelation supplies its ending. Revelation does this without ignoring either the importance of the Old Testament or the radical newness of the Christ event, narrating a series of God-given visions in ways that are reminiscent of Old Testament apocalyptic passages and yet provide a fresh glimpse of end-time realities.

---

86. John C. Thomas, *The Spirit of the New Testament* (Leiderdorp: Deo, 2005), 157–74.

87. First John 4:1–3; cf., e.g., Rev 1:10; 4:2; 17:3; 19:10 ("the spirit of prophecy"); 21:10; 22:6 ("the God of the spirit of prophecy").

88. See Kent D. Clarke, "Canonical Criticism: An Integrated Reading of Biblical Texts for the Community of Faith," in *Approaches to New Testament Study*, ed. Stanley E. Porter and David Tombs, JSNTSup 120 (Sheffield: Sheffield Academic, 1995), 209: a canonical reading "places emphasis on Revelation as the concluding chapter and final summation of the entire Bible."

89. In line with this, viewing Matt 1:1 (*biblos geneseōs* ["The book of the genealogy"]) as the title for the entire Gospel that it heads sets the story of Jesus as a counterpart to another "history of origins," the book of Genesis.

90. Robert W. Wall, "The Apocalypse of the New Testament in Canonical Context," in Wall and Lemcio, *New Testament as Canon*, 280; cf. Tobias Nicklas, "The Apocalypse in the Framework of the Canon," in *Revelation and the Politics of Apocalyptic Interpretation*, ed. Richard B. Hays and Stefan Alkier (Waco, TX: Baylor University Press, 2012), 143–53.

CHAPTER 3 CONCLUSIONS

The following comments may be made about the order(s) of the books that make up the New Testament. The ordering of books according to (decreasing) size is found a number of times, for example in the Pauline Epistles, both for the series of letters to churches (Romans-Thessalonians) and letters to individuals (1 Timothy-Philemon), and then also for 1-2 Peter and 1-3 John. This may appear to be an arbitrary rationale, but it influences reading. For example, Romans is given special prominence by being placed in premier position within the Pauline corpus.

Assumed common authorship did not ensure that Luke and Acts were placed side by side, nor was the Johannine corpus—John's Gospel, 1-3 John, and the Revelation of John—collected together in one place.[91] However, such authorial connections do imply the ready compatibility of the teaching that comes in the alternative generic forms of Gospel, Acts, and epistle. A different slant is given to Acts depending on whether it is followed by the Pauline Epistles or the Catholic Epistles. Hebrews placed either among (other?) Pauline letters or at the head of the Catholic Epistles acts as a link between these two epistolary collections. Alternative orders of biblical books warn the reader against prescribing any one order as determinative for interpretation.

GUIDELINES FOR INTERPRETING
THE ORDER OF THE NEW TESTAMENT

1. The wide distribution of the Johannine writings assists in unifying the disparate contents of the canon and promotes a reading of the New Testament as a whole from a Johannine perspective with its high Christology.

2. Revelation is given special prominence by putting it at the end of the canon. It is the goal of a narrative trajectory of the preceding books, recapitulating their key themes. With the book of Genesis, Revelation forms an envelope around the

---

91. There is no attempt to differentiate between the Johns in the titles, so that the reader would assume their canonical identity. "Revelation of John" is the earliest title used in manuscripts (ℵ, C); see Metzger, *Textual Commentary*, 662.

whole Bible, bringing God's saving purposes to a satisfying conclusion.

3. For the ordering of the books of the New Testament, considerations of genre dominate, resulting in the bringing together of the different books that make up the four-Gospel collection (plus Acts) and the corpora of Pauline and non-Pauline epistles (with Revelation). This shows that genre is the leading factor in the assemblage of New Testament canonical aggregations.

4. A story line thread also plays a part, so that the events of the life and ministry of Jesus are placed first (Gospels), then an account of the postascension spread of the message about Jesus (Acts), followed by letters addressed to churches that resulted from that proclamation (Letters), and completed by the final placement of Revelation, which encourages a hermeneutic stressing its futuristic orientation.[92]

5. The positioning of each New Testament book relative to other books in the canonical collection, whether in terms of the grouping in which it is placed or the book(s) that follow or precede it, has hermeneutical significance for the reader who seeks meaning in the text.

---

92. See Gregory Goswell, "Two Testaments in Parallel: The Influence of the Old Testament on the Structuring of the New Testament Canon," *JETS* 56 (2013): 459-74.

PART II

BOOK TITLES

4

TITLES OF OLD TESTAMENT BOOKS

INTRODUCTION

The titles assigned to the books of Scripture are an element of paratext that we make use of virtually every time we refer to any given portion of Scripture.[1] The title of a literary work is one of a number of paratextual elements that frame or package the material that forms the text proper. It is only too easy for those who read texts to overlook the influence of the paratext on the reading process. With this in mind, Kevin Jackson has called paratextual elements such as book titles "invisible forms," and he bemoans the fact that they are often unacknowledged and unexamined.[2] The title assigned to a work exercises a powerful influence on its reception.[3] That influence may be for good or for ill, for any given title may be appropriate or otherwise, and so a critical appraisal of this aspect of the paratext of Scripture is in order.[4] The titles of the biblical books deserve and require readerly attention.

---

1. An earlier version of material in this chapter can be found in Gregory Goswell, "What's in a Name? Book Titles in the Torah and Former Prophets," *Pacifica* 20 (2007): 262-77, © Gregory Goswell, 2007, reprinted by permission of SAGE Publications, https://doi.org/10.1177/1030570X0702000302; and Goswell, "What's in a Name? Book Titles in the Latter Prophets and Writings," *Pacifica* 21 (2008): 1-16, © Gregory Goswell, 2008, reprinted by permission of SAGE Publications, https://doi.org/10.1177%2F1030570X0802100102.

2. Kevin Jackson, *Invisible Forms: A Guide to Literary Curiosities* (New York: Thomas Dunne Books, 1999); see ch. 1 on titles.

3. Marie Maclean, "Pretexts and Paratexts: The Art of the Peripheral," *NLH* 22 (1991): 274-75.

4. Gérard Genette, "Structure and Functions of the Title in Literature," *CI* 14 (1988): 692-720; Genette, *Paratexts*, 76-94.

THE POSSIBLE FUNCTIONS OF A BOOK TITLE

Gérard Genette provides a useful interpretive grid in analyzing the possible functions of any given book title. There are a number of possible functions of a title.[5] One is to identify or designate the work, another to indicate its general contents or theme, a third to highlight it to the public, and a fourth to indicate its form or genre. Only the first is unavoidable; the other functions are optional and additional.

Identification is the first and main reason for naming a literary work, and a randomly chosen title is sufficient to fulfill this function, though it is unlikely that any book in the Bible received an arbitrary title, even though some titles (e.g., Leviticus, Ecclesiastes) probably mean little or nothing to many readers. For most readers, the names of the different Bible books usually serve no profounder purpose than that of mere identification, so that a book can be referred to in discussion or communication, or a biblical quotation identified as to source (e.g., John 3:16).

With regard to the second function, the relation between a title and the content of a literary work is extremely variable, and so, for example, the prophet Samuel only features in 1 Samuel, not 2 Samuel, and then mainly in 1 Samuel 1–16. In regard to subject matter or theme, titles inevitably simplify and are highly selective. Since no title can say everything that might be said about the subject of a text, a title may easily mislead readers as to what a text is about (e.g., the title "Kings" obscures the role played by prophets in the directing of Southern and Northern kingdoms).

The title has potentially a wider audience than the text itself, because more people read (or have heard of) the title of a book than have necessarily read the book (e.g., *Robinson Crusoe*), and the title of a work may even influence the opinion of others with regard to it.[6] The title "The Song of Songs" (= The Greatest Song) is a recommendation to the potential reader.

A fourth function of a title is to indicate and assert a work's form,[7] and this may be a variation on the second function, for example, Psalms, Proverbs, Lamentations, and Chronicles. If thematic (content-indicating) titles

---

5. For what follows, see Genette, "Structure and Functions," 708–9.

6. Genette, "Structure and Functions," 707.

7. Genette insists on the assertive nature of generic indications. See Gérard Genette, "Introduction to the Paratext," *NLH* 22 (1991): 268.

dominate the picture today, in classical usage generic (form-indicating) titles predominated.

Whether intentional or not on the part of those who affixed a title to a particular work, the optional second function, the descriptive, is inescapable in practice, for the assigned title is routinely seen as a key for interpretation of a literary work.

TORAH

Torah is the overarching title for a five-book collection. Some would explain the division into five sections as simply due to the practical necessity of not allowing the scrolls of antiquity to become long and unwieldy.[8] The Jewish name for the Pentateuch is Chumash, which recalls its five-book structure. The word *chomesh* ("a fifth") is a way of referring to one of the five books of the Moses (y. Meg. 74a), and the book of Exodus is called "the second fifth" (Sotah 36b). Moshe Greenberg suggests that the largely arbitrary subdivision of the whole is demonstrated by the fact that it is sometimes called "the five fifths of the Torah,"[9] which is equivalent to the Greek *hē pentateuchos (biblos)* (the "five-roll [book]"), from which comes "Pentateuch," through the Latin version *pentateuchus (liber)*. This logic is, however, questionable, and Rolf Rendtorff insists that each of the books has a distinctive character,[10] and the assigning of titles to each supports their integrity. For example, Genesis is structured by means of a repeated genealogical formula, "These are the generations of ..." (2:4; 5:1; 6:9; 11:27; etc.), which ties the various parts of this book into a unity, and the book closes with the death of Joseph, which brings the patriarchal era to an end (see Exod 1:6).

Placing the first five books under the title "Pentateuch" draws the reader's attention to its five-book structure and, properly understood, asserts the individuality of the books as well as their essential relation to one another. The name "Torah" does not have to suggest that Genesis to Deuteronomy contains nothing but legislation for the nation of Israel, though it does highlight the

---

8. E.g., Moshe Greenberg, *Introduction to Hebrew* (Englewood Cliffs, NJ: Prentice-Hall, 1965), 175. The same explanation is offered by some for the twenty-four books of Homer's *The Iliad* as representing an original division into twenty-four papyrus rolls as a physical necessity for the immense literary work.

9. E.g., Norman H. Snaith, *Sefer Torah, Nevi'im uKetuvim* (London: British and Foreign Bible Society, 1958).

10. Rendtorff, *Old Testament*, 131.

Sinaitic didactic portions given a central position in the corpus (Exod 20–23; Leviticus; Num 1–9). The usual English rendering "law" has a legalistic ring not present in the underlying Hebrew word, which is closer to "instruction."[11] Deuteronomy in its opening sentences classifies its contents in this way (1:5) and the description is broad enough to encompass the sermonic or hortatory character of the speeches of Moses. What happened is that the word first used to designate Deuteronomy (see Josh 1:8: "this book of the law") was later reapplied to the Pentateuch as a whole. This also suggests that all five books should be read through the theological lens provided by Deuteronomy.

Genesis

Following the ancient Near-Eastern custom,[12] the Hebrew titles of the first five books are incipits (openings), taken from the first (significant) word(s) of the books, so that Genesis is named bərēšît ("In the beginning"). As a book of beginnings, it describes a series of starts: the origin of the earth, of humanity, and of Israel in the persons of its patriarchal forebears, so that the title can be understood to designate the general theme of the book. In the Greek Bible the title of each book in the Pentateuch gives a rough characterization of its content. In the present case the Hebrew and Greek (*Genesis* = "Origin") titles do not differ greatly. This is not the case for the other four books. The Greek title is an abbreviation of *genesis kosmou*, "The Origin of the World" (the form in Alexandrinus)[13] and may be traced to the LXX rendering of Genesis 2:4: "This is the book of the origin [*geneseōs*] of the heavens and the earth," with the same Greek word used to translate the Hebrew *tôlədôt* ("generations") in the repeated genealogical formula. The names of four out of the first five books in the Greek Bible are, in effect, allusions to specific passages from the respective books.

---

11. Barnabas Lindars, "Torah in Deuteronomy," in *Words and Meanings: Essays Presented to David Winton Thomas*, ed. P. R. Ackroyd (Cambridge: Cambridge University Press, 1968), 117–36, who emphasizes the didactic character of the word "Torah."

12. See W. G. Lambert and A. R. Millard, *Atra-hasis: The Babylonian Story of the Flood* (Oxford: Clarendon, 1969), 32, 42–43, in which colophons refer to tablets by their first line of text.

13. A. Rahlfs, ed., *Septuaginta* (Stuttgart: Deutsche Bibelstiftung, 1935), 1:1.

Exodus

"Exodus" in the Hebrew canon is named (wə'ēlle) səmôt, "[Now these are] the names of," a reference to the names of the twelve sons of Jacob, though these names are not used much in the book itself. This is, however, the start of the *real* Old Testament, in that it is here that the twelve-tribe nation of Israel is produced (1:7) and the family of Jacob becomes "the people of Israel" (1:9).[14] The rest of the Old Testament is the story of this nation. The LXX title is *Exodos*, referring to "The Going Out [from Egypt]," and the fuller form of the title is found in Alexandrinus (*exodos Aigyptou*). The subscription in Alexandrinus takes the form of "The exodus of the sons of Israel from Egypt."[15] This tries to summarize the content of the book (a second function title), though it refers only to the material up to chapter 14 (or maybe ch. 18). The word appears in LXX 19:1 (*tēs exodou*) when the Israelites arrive at Mount Sinai,[16] which can be viewed as the immediate goal of the deliverance (see Exod 3:12), and 19:4 could be read as a poetic summarizing of the events in the preceding eighteen chapters. The Greek title is presumably an allusion to 19:1. This title throws the weight onto the first half of the book, yet the Sinai goal is perhaps even more important than the preceding rescue, with its covenant making (chs. 19–24) and provision for the ongoing worship of God (chs. 25–40).[17]

Leviticus

Leviticus in Hebrew is titled *wayyiqrā'* ("Then he [YHWH] called"), and this amounts to a generic description of the book as (divine) speeches (Genette's fourth function). The title is extracted from the first verse of the book ("[Then he] *called* Moses and spoke to him from the tent of meeting" [ESV]). This title gives no clue as to the content of the speeches. The LXX title is *Leuitikon* (in Vaticanus and Alexandrinus), an adjective modifying the word *biblion*, and thus "Levitical [and priestly] book/matters." On one level, the title is not

---

14. This is the first application of the word "people" ('am) to Israel in the OT.

15. Rahlfs, *Septuaginta*, 86, 158.

16. Philo uses the title *hē exagogē*, likewise meaning "The Going Out." See H. E. Ryle, *Philo and Holy Scripture* (London: Macmillan, 1895), xx–xxiv, cited in Beckwith, *Old Testament Canon*, 246.

17. See Graham Davies, "The Theology of Exodus," in *In Search of True Wisdom: Essays in Old Testament Interpretation in Honour of Ronald E. Clements*, ed. Edward Ball, JSOTSup 300 (Sheffield: Sheffield Academic, 1999), 137–52.

an obvious one, seeing that the word "Levites" (sg. *leueitēs*) is only found in Leviticus 25:32-33 (twice in each verse), but the priests arose from the tribe of Levi, and "Aaron and his sons" feature prominently in Leviticus.[18] The Vulgate designates it simply as *Leviticus*, a title that summarizes the content of the speeches with their religious orientation (Genette's second function). The Hebrew (Mishnaic) titles "Book of Priests" and "Book of Offerings" are, likewise, second function titles that characterize the contents as about regulations for worship.

Numbers

Numbers (Vulgate *Numeri*) shows that the Hebrew title is not necessarily the first word but instead what was seen as the first *significant* word, *bəmidbar* ("in the wilderness"), the opening words being "YHWH spoke to Moses *in the wilderness* of Sinai." Perhaps the first word *wayədabbēr* ("Then he spoke") was too similar to the opening of the previous book (and the following book, for that matter). Certainly, divine speeches in Numbers do not play the prominent part they do in Leviticus. The Hebrew title serves to foreground the years of wilderness testing occupying the central section of the book (chs. 11-21),[19] which gives the book its separate identity compared to the books on either side of it, for Numbers 1-10 shares the same location as Exodus 19-40, and Numbers 22-36 is situated "in the plains of Moab," just as is Deuteronomy. The LXX title *arithmoi* in Vaticanus and Alexandrinus, or "Numbers," highlights the census lists of the two generations (chs. 1, 26), which are seen by Dennis Olsen as the key to the book's structure,[20] so that an exegetical insight is provided by the Septuagintal title. The contrast between the two generations—their differing character and fate—is central to the implied message of the book about the requirement of faithfulness to inherit the promises.

---

18. John Ellington, "Translating Old Testament Book Titles," *BT* 34 (1983): 227.

19. See Allan A. MacRae, "The Book Called 'Numbers,' " *BSac* 111 (1954): 47-53.

20. Dennis T. Olsen, *The Death of the Old and the Birth of the New: The Framework of Numbers and the Pentateuch*, BJS 71 (Chico, CA: Scholars Press, 1985). The word *arithmos* is found in LXX Num 1:2 and fourteen times in total in Num 1 (vv. 2, 18, 20, 22, 24, etc.).

Deuteronomy

Deuteronomy is given the Hebrew title *dəbārîm* ("words"), derived from the book's opening ("These are the words ..."), because the book consists of speeches of a hortatory character by Moses. This fourth function title highlights the form in which divine revelation comes.[21] The LXX title *Deuteronomion* (Vaticanus, Alexandrinus) is usually explained as referring to the "Second Law," a repetition of the law by Moses before his death. It is dependent on Deuteronomy 17:18 (*misnē hattôrâ hazzōʾt*), which the LXX renders "this second law," whereas the Hebrew text really means "a copy of this law" (RSV). The Latin formulations of the five Pentateuchal titles have come into English through the Vulgate. The title of Deuteronomy, at least as commonly interpreted, refers to a second body of laws different and distinct from those given at Sinai. This reflects the hermeneutical problem of the relation between the laws as expounded in Deuteronomy and earlier forms promulgated at Sinai. Why are some laws different, and how different are they? The title, if understood in this way, would seem to encourage what has been a preoccupation both of traditional Jewish exegesis and modern critical analysis. The first approach is harmonistic, and the second tends to exploit differences.

It is not clear, however, that the Greek translators necessarily intended the title to mean "Second Law," and Rashi's commentary on Deuteronomy understands 17:18 to mean "two Torah scrolls" (*štê siprê tôrâ*), one to be placed in the king's treasure house and one to carry around for consultation. Seeing that the king in Deuteronomy is portrayed as a model citizen, it is not an inappropriate passage for the Greek title to highlight. The king sets an example by habitually reading the law, doing what all Israelites should be doing (6:7–9; 11:18–21). The king is engrossed in the study of the law "that he may learn to fear the LORD his God" (17:19), which is a key Deuteronomic virtue (see 4:10; 5:26 [29]; 6:2; 14:23). In this way the book's ethic of obedience is modeled by the king, who sets an example for all his Israelite "brothers."[22]

---

21. Peter C. Craigie draws attention to the importance of the Hebrew title as a self-description of the book as "a report of words which were spoken." See Craigie, *The Book of Deuteronomy*, NICOT (London: Hodder and Stoughton, 1976), 17–18.

22. For more, see Gregory Goswell, "The Paratext of Deuteronomy," in *Interpreting Deuteronomy: Issues and Approaches*, ed. David Firth and Philip Johnston (Nottingham: Inter-Varsity, 2012), 209–28.

FORMER PROPHETS

The books Joshua to Kings in the Hebrew canon (Ruth not included) are called the "Former Prophets," perhaps because the viewpoint taken of the history narrated is to a large extent that of the early prophets.[23] According to John Barton, the four books were designated prophecy because, though narrative, they are paradigmatic, and in that sense predictive, of God's ongoing dealings with his people. They "are an expression of the eternal shape of God's purpose for his people: a pattern of his chastisement and consolation."[24] Certainly, the history recounted becomes the basis for prophetic appeals to covenant loyalty. Reference is made to a *series* of prophets, for example, Deborah (Judg 4:4), Samuel (1 Sam 3:20), Nathan (2 Sam 7:2; 12:1), Gad (24:11), and Ahijah (1 Kgs 11:29), though it is only in the books of Samuel and Kings that prophetic figures become a *regular* feature of the narrative, and only really in Kings that the competition between prophets and kings is central to the theology of the narrative. So too, the prediction-fulfillment formula is only really prominent in the book of Kings. These four books are regularly in English called "Histories," for they are part of the sequential history recounted by the books Joshua to Esther in the Greek canon.

Joshua

The titles Joshua, Judges, Samuel, and Kings give the Former Prophets a leadership focus that is quite appropriate. The book divisions at significant deaths (Josh 1:1; Judg 1:1; 2 Sam 1:1; 2 Kgs 1:1) have the same effect. The title "Joshua" (LXX *Iēsous*) obviously refers to the main character and leader, who is mentioned in the first verse (Josh 1:1). The title implies that this is a book *about* Joshua and need not be taken as meaning that it was written by Joshua. After the description of his commissioning (1:1-9), the book is demarcated by an inclusio formed by speeches made by and to Joshua in the remainder of chapter 1 and in the final two chapters (23-24). Joshua 1-6 is a Joshua apology (see 6:27), accrediting him as the God-appointed successor to Moses.[25] Following that, Joshua leads in the conquest (chs. 7-12) and divides the land

---

23. John Barton, "'The Law and the Prophets': Who Are the Prophets?," in *The Old Testament: Canon, Literature and Theology: Collected Essays of John Barton* (Aldershot: Ashgate, 2007), 13.

24. See Mark A. O'Brien, "The 'Deuteronomistic History' as a Story of Israel's Leaders," *ABR* 37 (1989): 14-34.

25. See Dennis J. McCarthy, "The Theology of Leadership in Joshua 1-9," *Bib* 52 (1971): 165-75.

(chs. 13-21). All these features serve to underscore the leadership issue, as does the death notice with which the book starts: "After the death of Moses." The book closes with the recording of the death of Joshua (24:29-30), together with two other important burials.

The title foregrounds the role of Joshua, but alternative titles could have suggested other foci. Joshua 10:13 makes mention of a certain "Book of Jashar" (RSV), which is also quoted from in 2 Samuel 1:18. This lost book appears to be a collection of odes in praise of the exploits of select Israelite heroes. The RSV renders it as a proper name ("Jashar"), which, if related to "Jeshurun" (yəšurûn), a poetic name for Israel (Deut 32:15; 33:26-27), suggests some kind of national epic celebrating the acts of the incomparable God of Israel. Equally probable is the suggestion that it means "the upright [one]" (RSV margin), perhaps to be construed as a collective: "the Book of Heroes" (Moffatt). The book called the "Book of the Wars of the LORD" (Num 21:14) could possibly be the same book under a different title. Seeing that the book of Joshua attributes Israelite military success to God's blessing (e.g., 1:9, 15, 17), a title might have been chosen that highlights that rather than the human instrument YHWH chose to use in the conquest of Canaan.

Judges

Judges (LXX *Kritai*), whose title reflects the Hebrew name *šôpəṭîm*, is set in the post-Joshua situation (Judg 1:1; 2:6-10). The title makes the stories of the judges, six major and six minor (chs. 3-16), the highlighted feature (2:16). In this way, the main focus in the book of Judges is leadership. The English word "judge" suggests a *legal* figure, but the Hebrew word indicates the more general role of leader. The judges were not primarily concerned with legal matters but were fundamentally savior figures.[26] The unity of Israel and its twelve-tribe structure remains intact (but only just) at the end of the period (Judg 19-21), so that the institution of judgeship is shown to be functional. There is no implication in the presentation that the newfangled institution

---

26. A. Malamat, "Charismatic Leadership in the Book of Judges," in *Magnalia Dei: The Mighty Acts of God: Essays on the Bible and Archeology in Memory of G. Ernest Wright*, ed. F. M. Cross et al. (Garden City, NY: Doubleday, 1976), 152-68.

of kingship would be any better at solving the problems of the nation than
the well-tried office of the judge.[27]

Samuel

The book of Samuel (Vulgate *Liber Samuelis*) coincides with the Hebrew
naming of the book after the first of three major characters, Samuel, Saul,
and David, whose interconnected lives and fates are recounted. A partial
climax is found in Samuel's (supposed) farewell speech in 1 Samuel 12, but
Samuel is not accepting retirement (12:23). Samuel has important roles in
1 Samuel 13; 15–16, and he is mentioned again in 19:18–24. His death notice
only comes in 25:1, and even then he returns one more time to pronounce
Saul's doom (1 Sam 28). Samuel has, in effect, superintended the career of
Saul from its beginning to its end. Samuel is not featured at all in 2 Samuel,
but his epochal role in anointing Saul and David is justification enough for
the book to be named after him.[28]

On the other hand, A. F. Campbell sees the book(s) of Samuel as being
about David and oriented toward David (and his dynasty) from the beginning, and it is true that Samuel is less visible after he has anointed David, so
that Campbell asserts that "Samuel's life-work is finished by 1 Sam 16:13."[29] If
that is accepted, a more appropriate title for the book would be "David," but
this possibility may have been excluded by the fact that "David" was early on
used as a way of referring to the book of Psalms.[30] An alternative viewpoint is
provided by Diana Edel Viewing 1 Samuel 31 as an endpoint, however, turns
1 Samuel 9–31 into a story about Saul and not a section detailing the rise of
David (which does not end until 2 Sam 5). Perhaps nothing is to be gained
by adjudicating what is likely to be a perennial dispute among scholars, for
the good reason that there is a special interest in the book in the persons and
personal characteristics of all three protagonists.

---

27. For a more extensive argument along these lines, see Gregory Goswell, "The Attitude
to Kingship in the Book of Judges," *TJ* 40 (2019): 3–18.

28. Stanley D. Walters suggests that the title "Samuel" is a hermeneutical guide, alerting the
reader to the prophetic outlook of the narrative, so that "royal ideology must be subservient to
prophetic ideology." See Walters, "Reading Samuel to Hear God," *CTJ* 37 (2002): 68.

29. A. F. Campbell, *1 Samuel*, FOTL 7 (Grand Rapids: Eerdmans, 2003), 25.

30. E.g., 2 Macc 2:13–15; Heb 4:7; and 4QMMT as reconstructed in E. Qimron and J. Strugnell,
Qumrân Cave 4.V: Miqsat Maʿase ha-Torah, DJD 10 (Oxford: Clarendon, 1984), 59.

The alternative names given to the book of Samuel in the Greek (and Latin) tradition, the First and Second Books of "Reigns" or "Kingdoms," are approved by some commentators as "more apposite,"[31] for this title highlights the transition to kingship that is plotted in the book(s) of Samuel and throws the focus on Saul and David as the first two kings. The presentation does not, however, have to be understood as a blanket endorsement of kingship as a divine institution for the present or the future. It more likely looks back without nostalgia to a bygone age when kings reigned in Judah and Israel. Samuel is a theological endorsement of human kingship that was rejected during the period of the judges, yet the book is alive to the dangers of this institution.

Kings

The book of Kings (Vulgate *Liber Regum*) is the Third and Fourth Books of Kingdoms in the LXX (*basileiōn*) and Vulgate (*Regnorum*), corresponding to the Hebrew title *məlākîm* ("Kings"). In the 1518 folio edition of the Bomberg Rabbinic Bible, the book is not divided, but there is a marginal note (in Hebrew) at 2 Kings 1: "Here the Greeks and Latins begin the Fourth Book of Kings." In the quarto edition of 1521, there is at 2 Kings 1 the marginal note "Book Four."[32] The evident relation of Samuel and Kings is signaled in the Greek Bible, and following that, the Latin Bible, by their counting Samuel and Kings as four books of "Kingdoms." In the first two chapters of Kings, aged David dies (1 Kgs 1:1: "Now King David was old, gone in years"), so that it begins virtually "after the death of David" (see 1 Kgs 2:10–12) and is occupied with the reigns of the kings of both Judah and Israel in the post-David era.

The division between the books of Samuel and Kings is not arbitrary, since 2 Samuel 21–24 closes the book by reviewing the flow of the preceding narrative.[33] Leonhard Rost's theory of the succession narrative, presented in The Succession to the Throne of David, sees that narrative including and culminating with 1 Kings 1–2, but this approach has to be rejected for not giving enough credence to the canonical boundary between the books of Samuel and

---

31. E.g., Ralph W. Klein, *First Samuel*, WBC 10 (Waco, TX: Word Books, 1983), xxv.

32. G. F. Moore, "The Vulgate Chapters and Numbered Verses in the Hebrew Bible," in *The Canon and Masorah of the Hebrew Bible: An Introductory Reader*, ed. Sid Z. Leiman (New York: Ktav, 1974), 816.

33. Brevard S. Childs, *Introduction to the Old Testament as Scripture* (London: SCM, 1979), 273–75.

Kings. The LXX division (and that of the Vulgate following it) is at 2 Kings 1:1
("After the death of Ahab"). This evil king is described in superlative terms
(1 Kgs 16:30: "Ahab the son of Omri did evil in the sight of YHWH more than
all that were before him"), so that after the death of the *worst* northern king
there is perhaps hope for the nation. It may thus be viewed as a favorable
turning point.[34] All this construes the book as one chronicling the reigns of
successive kings,[35] yet the prophets are equally prominent (or nearly so) in
the book named Kings. There is a series of named prophets (e.g., Nathan, Gad,
Abijah) and especially a large amount of material on Elijah and Elisha, and
the book may be analyzed in terms of the repeated pattern of confrontations
between kings and prophets.[36] The expression in 2 Maccabees 2:13-15, "the
books about kings and prophets," probably refers to Samuel and Kings, and
all in all a more apt title for Kings would be "Kings and Prophets."[37]

LATTER PROPHETS

The Latter Prophets has four large books: Isaiah, Jeremiah, Ezekiel, and the
Twelve. Unlike the Former Prophets, whose books are named after main characters (e.g., Joshua, Samuel) or content (e.g., Judges, Kings), the books of the
Latter Prophets are named after the prophetic mouthpiece used by God (e.g.,
Isaiah, Jeremiah, Micah). The common titles of the separate books (Isaiah,
Jeremiah, Amos, etc.) are justified by the superscriptions that head most of
them (e.g., Isa 1:1; Jer 1:1-3; Amos 1:1). Alexandrinus in its subscriptions to the
three great prophetic books has "Isaiah the prophet" and so on.[38] The titles
amount to abbreviations of long superscriptions and so do not give all the
information that the superscriptions do. For example, kings are mentioned
by name in a number of the superscriptions but do not make it into the titles.
The abbreviated titles imply "Isaiah's message" and so on.

---

34. T. R. Hobbs, "2 Kings 1 and 2: Their Unity and Purpose," *SR* 13 (1984): 334.

35. The titles for the sources used confirm such an orientation, e.g., "Book of the Acts [*dibrê*] of Solomon" (1 Kgs 11:41), "Book of the Chronicles of the Kings of Israel" (1 Kgs 14:19), "Book of the Chronicles of the Kings of Judah" (2 Kgs 8:23).

36. E.g., Victor H. Matthews, "Kings of Israel: A Question of Crime and Punishment," in *SBL 1988 Seminar Papers*, ed. David J. Hull (Atlanta: Scholars Press, 1988), 517-26.

37. A similar title is used by A. F. Campbell for the book *Of Prophets and Kings: A Late Ninth Century Document (1 Samuel 1–2 Kings 10)*, CBQMS 17 (Washington, DC: Catholic Biblical Association of America, 1986).

38. Rahlfs, *Septuaginta*, 566, 656, 748, 770, 863.

It cannot be said, however, that the personal figure of the prophet is prominent in most of the books so named. Isaiah features in his prophecy only in chapters 6-8; 20; and 36-39. Jeremiah as a character is mainly found in chapters 26-29 and 32-44. His prophetic book provides a "biography of the word," not of Jeremiah himself, who is featured only as the bearer of the word, and he suffers because God's word is rejected. Ezekiel features in his call in Ezekiel 1 and his prophetic actions in chapters 4-5 and 12, but in quite a different way from Jeremiah, whose ministry was a very public one. Ezekiel's disconnection with his situation has led to scholarly debate over his location.[39] The result is that Ezekiel as a character is not as prominent in the book named after him as is Jeremiah in his book.

In Hosea 1-3 the pattern of Israel's history is reflected in the marriage relationship of Hosea and Gomer. Gomer's sin, punishment, and restoration symbolizes God's dealings with Israel. The prophet Amos only features in Amos 7:10-17, which is part of the larger theme of the silencing of the prophets (2:12; 3:8; 5:13).[40] The priest Amaziah urges Amos to flee to Judah and preach there, not in Bethel. The little prophecy of Jonah is in reverse proportions to other prophetic books, being a narrative *about* the prophet, with the oracle of Jonah (3:4) limited to five words (in Hebrew). The prophet's own character and psychology are the focal point of the book. Jonah is a prophetic caricature or parody.[41] On the whole, then, little information is provided about the prophets as people, and Joel, Obadiah, Nahum, Habakkuk, and Malachi are names only. In the case of Malachi (Heb. "my messenger"), we may not even know that. The titles put the focus on the prophetic mouthpiece, but the books are not reflective of a biographical interest per se, and with the exception of the book of Jonah, they largely consist of an anthology of the oracles of the prophets.[42]

The failure of the brief titles to specify to whom the prophet speaks— whether to Judah, to Israel, or to the exiles—which is often in the

---

39. John F. Kutsko, *Between Heaven and Earth: Divine Presence and Absence in the Book of Ezekiel*, BJSUCSD 7 (Winona Lake, IN: Eisenbrauns, 2000), 15-18.

40. P. R. Ackroyd, "A Judgment Narrative between Kings and Chronicles? An Approach to Amos 7:9-17," in *Canon and Authority: Essays in Old Testament Religion and Theology*, ed. George W. Coats and Burke O. Long (Philadelphia: Fortress, 1977), 71-87.

41. Robin Payne, "The Prophet Jonah: Reluctant Messenger and Intercessor," *ExpTim* 100 (1989): 131. The book of Jonah amounts to a manual on how *not* to be a prophet!

42. See Luke 3:4: "the book of the words of Isaiah the prophet" (cf. Luke 4:17, 20).

superscription, is a feature that helps to universalize their message. With regard to the individuals whom the prophetic scrolls invoke as the eponyms, it is not necessarily the case that those who appended the prophets' names to the respective books viewed the prophets as the authors of their books.

The titles are not straightforward claims about authorship. Certainly, the book of Jonah's highly critical stance toward its protagonist does not suggest that Jonah himself is a likely candidate for author.

In the Hebrew Bible the prophets Hosea to Malachi are combined together in one book as "the Twelve Prophets." Consistent with this understanding, Epiphanius (*De Mensuris et Ponderibus* 23) transliterates in Greek letters the Hebrew title when referring to this part of the canon (*dathariasara*). As part of a review of Old Testament worthies, Sirach 49:10 mentions "the bones of the twelve prophets [*tōn dōdeka prophētōn*]." This wording reflects the view that the twelve prophetic books are a collection. This Hebrew designation also appears in the Babylonian Talmud (b. B. Bat. 14b) and is matched by *dōdekaprophētōn* in the LXX (Vaticanus, Alexandrinus). Acts 7:42 refers to the Book of the Twelve under the title "the Book of the Prophets" (*en biblō tōn prophetōn*) in introducing a quotation from Amos 5:25–27. The Vulgate designates them *Prophetae Minores*, represented in English by the "Minor Prophets." This common designation refers only to the relative brevity of the individual books, not to their importance. It probably derives from Augustine (*City of God* 18.29). In the Jewish canonical lists, the Twelve Prophets are always counted as one book. The limitation of their number to twelve (one prophet per tribe?) appears to express completeness, that is, there are twelve and no more, marking and asserting the end of Old Testament prophecy.[43] Not only is Malachi the last canonical prophet, but there is also no expectation of any beyond him.

WRITINGS

The naming of the third part of the Hebrew canon, "the Writings" (*hak-kətûbîm*), reflects its *disparate* contents, with this group of books being the most diverse and heterogeneous of the three groupings in the Tanak in terms

---

43. Conrad, "End of Prophecy."

of form and content.[44] The term "Hagiographa," as an alternate name for the Writings, corresponds to the expression *kətûbê haqqôdeš* (the Holy Writings), used by the Jews in antiquity for the books of the third division of their canon.[45] A general expression such as that also allows this section of the canon to encompass works belonging to many genres.

Psalms

Psalms (Vulgate *Liber Psalmorum*) is in Hebrew [*sēpēr*] *təhillîm*, that is "[book of] praises," though the word occurs (in the singular) only once in a title to an individual psalm (Ps 145, "Praise of David"). Philo and Josephus use the Greek word *hymnoi* ("hymns"), apparently in reference to the book (Philo, *Contempl.* 25; Josephus, *Ag. Ap.* 1.38-41), and this could go back to *təhillîm*. The title corresponds with its designation in the New Testament, the "book of psalms" (*biblos psalmōn*) (Luke 20:42; Acts 1:20). Melito calls it *Psalmōn Dabid* ("The Psalms of David"), and this makes the Davidic connection explicit (Eusebius, *Hist. eccl.* 4.26). The LXX (Vaticanus, Sinaiticus) calls it *psalmoi*, which word in the Greek versions is used to render another Hebrew word, *mizmôr* ("song, melody"), found often in the titles of individual psalms (e.g., Pss 47-51). This word makes the book an anthology of hymns to be sung to musical accompaniment. Praise is where the Psalter *ends* (Pss 146-50), but it is not an obvious name for the book when the reader commences, for the early psalms are mostly laments (e.g., Pss 3-7). However, the first four books of the Psalter end with short doxologies (41:13; 72:18-19; 89:52; 106:48), and the Psalter as a whole closes with five hallelujah psalms that are all praise (Pss 146-50).[46]

The title is also in some tension with the book's setting among wisdom books and the positioning of Psalm 1 as an *introduction*, but it has the virtue of keeping alive the memory of its use in communal praise (as reflected in some psalm titles).[47] The Hebrew title *təhillîm* emphasizes the feature of praise that

---

44. David Noel Freedman, *The Unity of the Hebrew Bible* (Ann Arbor: University of Michigan Press, 1991), 75.

45. Harry M. Orlinsky, "Prolegomenon: The Masoretic Text: A Critical Evaluation," in *Introduction to the Massoretico-Critical Edition of the Hebrew Bible*, by C. D. Ginsburg (New York: Ktav, 1966), xl.

46. For the significance of the Psalter ending with praise, see Walter Brueggemann, "Bounded by Obedience and Praise: The Psalms as Canon," *JSOT* 50 (1991): 63-92.

47. See Harry P. Nasuti's discussion of the title, *Defining the Sacred Songs: Genre, Tradition and the Post-Critical Interpretation of the Psalms*, JSOTSup 218 (Sheffield: Sheffield Academic, 1999), 194-96.

is found in almost all the psalms, even the psalms of lament (e.g., 3:3; 7:11). It is a faith statement to the effect that in the good purposes of God lament will eventually give way to praise. Another English title, "Psalter," comes from Alexandrinus, which gives this book the title *psaltērion*,[48] meaning "stringed instrument," on the assumption that the psalms are songs to be sung to the lyre. This word is used in the Greek Psalter to translate the Hebrew words *kinnôr* (e.g., LXX Pss 48:4 [Eng. 49:4]) or *nebel* (e.g., LXX Pss 32:2 [Eng. 33:2]; 56:8 [Eng. 57:8]). Such a naming also construes the Psalter as a book of praise.

Job

The book of Job matches its Hebrew name, referring not to the putative author of the work but to its main character, the long-suffering Job, who is a wisdom model (1:1: "one who feared God"; cf. the motto of Prov 1:7). Job's fascinating, at times hair-raising, speeches mean that his character is at the forefront of the reader's attention, for the book is no academic and disembodied discussion of suffering and evil.

Proverbs

"Proverbs" (Vaticanus *Paroimiai*) corresponds to the Hebrew *mišlê* ("the Proverbs of [Solomon]") as in the superscription (1:1),[49] and the singular noun *māšāl* ("proverb") is used in 1:6 along with a number of close synonyms. This title inevitably throws the emphasis on chapters 10–31 as the *body* of the book, with chapters 1–9 viewed as introductory. Indeed, it is of the final twenty-one chapters that we tend to think when the book of Proverbs is mentioned. An acceptance of this title may reverse the canonical focus, seeing that chapters 1–9 appear to serve as a hermeneutical guide to the rest of the book, that is, chapters 10–31 are to be read through the lens of chapters 1–9, which place a profound theological nuance on the individual proverbs, many of which make no reference to God.[50] The inclusion of the name of Solomon in the title (either as author or collector or both) also suggests a religious

---

48. This is the name given in the Bryennios list. See J.-P. Audet, "A Hebrew-Aramaic List of the Books of the Old Testament in Greek Transcription," *JTS* 1 (1950): 136.

49. Alexandrinus gives the fuller title *Paroimiai Solomōntos*, and Sinaiticus adds *Solomōntos* in the subscription; see Milne and Skeat, *Scribes and Correctors*, plate 4.

50. The Hebrew (Mishnaic) title *sēpēr ḥokmâ* ("Book of Wisdom") classifies Proverbs as in the genre of wisdom literature and perhaps identifies it as the apotheosis of wisdom thinking.

orientation for the book as a whole, given that this king's supreme wisdom in Kings is depicted as God-given (1 Kgs 3:3–14).[51]

Ruth

The book received this title, Ruth (LXX *Routh*; MT *rût*), despite the fact that the book depicts the crisis of Naomi, who is left without husband and sons (1:3–5), the plot moving from her emptiness (1:21) to her fullness (4:17). All the other characters—her husband, her sons, her two daughters-in-law, Boaz, even the son whom Ruth bears—stand in relation to Naomi (1:3, 5–6; 2:1; 4:17). All this tends to focus the story from Naomi's perspective.[52] On the other hand, Boaz is the best-connected character in terms of the number of links with other persons (starting in 2:1), including David.[53] Why, then, was the book called Ruth? It is the figure of Ruth who captures the reader's interest, because it is she who features in every scene in the book except that at the city gate, and there she is the subject of conversation in that all-male situation. The main theme of the book is the manner and method by which Naomi's hopeless condition is reversed, and it is through loyal and active Ruth that the reversal takes place, and Ruth (and Boaz) embody an ethic of kindness (*ḥesed*), so the book of Ruth can be considered aptly named.

The Song of Songs

The name Song of Songs, in Hebrew *šîr haššîrîm* (= the greatest song),[54] would appear to be a recommendation of it as the song of supreme beauty (GNB 1:1) or artistic merit (Genette's third function), and it takes the same form in the Latin (*Canticum Canticorum*).[55] The alternative English title "The Song of Solomon" (AV), which amounts to a differently worded abbreviation of the superscription, makes a Solomon connection, and this links the song to other canonical wisdom productions such as Proverbs and Ecclesiastes (see Prov

---

51. Melito expands the title as *Solomōntos Paroimiai, hē kai Sophia* ("The Proverbs of Solomon, which is also Wisdom") (Eusebius, *Hist. eccl.* 4.26.12–14).

52. Adele Berlin, *Poetics and Interpretation of Biblical Narrative*, BLS 9 (Sheffield: Almond, 1983), 83–110.

53. As demonstrated by John T. Dekker and Anthony H. Dekker, "Centrality in the Book of Ruth," *VT* 68 (2018): 41–50.

54. Ronald J. Williams, *Hebrew Syntax: An Outline*, 2nd ed. (Toronto: University of Toronto Press, 1976), §47.

55. Likewise, the usual German title, *Hohelied*.

1:1; Eccl 1:1). Solomon is not, however, the lover depicted, despite his considerable reputation, even notoriety, in this field (see 1 Kgs 11:1–3). The LXX title (Vaticanus) is simply *Asma* ("Song"), and this is a generic designation, but Sinaiticus has a more literal rendering of the Hebrew title (*Asma asmatōn*). The wisdom connection via Solomon's name implies that the Song is more than an effusive outpouring of sentiment but is a means of instruction, for example, the urging in the refrain-like verses at 2:7; 3:5; and 8:4 ("that you stir not up nor awaken love until it please" [RSV]).

Ecclesiastes

Ecclesiastes in Hebrew bears the title *qōhelet*, drawn from the superscription in Ecclesiastes 1:1 ("The words of Qoheleth"). The term is used in 1:1–2; 7:27; and 12:8–10. It comes from the Hebrew root *qāhal* ("to collect"), and this Hebrew participial form is an occupational designation. Ecclesiastes 12:9 may imply "assembly of pupils" (he collects students).[56] The English title "Ecclesiastes" comes from the Greek, meaning "member of the assembly," but the title may refer to the author as an "assembler (of proverbs)," also due to what is said about him in 12:9, and this may be the best suggestion for what the Hebrew word means. This draws attention to the presence of proverbial material in the book (e.g., 7:1–13) and helps to relate Ecclesiastes to the book of Proverbs as a partner book.

There are also Solomon-like descriptions in the book (1:1, 12, 16; 2:4–11), though a claim to have wisdom "surpassing all who were over Jerusalem before me" sounds a little odd (1:16; 2:7, 9 ESV), seeing that Solomon was only preceded by *one* such king, David, his father. It may, however, be a stock phrase that is not meant to be taken literally (see 1 Chr 29:25). It seems clear enough that the reader is meant to think of Solomon, the consummate wise king who had everything, yet it has also been suggested that this first-person narrative is in the form of a fictional autobiography (one can make a strong case for comparison with Akkadian fictional autobiographies).[57] The Solomonic connection asserts that Ecclesiastes, for all its oddities, is orthodox

---

56. Qoheleth Rabbah 1:2 adopts this explanation (referring to 1 Kgs 8:1: "Then Solomon assembled [*yaqhēl*] the elders of Israel ...."

57. C. L. Seow, "Qohelet's Autobiography," in *Fortunate the Eyes That See: Essays in Honor of David Noel Freedman in Celebration of His Seventieth Birthday*, ed. Astrid B. Beck et al. (Grand Rapids: Eerdmans, 1995), 275–87.

and *official* wisdom literature rather than "wisdom in revolt,"[58] and its teaching is compatible with the book of Proverbs.

Lamentations

The book in Hebrew is named after its first word, *'êkâ*, being the characteristic lament "Ah, How!" which is found again in prominent position in Lamentations 2:1 and 4:1. The LXX, however, named it after its content, "Laments [of Jeremiah]" (*Thrēnoi*),[59] as did the Vulgate *Threni*, with the interpretation "The lamentations of Jeremiah the prophet" (*Threni, id est lamentationes Jeremiae Prophetae*), and the English title (KJV) is derived from the Latin. The title in Latin (*Lamentationes Jeremiae Prophetae*) is an authorship claim, and this is followed by the Vulgate and hence the English versions. The book is appropriate to the image of the suffering prophet as depicted in the book of Jeremiah. Jeremiah was an acknowledged composer of laments (2 Chr 35:25: "Jeremiah composed laments for Josiah"). He was a prophet adept at mourning (Jer 9:1: "Oh that my head were waters, and my eyes a fountain of tears, that I might weep day and night for the slain of the daughter of my people!" [ESV]). A verse such as Lamentations 3:14 sounds like Jeremiah (see Jer 20:7), and the similarity of the suffering of the man in chapter 3 generally to Jeremiah is plain. We are on the lookout for such similarities, given the Greek placement of the book after that of Jeremiah. This book, like the prophecy of Jeremiah, helps the reader to a right understanding of the catastrophe that befell Jerusalem and is indeed a vindication of the teaching of that prophet who predicted the city's downfall, but it also makes plain the prophet's heartfelt sympathy for the suffering of God's people under judgment.[60] All the titles normally assigned obscure the surge of hope that is found in the central part of the book (3:20-33).

---

58. Eric S. Christianson argues against the common supposition that the Solomonic guise is limited to the first two chapters of Ecclesiastes. See Christianson, *A Time to Tell: Narrative Strategies in Ecclesiastes*, JSOTSup 280 (Sheffield: Sheffield Academic, 1998), 128–72.

59. In Vaticanus and Alexandrinus *ieremiou* ("of Jeremiah") is added as a subscript. This amounts to an abbreviation of the superscription added in the Greek version of Lamentations: "And it came to pass after Israel was taken captive and Jerusalem laid waste, Jeremiah sat weeping and lamented this lament [*ethrēnēsen ton thēnon touton*] over Jerusalem and said ...").

60. Gregory Goswell, "Assigning the Book of Lamentations a Place in the Canon," *JESOT* 4 (2015): 1–19.

Esther

Naming the book "Esther" highlights the heroine of the book rather than sharing the attention between Esther and Mordecai, despite the fact that chapter 10 depicts Mordecai in semiroyal terms.[61] The assigned title is appropriate, given the book's puncturing of male pride (e.g., 1:12, 22); in particular, Haman is mercilessly mocked. The book is very positive about the role of women and undercuts male chauvinism.[62] Esther's initiative is highlighted (e.g., 4:16), so the book is aptly named "Esther." God's control of events is not stated in the book, probably so that the roles of Mordecai and Esther might take center stage. The omission of references to God must be intentional and serves a function in the narrative. The book parades and applauds human initiative in a crisis.[63]

An alternative title for the book is found in the treatise *Adath Deborim* by Joseph of Constantinople (AD 1207), "Ahasuerus,"[64] which is presumably an excerpt from the opening words of the book ("In the days of Ahasuerus"), and the king's name is used more often than any other name in the book. The book opens with this king's marital problems, the disobedience of Queen Vashti, and her deposition. This clears the way for Esther to enter court life as her replacement. There is a final reference to the fuller record of the reign of Ahasuerus in "the Book of the Chronicles of the kings of Media and Persia" (10:2; cf. 6:1). On this reading the book amounts to an account of the reign of Ahasuerus told from a certain highly pro-Jewish viewpoint, the dominant narratorial concern being the welfare of the Jews in his kingdom and the role that Mordecai and Esther had in serving both the Persian king and the Jewish people.

---

61. Second Maccabees 15:35 refers to Purim as "Mordecai's day," perhaps due to the prominence in 9:20-22 of Mordecai's letter, which contains instructions concerning the feast.

62. Bruce W. Jones, "Two Misconceptions about the Book of Esther," *CBQ* 39 (1977): 171-81.

63. Berg, *Book of Esther*; Gregory Goswell, "Keeping God Out of the Book of Esther," *EvQ* 82 (2010): 99-110.

64. The text of this note is supplied by Ginsburg, *Introduction*, 3 n. 1, though the name *magillat 'estēr* ("Scroll of Esther") (as also in B. Bat. 15a) is used in the same discussion.

Daniel

In the book of Daniel, so named in the Hebrew Bible, Daniel's name quickly comes to prominence over the other three named youths in chapter 1, who nevertheless have a chapter of their own (Dan 3). Daniel is named first in an alphabetical (in Hebrew) listing of the four youths (1:6). He is the spokesperson for the youths (1:8), and there is special reference to his understanding of visions and dreams (1:17). The three friends play a subsidiary role in Daniel 2, being enlisted to pray along with Daniel (2:17), but they are not mentioned at all in the court tales narrated in Daniel 4–6. As well, Daniel alone is the recipient of visions in chapters 7–12, and most of this section is written from the first-person perspective of Daniel. The title perhaps suggests that he is seen as a prophetic mouthpiece, just as other prophets have books named after them.[65] In line with this, the subscription in Alexandrinus reads "[the end of] Daniel the prophet."

Ezra-Nehemiah

The title "Ezra-Nehemiah" subverts the ideology of the book that would focus on the part played by the people, so that the title is antithetic to the work.[66] In Baba Batra 15a, Ezra-Nehemiah (named "Ezra") is considered to be one book.[67] The division into two parts is found first at the time of Origen (AD 185–253), for the reason that Nehemiah 1:1 is construed as an entirely new beginning ("The words of Nehemiah the son of Hacaliah"). However, literary and theological features show the unity of the larger work, so that this is to be understood as the heading for the second half of a united work. In a Hebrew manuscript of AD 1448 the division into two books was introduced, and this has been retained in modern Hebrew Bibles. In the 1518 folio edition of Bomberg the beginning of Nehemiah is indicated by the numeral i., but the running title at the top of pages, "Ezra," is carried on. In the quarto edition of 1521, we find the marginal note at Nehemiah 1, "The Book of Nehemiah," but

---

65. 4QFlorilegium 2:3 reads, "As is written in the book of the prophet Daniel," which is identical in form to the way in which it earlier refers to the prophecies of Isaiah and Ezekiel (see Allegro, *Qumrân Cave 4.1*, 53–54).

66. Eskenazi, *In an Age of Prose*.

67. So too by Josephus (*Ag. Ap.* 1.8), Melito of Sardis (Eusebius, *Hist. eccl.* 4.26) and Jerome (*Prologus Galeatus*).

still the running title for the second half of the book is "Ezra."[68] In Hebrew
Bibles the Masoretic notes at the end of the Nehemiah list the middle verse
as Nehemiah 3:32, which obviously views Ezra-Nehemiah as a unified whole.
The Vulgate calls Nehemiah the second book of Ezra (*liber secundus Esdrae*). In
the LXX editions of Swete and Rahlfs the two are united under the title *Esdras
B*, the Ezra and Nehemiah parts being chapters 1–10 and 11–23, respectively.[69]

Either title directs undue attention to the figure of Ezra, who does, however, feature in both parts of the united work (Ezra 7–10; Neh 8; 12:36). Both
in Ezra 9:1 and Nehemiah 8:1, it is the people who take the initiative and urge
Ezra to act. The title is a misnomer, for it fails to reflect that the main character of the book is the people, given the many lists of names and genealogies within it (e.g., Ezra 2; Neh 3; 7) and the fact that it ends with the failure
of the people to reform themselves as they pledged they would (Neh 13:4–31;
cf. ch. 10).

The achievements narrated in the book are those of the people themselves,
and the final failure is attributed to them as well.

Chronicles

"Chronicles" has the same meaning as the Hebrew *sēper dibrê hayyāmîm* ("the
book of the events of the days"), hence "annals" or "chronicles," for it chronicles a history that stretches from Adam (1 Chr 1:1) to the establishment of the
Persian Empire (2 Chr 36:20). *Adath Deborim* uses the alternative title "Adam,
Seth, Enosh," these being the first three words of 1 Chronicles 1:1 (an incipit),
which title would alert the reader to the universal history provided in this
work, with the point made that world history finds its divinely intended culmination in the prospect of the rebuilt temple in Jerusalem (2 Chr 36:22–23).
This title leads the reader to view the book as recapitulating Old Testament
history and providing a parallel to the primary history (Genesis to Kings).
As seen from 1 Chronicles 27:24, the term *dibrê hayyāmîm* is used in the
sense of (royal) annals (see Esth 2:23; 6:1; 10:2; Neh 12:23), so this is a fourth-
function (generic) title.[70]

---

68. Moore, "Vulgate Chapters," 816.

69. The title in Alexandrinus is *Ezras B hiereus* ("Ezra B priest").

70. Gary N. Knoppers and Paul B. Harvey Jr., "Omitted and Remaining Matters: On the
Names Given to the Book of Chronicles in Antiquity," *JBL* 121 (2002): 227–43.

The Greek Bible calls Chronicles "[The books] of the things left out" (= Omissions; *Paraleipomenōn*), the name apparently displaying the LXX translators' conception of the work. This is reflected in the alternative Latin naming *Liber Paralipomenon*.[71] It refers to the fact that in a number of passages Chronicles supplements the account of the history in Samuel and Kings. Such a name is misleading, for it obscures the fact that Chronicles also repeats and eliminates material from Samuel and Kings, and, more importantly, it fails to do justice to the Chronicler's own purpose in writing, which determined his selection and ordering of material. The influence of this misnomer in the Greek Bible and Vulgate on the Christian church has contributed to the undervaluing and subsequent neglect of this book until recent times.

A more expansive title is given in Alexandrinus, "the things omitted regarding the kings of Judah," and those texts of the Peshitta Syriac that follow Alexandrinus have as their inscription "the book of Chronicles, namely, the book remembering the days of the kings of Judah."[72] This alerts the reader that Chronicles only traces the line of southern kings. It would be wrong, however, to see the Chronicler as uninterested in the Northern Kingdom, for occasions when northerners come south to worship in Jerusalem and when royal reforms include areas of the north are highlighted (e.g., 2 Chr 11:13–17; 15:8–15; 19:4). In this way the ultimate reunion of all God's people, north and south, is anticipated. Chronicles is not to be viewed simply as a history of the Southern Kingdom.

CHAPTER 4 CONCLUSIONS

It is clear from the material marshaled in this chapter that the title given to a book fulfills certain functions and that titles constrain interpretation. Genette has provided a useful interpretive grid in analyzing the possible functions of any given book title, and I have sought to apply his postulated four functions of titles to the names assigned to biblical books. Titles are a powerful way of shaping the interpretation of texts, hence the importance

---

71. Jerome (*Prologus Galeatus*) suggests that a more representative title would be *Chronicon totius divinae historiae* ("a chronicle of the whole of sacred history"), expressive of the universal scope of the work (see PL 28:554).

72. Rahlfs, *Septuaginta*, 752, 811, 873; W. E. Barnes, *An Apparatus Criticus to Chronicles in the Peshitta Version with a Discussion of the Value of Codex Ambrosianus* (Cambridge: Cambridge University Press, 1897), 1.

of considering the issue in relation to the biblical text. It is plain, then, that the title assigned to a biblical book deserves serious consideration when its meaning is sought.

GUIDELINES FOR INTERPRETING
THE TITLES OF THE OLD TESTAMENT BOOKS

1. Make an effort to discover alternative titles that have been applied to the books of the Old Testament. Commentaries often supply this information.

2. Do more than critique the traditional titles assigned to the Old Testament books. Instead, consider whether the titles may supply an insight or present a viewpoint that may contribute to a richer understanding of the work.

3. The basic (and minimal) function of a book title is that of identification and so also of differentiation of one book from another. In practice, however, no biblical book title merely functions as an identification tag.

4. A second function is to indicate a book's contents, and this clearly has hermeneutical implications. The titles of the Pentateuchal books in the Greek canon (*Genesis*, *Exodos*, etc.) suggest what the different books are about but do not always adequately sum up their global contents. The title "Kings" obscures the vital role of the prophets in the presentation. The titles of Esther and Ruth accurately suggest that a female protagonist is central to the book's presentation.

5. A third possible function of a title is to highlight it to the public. The title "Song of Songs" (= The Greatest Song) is a recommendation of the book to its potential readership. By way of contrast, "Omissions" (the Greek title of Chronicles) is, in part, responsible for the scholarly neglect suffered by Chronicles relative to Kings until recent years.

6. A fourth function is to indicate a book's form or genre, and the titles of many biblical books fall under this category, for example, Chronicles (or Diaries), Praises (= Psalms), Proverbs, and Lamentations.

5

TITLES OF NEW TESTAMENT BOOKS

INTRODUCTION

The postauthorial titles of the books of the New Testament are a valuable but fallible commentary on the literary texts to which they are attached, constraining interpretation, sometimes in ways that are in tension with the texts themselves.[1] Making use of the categories provided by Genette, in this chapter I will survey the titles assigned to the books of the New Testament and explore their hermeneutical implications.[2]

THE GOSPELS

The titles attached to the four Gospels provide direction to the reader for interpreting the books they head. They do not use the term "gospel" (*euangelion*) as the name of a literary genre but identify each book as containing "the

---

1. An earlier version of material in this chapter can be found in Gregory Goswell, "What's in a Name? Book Titles in the New Testament," *Pacifica* 21 (2008): 160-74, © Gregory Goswell, 2008, reprinted by permission of SAGE Publications, https://doi.org/10.1177%2F1030570X0802100203.

2. See Garrick V. Allen and Kelsie G. Rodenbiker, "Titles of the New Testament (TiNT): A New Approach to Manuscripts and the History of Interpretation," *EC* 11 (2020): "Titles are not stable entities. Their variance in wording, form, and aesthetics provides substantial and unexplored data for important disciplinary questions, and analyzing titles helps us to create new contexts for interpreting the New Testament" (265); "They are avenues to comprehending the ways that real communities interpreted and contextualized their sacred texts" (269). For Genette's categories, see the explanation of this interpretive grid in the previous chapter. For an effort to adapt Genette's understanding to ancient manuscripts where the paratext is not supplied by the authors, see Peter Andrist, "Toward a Definition of Paratexts and Paratextuality: The Case of Ancient Greek Manuscripts," in *Bible as Notepad: Tracing Annotations and Annotation Practices in Late Antique and Medieval Biblical Manuscripts*, ed. Liv Ingeborg Lied and Marilena Maniaci, MB 3 (Berlin: de Gruyter, 2018), 130-49.

Gospel according to X," for example, *euangelion kata Iōannēn* ("The Gospel according to John").[3] The form of the titles prompts the reader to view each book as one witness among others to the one "gospel," the proclamation of what God has done in and through Jesus Christ. The titular uniformity renders it highly unlikely that they were independently formulated by the evangelists themselves. The similarity also renders unlikely the view of Martin Hengel that the Gospels were given their titles *before* they were combined in the canon of the four Gospels.[4] As well, we could imagine, for example, that the writer of Luke's Gospel may not have entirely approved the title assigned his work, given that Luke 1:1-4 reads like an apology for the work compared to earlier attempts to write about the life of Jesus. It is not clear, however, that the author of the Third Gospel intended to render obsolete earlier written records of the life and teaching of Jesus. His description of the work of his predecessors as an "attempt" (1:1, *epecheirēsen*) does not denigrate their efforts but points only to the challenging nature of the task.[5] The other implication to be drawn is that in what he himself wrote, the author of Luke's Gospel strove to do his best.[6]

Accepting for the purposes of argument the chronological priority of Mark, the incorporation by the author of Matthew of most of the material of Mark's Gospel could indicate that he intended that his Gospel should supersede it. In the same way the very different approach of the Fourth Gospel compared to the Synoptics could be construed as an implicit critique of the other approach taken. We do not need, however, to understand the titles as subverting the works to which they were later appended. The titles affixed

---

3. For details, see NA[27], 719, 721, 727, 732. Three older papyri display the long form of the titles, 𝔓[66] for John, 𝔓[75] for Luke and John, and 𝔓[64] for Matthew (NA[27], 247). Von Soden is not entirely correct, therefore, when he says that the overall tendency has been to expand rather than to abbreviate the titles (see *Die Schriften des Neuen Testaments I*, 295, 297-99, 301-27). For the early attestation of the names of the evangelists in the assigned titles (opening titles, running titles, and end titles), see Simon J. Gathercole, "The Titles of the Gospels in the Earliest New Testament Manuscripts," *ZNW* 104 (2013): 33-76.

4. Martin Hengel, *Studies in the Gospel of Mark* (London: SCM, 1985), 64-84; cf. Richard Bauckham, "The Gospel of Mark: Origins and Eyewitnesses," in Bird and Maston, *Earliest Christian History*, 146-48.

5. I. Howard Marshall, *The Gospel of Luke: A Commentary on the Greek Text*, NIGTC (Exeter: Paternoster, 1978), 41.

6. See Oscar Cullmann, "The Plurality of the Gospels as a Theological Problem in Antiquity," in *The Early Church: Studies in Early Christian History and Theology*, ed. A. J. B. Higgins (London: SCM, 1956), 43-44.

to the Gospels, however, prevent the hegemony of any one Gospel over the other three. They instruct the reader that the four Gospels are not to be seen as rivals but as complementary. "Gospel" is not a literary designation in Mark 1:1.[7] Rather, it appears to be saying, given the quotation from Isaiah 40:3,[8] that the gospel spoken by Isaiah (see Isa 52:7: "who brings good tidings" [LXX *euangelizomenou*]) is beginning to be fulfilled in the appearance of John the Baptist preaching about "he who comes after [him]" (Mark 1:7–8) and in Jesus's preaching of the nearness of the kingdom of God. It is perhaps a short step to calling documents that contain the gospel "Gospels," but it is a further step nonetheless.[9]

We will consider the four Gospels in turn. Matthew is introduced as a "book" (1:1, *biblos*). The superscription, "The book of the genealogy of Jesus Christ, the son of David, the son of Abraham" (on analogy with Gen 5:1 LXX), may be intended to cover no more than the genealogy (Matt 1:2–17). The repetition (in reverse order) in 1:2–17 of the triad of names found in the opening line could be construed as evidence for limiting the intent of the superscription to this passage: Abraham (1:2), David (1:6), and Jesus, who is called the Christ (1:16).[10] W. D. Davies and Dale Allison, however, opt for the view of Matthew 1:1 as the title for the entire gospel,[11] with the introductory use of *biblos geneseōs* ("The book of the genealogy") intended to set the story of Jesus as a counterpart to another "history of origins," the book of Genesis. If that is the intention, it signals that this book tells of the renewal of creation through the person and work of Jesus (see Matt 19:18, *palingenesia*).

To reiterate a point already made, even in the case of Mark, where the word "gospel" occurs in the first line of the work, there is nothing to suggest that the Evangelist saw "gospel" (*euangelion*) as a literary designation. Eugene Boring argues that in the opening line of this discourse about Jesus

---

7. Helmut Koester, "From the Kerygma-Gospel to Written Gospels," *NTS* 35 (1989): 370.

8. It is the Isaiah part of the composite quotation in Mark 1:2–3 that is highlighted: "As it is written in Isaiah the prophet."

9. See Denis Farkasfalvy, "The Apostolic Gospels in the Early Church: The Concept of Canon and the Formation of the Four-Gospel Canon," in *Canon and Biblical Interpretation*, ed. Craig Bartholomew et al., SHS 7 (Milton Keynes: Paternoster, 2006), 111–22, who shows that this is no arbitrary shift in meaning. For evidence of the first uses of "Gospel" as a literary designation, see McDonald, *Biblical Canon*, 261, 262, 265, 337, 346.

10. As noted by W. D. Davies and Dale C. Allison Jr., *The Gospel according to Saint Matthew*, ICC (Edinburgh: T&T Clark, 1988), 1:149.

11. Their reasons are given in Davies and Allison, *Gospel according to Saint Matthew*, 150–54.

Christ, the author titled it the *archē*, that is, it is the "rule" or "normative state-ment" for preaching the "gospel of Jesus Christ," and as such the beginning and foundation for the church's contemporary preaching of this message.[12] It is not clear, however, that the word can mean that.[13] The Gospel of Luke (and Acts for that matter) is designated a "narrative" (Luke 1:1, *diēgēsis*) that gives an "orderly account" of the events that have taken place, describing what God began to do through Jesus and Jesus continued to do (through the apostles). The closest we come to a designation for the Fourth Gospel is the reference to the "testimony" to Jesus (John 21:24, *martyria*) made available to the readers through what is written. Rudolf Schnackenburg does not see the written form as here called a "testimony"; rather, the reliable testimony of the beloved disciple comes through what is written,[14] and Schnackenburg is probably correct in making such a distinction.

As for the names mentioned in each Gospel title, the texts of the books do not explicitly divulge the names of their authors. For example, the Fourth Gospel does not disclose the name of "the beloved disciple" whose testimony that Gospel preserves (John 21:24).[15] The names of John and his brother James are notably absent from the Fourth Gospel, though there is one mention of "the sons of Zebedee" in 21:2. On the other hand, Peter is called "Simon, son of John" (John 1:42; 21:15, 16, 17), significantly in the final chapter when he is being compared and contrasted with the (still) unnamed beloved disciple. This could be viewed as hinting at the identity of the beloved disciple, who is identified as the source behind the Johannine tradition and perhaps the one who wrote the Gospel.[16] This discussion of the titular labeling of the Gospels according to the names of their reputed authors (e.g., "The Gospel according to John") is not to be misconstrued as arguing for or against any specific historical identification of the authors. That is a strictly historical

---

12. M. Eugene Boring, "Mark 1:1–15 and the Beginning of the Gospel," *Semeia* 52 (1990): 53.

13. See G. Delling, "*archō*," *TDNT* 1:478–89.

14. Rudolf Schnackenburg, *The Gospel according to John*, vol. 3, *Commentary on Chapters 13–21* (Tunbridge Wells: Burns & Oates, 1982), 373.

15. For more, see Armin D. Baum, "The Original Epilogue (John 20:30–31), the Secondary Appendix (21:1–23), and the Editorial Epilogues (21:24–25) of John's Gospel: Observations against the Background of Ancient Literary Conventions," in Bird and Maston, *Earliest Christian History*, 229–33.

16. See Raymond E. Brown, *An Introduction to the Gospel of John*, ed. and updated by Francis J. Moloney (New York: Doubleday, 2003), 191–92, and comments by the editor on 191 n. 6.

investigation, whereas the present discussion concerns the hermeneutical effects of attaching certain names (Matthew, Mark, etc.) to literary works that are in fact anonymous.

The Matthew in the title of the First Gospel is obviously intended to refer to the disciple by the same name (Matt 10:3: "Matthew the tax collector"), whose call is described in 9:9–13. The implication of the title, then, is that the book provides a firsthand account of many of the things narrated. In Mark and Luke it is not made clear that "Levi" who is called to follow (Mark 2:14; Luke 5:27) is to be identified with the "Matthew" listed among the Twelve (Mark 3:18; Luke 6:15). Only in the Gospel of Matthew is this clarified.

The name Mark in the title of the Second Gospel is presumably intended to refer to the youthful resident of Jerusalem who bore that name (Acts 12:12) and who was the coworker of Peter (1 Pet 5:13) and Paul (Acts 12:25; Col 4:10; Phlm 24; 2 Tim 4:11). In this way, the name of Mark, once it was used in the assigned title of the Second Gospel, serves to link the letter writers Peter and Paul with the Gospel collection, so that its effect is to suggest the harmony of the different witnesses enshrined in the New Testament.[17]

That the author of Luke's Gospel is the coworker of Paul is implied by his second volume (Acts), wherein the "we passages" report certain events in which the author was personally involved (Acts 16:10–17; 21:1–18; 27:1–28:16).[18] As well, the name of Luke is found in Colossians 4:14; 2 Timothy 4:11; and Philemon 24. Thus, the title of the Third Gospel helps to bridge between the four-Gospel corpus and the Pauline Letters, and disallows any interpretation that views Paul as slighting the importance of the historical record of Jesus's life (a misunderstanding of 2 Cor 5:16)[19] or as needlessly complicating or even corrupting the gospel first proclaimed by Jesus.

The author of the Fourth Gospel, named as John in the assigned title, also has to his credit three epistles (1–3 John) and the book of Revelation (see Rev 1:1, 4, 9), and this is a further way in which Gospels and epistles are shown to be alternate mediums for the same message, centered on Jesus Christ. The

---

17. For more, see Goswell, "Authorship and Anonymity," 733–49.

18. Though disputed, this is still the most likely explanation.

19. See the discussion of C. K. Barrett with reference to the Bultmann school that viewed Paul as having no interest in the "Jesus of history." See Barrett, *The Second Epistle to the Corinthians*, 2nd ed., BNTC (London: Black, 1973), 171. Origen viewed Paul in 2 Cor 8:18 as referring to and commending Luke and his Gospel (Eusebius, *Hist. eccl.* 6.25.6).

identification is favored by the fact that there is no attempt to differentiate between these Johns in the titles, so that the reader is meant to assume their identity. The similar idioms used (e.g., John 1:1, 4, 14; cf. 1 John 1:1) would serve to confirm the assumption. So too, the "I am" sayings of Revelation (e.g., Rev 1:17; 2:23; 21:6; 22:13, 16) can be compared to those in the Fourth Gospel. All in all, the titles of the four Gospels, incorporating as they do the names of their reputed authors, assist in giving the impression of the unity of the New Testament witness to Jesus Christ. To reiterate what is said above, this discussion of the authors of the Gospels is not assessing historical claims but seeks to elucidate the hermeneutical effects of the postauthorial titles found at the head of the four Gospels.

Each evangelist wrote his composition as a standalone literary work depicting the life of Jesus Christ in distinctive ways. Redaction criticism promoted the understanding that this was because each evangelist wrote for a different audience, each of which had differing needs.[20] It is questionable, however, whether we can use the Gospels to build up a profile of specific communities to which they were written. What the four Gospels have in common is greater than their differences, which redaction criticism has perhaps overplayed. As part of the canonical process, all four Gospels were collected together and given the same *inscriptio*: "The Gospel according to X." Certainly, the titles attached to each of the four make no mention of different addressees, so that these books now function as the Gospel for God's people everywhere. This need not be viewed as a radically new function but, if we follow Bauckham, as confirmation of what they always were. The canonical designation given to each book ("The Gospel according to X") further suggests that each evangelist writes from his own perspective so that the multifaceted story of Jesus would be incomplete if the other Gospels were excluded from consideration. All four Gospels are needed for a complete picture of the words and work of Jesus Christ. The titles of the Gospels assert that the exclusive

---

20. This understanding has been critiqued. See the essays in the volume edited by Richard Bauckham, *The Gospels for All Christians: Rethinking the Gospel Audiences* (Edinburgh: T&T Clark, 1998). There are good grounds for supposing that the Gospels were written for a wide readership and not just for a particular community with peculiar needs. This volume makes no mention of the Gospel titles in the arguments marshaled.

use of any one of the four is illegitimate. The reader is warned against the danger of playing favorites.[21]

ACTS

Presumably for the author of Luke's Gospel, his second volume comes under the designation of a "narrative" (Luke 1:1, *diēgēsis*) given in the prologue of his first volume. The way in which Acts 1:1 connects this second volume with the first implies this. "The Acts of the Apostles" did not receive that title until the latter part of the second century and it is first attested in the anti-Marcionite prologue to Luke. The intention behind the title may be to argue that Paul was not the only faithful apostle of Christ, even if more is said about him than about others in Acts.[22] Such a title would seem to be in tension with the book it heads. The name *praxeis [tōn] apostolōn* (Acts of the Apostles), or just *praxeis* (Acts),[23] is attested since the time of Clement of Alexandria and Irenaeus. The Muratorian Canon (line 34), consistent with its anti-Marcionite stance, calls it *acta omnium apostolorum* ("the acts of *all* the apostles"), for Paul is not the only apostle featured, and the other apostles are also accredited. Cyril of Jerusalem calls it "the Acts of the Twelve Apostles" (*Catechetical Lectures* 4.36). According to W. G. Kümmel,[24] the title "The Acts of the Apostles" is scarcely original and does not fit the contents of the book, for the apostles are not the main characters of the book.

All the apostles are named in chapter 1, and there is the expressed concern to make up the number of the Twelve after the death of Judas (1:15-26). Peter, James, and John are strongly featured up to the Jerusalem conference in Acts 15, which is a major turning point in the book, and Paul is especially prominent in Acts, but the other apostles as individuals receive no attention. Stephen and Philip (Acts 6-8) are not even apostles but nevertheless play an important role in preparing for the gentile mission. The apostles as a group fade out of prominence, some of the last references being 9:27; 11:1; 15:2, 4.

---

21. See Wall, "Problem of the Multiple Letter Canon," esp. 4-5. I acknowledge my substantial dependence on him for this and the following section.

22. F. F. Bruce, *Commentary on the Book of the Acts: The English Text with Introduction, Exposition and Notes*, NICNT (Grand Rapids: Eerdmans, 1954), 17.

23. See NA[27], 320, 735 for details.

24. W. G. Kümmel, *Introduction to the New Testament*, rev. ed., trans. Howard Clark Kee (London: SCM, 1975), 159 n. 149.

Peter is their usual spokesman, and the others have no voice. Barnabas and Paul are twice called "apostles" (14:4, 14), but in the restricted sense of church representatives.[25] No doubt the debate will continue over the purpose of Acts, but this must be resolved in some way around the purpose of the dominating presence of Paul within the book (especially in Acts 13-28), with due weight given to the extensive parallels between Paul and the Lukan Jesus (e.g., their final journey to and trials in Jerusalem).[26]

Further, as noted by David Trobisch,[27] "Acts" as a fourth function title (according to Genette's scheme) does not conform well to the ancient literary genre described as "Acts" (*praxeis*), for typically the mighty deeds of only one hero are narrated, not those of several heroes, and the usually noble death of the figure is narrated. On that count, apocryphal books such as Acts of John, Acts of Peter, and Acts of Andrew better conform to the genre.[28] The narrative of Acts closes before the martyrdom of Paul, though Luke knew of it, given the predictions recorded in Acts 20:23 and 21:11. The ill-fitting generic title turns the book into a celebration of apostolic achievements.[29] In tension with such an orientation, the summaries scattered through Acts (e.g., 6:7; 9:31; 12:24) suggest that it chronicles the spread of the word to the seat of empire, Rome, God having used different agents to bring this about. On the other hand, the reference in the title to "apostles" (plural) prepares for the letters attributed to various apostles (Paul, Peter, John) that follow in the canonical ordering of the New Testament materials.

The opening verses of Acts (1:1-2) summarize the scope and thrust of Luke's Gospel as "all that Jesus began [*ērxato*] both to do and to teach" and suggest (allowing the auxiliary Greek verb its full force) that this second volume recounts what Jesus *continued* to do and teach through his Spirit-empowered

---

25. In Acts 14:14 the order is "the apostles Barnabas and Paul," which can perhaps be taken as support for the interpretation suggested.

26. A. J. Mattill Jr., "The Jesus-Paul Parallels and the Purpose of Luke-Acts," *NovT* 17 (1975): 15-46.

27. Trobisch, *First Edition*, 39.

28. E. Hennecke and W. Schneemelcher, *New Testament Apocrypha*, English translation ed. R. McL. Wilson (Philadelphia: Westminster, 1964), 2:188-531.

29. With regard to the effect of the commonly assigned title of Acts on the reading process, Robert W. Wall states: "The effect of recognizing the superscription of Acts as a canonical property is to call attention to a new set of orientating concerns for readers of Acts as Scripture." See Wall, "The Acts of the Apostles," *NIB* 10:29.

witnesses.[30] Such a view of the book is supported by references to the activity of the risen Christ in its pages (e.g., 9:5; 16:7; 22:18; 23:11), as well as by the Christlike character and actions of a number of its leading participants (e.g., Stephen, Philip, Peter, Paul).[31] The common title of the book fails to reflect this aspect, so that a modification such as "The Acts of [Jesus Christ through] the Apostles" might be suggested, or even "The Acts of the Holy Spirit," if it is kept in mind that he is "the Spirit of Jesus" (16:6–7) and that he works mainly through Spirit-empowered messengers.

LETTERS

Each of the letters of the New Testament was written to address a certain audience concerning particular church problems. The "letter" of James is categorized in this way by the assigned title, but is generically more homily than letter.[32] There is, however, a salutation ("Greeting") to diaspora Jewish Christians in James 1:1,[33] so that it certainly purports to be a letter. First John is a written homily.[34] The same applies to the "epistle" to the Hebrews,[35] noting the self-description supplied in Hebrews 13:22 ("my word of exhortation"), coinciding with the reference to the diaspora synagogue sermon of Paul and Barnabas in Acts 13:15. Hebrews is not, however, totally devoid of letter characteristics, for example, the giving of news (13:23) and final greetings (13:24).[36] First John lacks major elements of an epistolary form (e.g., prescript and postscript), whereas 2 John and 3 John conform to the conventions of

---

30. C. K. Barrett, *The Acts of the Apostles*, vol. 1, ICC (Edinburgh: T&T Clark, 1994), 66–67. The phraseology at the end of John's Gospel (21:25: "many other things that Jesus did" [*alla polla epoiēsen ho Iēsous*]) may be compared to Acts 1:1 (*hōn ērxato ho Iēsous poiein*).

31. E.g., David P. Moessner, "'The Christ Must Suffer': New Light on the Jesus-Peter, Stephen, Paul Parallels in Luke-Acts," *NovT* 28 (1986): 220–56.

32. This genre identification is preferable to that of paraenesis that was popularized by the influential commentary by Martin Dibelius. See the discussion of Douglas J. Moo, *The Letter of James*, PNTC (Grand Rapids: Eerdmans, 2000), 8.

33. For the genre of James, see Karl-Wilhelm Niebuhr, "Der Jakobusbrief im Licht frühjüdischer Diasporabriefe," *NTS* 44 (1998): 420–43. Niebuhr interprets James within the diaspora letter tradition of Jer 29, the Epistle of Jeremiah, 2 Macc 1–2, and 2 Bar 78–86.

34. However, see Fred O. Francis, "The Form and Function of the Opening and Closing Paragraphs of James and 1 John," *ZNW* 61 (1970): 110–26.

35. It is called an epistle, for example, by Clement of Alexandria, as quoted in Eusebius, *Hist. eccl.* 6.13.4–8; 6.14.1–3.

36. See James Swetnam, "On the Literary Genre of the 'Epistle' to the Hebrews," *NovT* 11 (1969): 261–69.

the ancient letter tradition.[37] First John is not, however, without epistolary characteristics, for there is the repeated "I write this to you ..." (2:1, 7, 12, 21, 26; 5:13). The letter form of 1 Peter is only really manifest at the beginning (1:1-2) and end (5:12-14). Only the opening of 2 Peter sounds like a letter (1:1-2), though it makes the explicit claim to be a letter (3:1: "This is now the second letter that I have written to you" [RSV]).

Whatever the differences between these literary productions, their assigned titles designate each as a "letter" (*epistolē*), and this generic designation embodies a certain hermeneutical agenda. Those who affixed these titles understood a religious "letter" as written to provide practical remedy for pastoral problems.[38] The letter genre identifies problems afflicting churches and suggests ways to resolve them, as is plainly to be observed in the shorter letters to the churches in Revelation 2-3.

Pauline Epistles

According to the assigned titles, the Pauline Epistles all have the same principal author (Paul) and so are named according to whom they were addressed, for example, Romans (*Pros Rhōmaious*), Corinthians (*Pros Korinthious*). This pattern requires Ephesians to be addressed to one particular church, even if, as the theory goes, it was once a circular letter.[39] At minimum these titles serve Genette's first function, to identify or designate a work, differentiating it from others, for the different place designations in the titles suggest nothing about the contents of the different letters. At the same time, the names of the different churches in the titles are, in effect, cross-references to accounts given in Acts about the different churches that have letters written to them (e.g., the founding of the church in Philippi in Acts 16). The only exception to this is Colossians, for the churches of the Lycus Valley were not founded

---

37. See Robert W. Funk, "The Form and Structure of II and III John," *JBL* 86 (1967): 424-30.

38. Wall, "Multiple Letter Canon," 4-5.

39. The phrase *en Ephesō* ("in Ephesus") of Eph 1:1 is absent from 𝔓⁴⁶, Sinaiticus, and Vaticanus. See Ernest Best, "Ephesians i.1," in *Text and Interpretation: Studies in the New Testament Presented to Matthew Black*, ed. Ernest Best and R. McL. Wilson (Cambridge: Cambridge University Press, 1979), 29-41. No named individuals are greeted in the letter. An example of the opposite text-critical move is the well-supported words "in Rome" (*en Rhōmē*) in Rom 1:7, which are absent in a few less important witnesses (see Rom 1:15). This may reflect the view of copyists that Paul's "treatise" was of more than local application.

by Paul (see Col 2:1). These accounts in Acts provide the reader with background information about the churches that have letters addressed to them.

The titles of four Pauline letters classify them as addressed to individuals: 1 and 2 Timothy, Titus, and Philemon. On the other hand, the instructions about the organization of church life given by Paul in 1 Timothy and Titus, and the character of 2 Timothy as a "testament" of Paul, make their wider application obvious.[40] As well, the formality of the openings of the Pastoral Epistles (1 Tim 1:1; 2 Tim 1:1; Titus 1:1–3) suggests that Paul is, in fact, addressing church situations through his envoys, so that these letters are not so very different in character from those whose titles mark them as written to churches. This is confirmed by the use of second-person *plural* pronouns in final blessings ("Grace be with you [*hymōn*]") in 1 and 2 Timothy, with the addition of "all" in Titus ("Grace be with you all").[41] Similarly, exclusive mention of Philemon in the title brings it into line with Paul's letters to Timothy and Titus, but an alternative and longer title would have been possible given that it was addressed not only to Philemon but also to "Apphia our sister and Archippus our fellow soldier, and the church in [Philemon's] house" (Phlm 2).

The title supplied to the anonymous book "To the Hebrews" (*Pros Hebraious*), whether it originally was written for a mixed audience or not, situates the book within Jewish Christianity.[42] It is thereby connected with the Catholic Letters rather than with the Pauline Letters, seeing that Paul was entrusted with the gospel "to the uncircumcised" rather than "to the circumcised" (Gal 2:7–9; Acts 9:15; 22:21; 26:17), and indeed its position in modern printed editions (following the Vulgate order) is in front of the Catholic Epistles. On the other hand, the title "To the Hebrews" is a connection to (other?) Pauline letters that name the letters by addressee and separates it from the Catholic Epistles, which are named by reference to their authors. The letter does have specific referents (Heb 10:32–4), but the details of their identity and location remain vague.

The addressees are not named "the Hebrews" within the book itself, so that the title appears to have been coined on analogy with the titles of the

---

40. The suggestion is that of Dahl, "Particularity of the Pauline Epistles," 266.

41. James W. Aageson, "The Pastoral Epistles, Apostolic Authority, and the Development of the Pauline Scriptures," in Porter, *Pauline Canon*, 8–9.

42. John Dunnill, *Covenant and Sacrifice in the Letter to the Hebrews*, SNTSMS 75 (Cambridge: Cambridge University Press, 1992), 13–39.

(other) Pauline letters. Therefore, according to Trobisch, the title of the anonymous Letter to the Hebrews implies the name of Paul.[43] Likewise, as noted by Trobisch,[44] the title of 2 Corinthians represents a narrowing, in conformity to other Pauline titles, for it is addressed not only to the Corinthians but also to "all the saints who are in the whole of Achaia" (2 Cor 1:1). So too, the letter to the "Galatians" is destined for more than one church (on the South Galatian theory, churches in the cities of Antioch of Pisidia, Iconium, Lystra, Derbe), for this is not a *city* name. What this shows is that the titles have been manipulated to apportion the Pauline corpus into letters to churches and letters to individuals.

These titles need to come into consideration in the formulation of any theory as to how and when the Pauline corpus was produced.[45] An embryonic form of that corpus may be alluded to in the terse mention of "the books [*ta biblia*], and above all the parchments [*tas membranas*]" (2 Tim 4:13 RSV) that Paul wishes to retrieve (along with his coat). These two terms may refer, in turn, to Old Testament scrolls owned by Paul (see Luke 4:20; Gal 3:10; Heb 9:19) and to copies of Paul's own letters that he had retained in the form of a codex notebook, which, in effect, would be an early Pauline corpus.[46] Chris Stevens argues, on the basis of the textual uniformity of the Pauline corpus after AD 200, for Paul's personal involvement in preparing a corpus for circulation on the basis of duplicate copies of his letters that he had kept in his possession.[47]

Many of the epistles also in the course of time acquired subscriptions (*hypographai*) appended to the end of the books. These were originally brief, but over time they were elaborated; for example, the earliest subscription for Romans is simply *pros Rhōmaious* ("To the Romans" [‫א‬, A, B*, C, D*]), and an example of a later elaboration is *pros Rhōmaious egraphē apo Korinthou* ("To the

43. Trobisch, *First Edition*, 59.

44. Trobisch, *First Edition*, 40.

45. On the different theories of the formation of the corpus of Pauline Letters, see Stanley E. Porter, "When and How Was the Pauline Canon Compiled? An Assessment of Theories," in Porter, *Pauline Canon*, 95–127.

46. Kruger, *Question of Canon*, 93–94; cf. E. Randolph Richards, "The Codex and the Early Collection of Paul's Letters," *BBR* 8 (1998): 161–62.

47. Chris S. Stevens, *History of the Pauline Corpus in Texts, Transmissions and Trajectories: A Textual Analysis of Manuscripts from the Second to the Fifth Century*, TENTS 14 (Leiden: Brill, 2020), 185–211, esp. 205.

Romans, written from Corinth" [B2b, Db]).[48] The claims of the subscriptions are sometimes contradicted by the contents of the letters to which they are appended. For example, some subscriptions to 1 Corinthians say that it was written from Philippi in Macedonia (yet see 1 Cor 16:8, 19).[49]

The gathering of the Pauline Epistles into a corpus, and the Vulgate titles that reflect this as an established fact (*Epistola Pauli ad Romanos, Epistola Pauli ad Corinthios Prima*, etc.), obscure the involvement of others in the production of the letters so designated. Perhaps all of Paul's letters were written by the hand of an amanuensis.[50] This is made explicit in the case of his Letter to the Romans (16:22: "I Tertius, the writer of this letter, greet you in the Lord" [RSV]). The noted presence of others (16:21) may also imply that they had some involvement in the framing of the letter. When Paul writes a final part of a letter with his own hand (1 Cor 16:21; Gal 6:11; Col 4:18; 2 Thess 3:17; Phlm 19), the involvement of a scribe is also made plain. As well, most of his letters were coauthored:[51] First Corinthians 1:1 (Paul and Sosthenes); 2 Corinthians 1:1 (Paul and Timothy); Philippians 1:1 (Paul and Timothy); Colossians 1:1 (Paul and Timothy); 1 Thessalonians 1:1 (Paul, Silvanus, and Timothy); 2 Thessalonians 1:1 (Paul, Silvanus, and Timothy); and Philemon 1 (Paul and Timothy). By only mentioning the name of one addresser (Paul), the titles imply that the teaching and instructions derive exclusively from one apostolic personality. The clipped titles also obscure links to non-Pauline letters, especially 1 Peter, which has connections with the Pauline circle in the person of Silvanus as letter carrier (5:12).[52] Fuller epistolary titles would have encouraged a fruitful conversation between the Pauline and Petrine corpora (see 2 Pet 3:15-16).

---

48. Metzger provides information about these in *Textual Commentary*, at the close of his notes on each epistle, and I am dependent on him for this example. For Alexandrinus, see Milne and Skeat, *Scribes and Correctors*, plates 39-42.

49. See Metzger, *Textual Commentary*, 504.

50. E. Randolph Richards, *The Secretary in the Letters of Paul*, WUNT 2/42 (Tübingen: Mohr Siebeck, 1991), 189-94.

51. For a helpful discussion of this feature, see Murray J. Harris, *The Second Epistle to the Corinthians: A Commentary on the Greek Text*, NIGTC (Grand Rapids: Eerdmans, 2005), 130-32; Richards, *Secretary in the Letters*, 153-58, esp. 154: "The practice of including others in the address as a 'nicety' is not supported by the evidence." The named coauthors aided Paul in some way in writing the letters; see also Prior, *Paul the Letter-Writer*, 37-59.

52. E. Randolph Richards, "Silvanus Was Not Peter's Secretary: Theological Bias in Interpreting *dia Silouanou ... egrapsa* in 1 Peter 5:12," *JETS* 43 (2000): 417-32.

Catholic Epistles

Seven epistles (James, 1-2 Peter, 1-3 John, and Jude) are grouped together under the title "Catholic Epistles" (*katholikai*),[53] used in the sense of universal, reflecting the fact that (except for 2-3 John) they are not addressed to any named church or individual and so are named according to who *wrote* them. The lack of reference to any particular church in their titles, unlike in the case of the Pauline Epistles, implies their universal application. This understanding is supported by the breadth of the readership addressed (e.g., Jas 1:1: "To the twelve tribes in the Dispersion"; 1 Pet 1:1: "To the exiles of the Dispersion in Pontus, Galatia, Cappadocia, Asia, and Bithynia"), though the addressees are not strictly without geographical limitation. The implication is that 2 Peter was written to the same wide readership as the first letter (3:1). James presents itself as an encyclical to diaspora believers, and that claim (according to Bauckham) means resisting the tendency in some scholarly circles to envisage a specific "community of James."[54] First John addresses a church where a group has seceded (1 John 2:19), but the error of those who departed is not clearly profiled. The secession is described as being typical of "the last hour" (2:18) so that it is relevant to all churches, both present and future. As well, 1 John 2:19 alludes to more than a local dispute, given the generalizing reference to "many antichrists" (2:18) and "many false prophets" (4:1; see 2 John 7, "many deceivers"). There is the danger of allowing a hypothetical construct to play too determinative a role in the exegesis of this letter. It would be a mistake to turn the whole letter into antisecessionist polemic.[55] Indeed, the lack of specifics facilitates its (now) general application within the corpus of Catholic Epistles.

The James and Jude in the titles are presumably the (half-)brothers of Jesus (see Mark 6:3), and this is corroborated by the authors' self-reference not as apostles but as "servants" of Jesus Christ (Jas 1:1; Jude 1). Use of their names is another link between the Epistles and the Gospels and Acts (see Acts 1:12-14; 15:6-21). In this little corpus of seven books, the apostles of Christ

---

53. For details, see NA²⁷, 588, 598, 608, 615, 625, 627, 628, 743-45.

54. Bauckham, *James*, 25-28.

55. See Hansjörg Schmid, "How to Read the First Epistle of John Non-Polemically," *Bib* 85 (2004): 24-41, for a survey and evaluation of previous work starting with that of Judith Lieu. Schmid then proposes his own nonpolemical reading of 1 John, the apocalyptic context of the "opponents" motif, making that motif a standing reminder of the possibility of failure.

(Peter/John) and the family of Jesus (James/Jude) form a chorus in witness to him. The prominence of Peter in both the Gospels and Acts is another unifying factor between the different parts of the New Testament. Petrine authorship is claimed in 1 Peter 1:1, yet the letter also manifests connections with the Pauline circle in the persons of Silvanus and Mark, mentioned in 5:12–13. There is, likewise, the approving mention of the writings of Paul in 2 Peter 3:15–16. Peter is thus a key unifying link between different parts of the epistolary corpus of the New Testament.

REVELATION

The title "Revelation" (*Apokalypsis*) is an incipit, taken from the first Greek word in the book (1:1: "The revelation of Jesus Christ"), with Revelation 1:1–2 amounting to a superscription for the book. The sense of the opening words is that this writing contains "the revelation *from* Jesus Christ,"[56] who is the mediator of God's revelation to believers. This title would appear to separate it from the letter category, even though it can be said to start with seven letters to churches (chs. 2–3). In Codex Sinaiticus and Codex Ephraemi the book is titled "The Revelation of John" (*Apokalypsis Iōan[n]ou*), and this is the form found in the subscription in Alexandrinus, for John is the prophetic mouthpiece used by the Lord Jesus to speak to the churches (see 1:1: "which he made known to his servant John"; cf. RSV book title: "The Revelation to John"). This simple title later received many additions and elaborations, some titles aiming to affirm the orthodoxy and authority of the book by linking it to the author of John's Gospel.[57] The title "Revelation" (or Apocalypse) was later understood as a genre designation, and indeed it has given its name to a genre (apocalyptic), but in the book itself this is the only time the term is used. John is not describing his composition as belonging to the literary type called "apocalypse," nor does it appear that noncanonical apocalyptic works

---

56. David E. Aune argues that *Apokalypsis Iēsou Christou* is a subjective genitive, with this interpretation supported by the succeeding clause, "which God gave him." See Aune, *Revelation 1–5*, WBC 52a (Dallas: Word, 1997), 6. The opening verses outline a communicative chain: from God to Jesus Christ to his angel to his servant John to the churches.

57. For details, see Bruce M. Metzger, *The Text of the New Testament: Its Transmission, Corruption and Restoration*, 2nd ed. (Oxford: Clarendon, 1968), 205; cf. Garrick V. Allen, "Paratexts and the Reception History of the Apocalypse," *JTS* 70 (2019): 617: "The titles also tend to connote (heavy-handedly) that the author is also the author of the Gospel of John, a feature that becomes more ensconced as the tradition develops until the advent of critical scholarship."

(mostly to be found in the Pseudepigrapha) are the context within which the writer wishes his own work to be interpreted.[58]

It is likely that *apokalypsis* is an allusion to Daniel 2 (LXX/Theodotion),[59] wherein the verb *apokalyptō* ("to reveal") is used up to six times. The writer of Revelation draws heavily on Daniel, as also on other Old Testament prophetic works. Within the book itself, this writing of John is termed a prophecy (Rev 1:3: "the words of the prophecy"), and there is the similarly worded 22:7, 10, and 18 (each reading "the words of the prophecy of this book") and 22:19 ("the words of the book of this prophecy") that form an inclusio around the book as a whole. As well, the verb "to prophesy" (*prophēteuein*) is used in 10:11 to describe the writer's prophetic task: "I was told, 'You must again prophesy about many peoples and nations and tongues and kings' " (RSV).[60] There is no actual quotation from the Old Testament prophets in Revelation, nor of any Old Testament book for that matter, but prophetic images, allusions, and phraseology form the warp and woof of the work.[61] The common title as an incipit is innocent enough, but it has often been understood in a way that obfuscates the book's main connection, which is to Old Testament prophecy.

OLD TESTAMENT/NEW TESTAMENT AS TITLES

Names are never without significance, and this applies to the possible import of the names commonly attached to the two major sections of the Bible, Old Testament and New Testament. Use of the term "Old Testament" as a name for first part of the Bible is value laden and is an overtly Christian way of

---

58. A point made by Bruce W. Jones, "More about the Apocalypse as Apocalyptic," *JBL* 87 (1968): 325 n. 1.

59. The suggestion is that of G. K. Beale, *The Book of Revelation: A Commentary on the Greek Text*, NIGTC (Grand Rapids: Eerdmans, 1999), 181.

60. See David Aune's arguments in favor of the prophetic character of Revelation in *Prophecy in Early Christianity and the Ancient Mediterranean World* (Grand Rapids: Eerdmans, 1983), 274–88. Other passages of relevance to the evaluation of the author as a prophet include Rev 1:1, 10; 4:1-2; 17:3; 19:10; 21:10; 22:9. These refer either to his Spirit endowment or to him under the title of "servant."

61. See G. K. Beale, *John's Use of the Old Testament in Revelation*, JSNTSup 166 (Sheffield: Sheffield Academic, 1998); Barbara Aland et al., eds., *The Greek New Testament*, 4th rev. ed. (Stuttgart: Deutsche Bibelgesellschaft, 2001), 891-901, esp. 896-900, for allusions and verbal parallels of prophetic books in Revelation; H. B. Swete, *The Apocalypse of St John*, 3rd ed. (London: Macmillan, 1909), cxl-clviii, which identifies half the uses as from Psalms (27 times), Isaiah (46), Ezekiel (29), and Daniel (31) (cliii n. 1). See Richard Bauckham, *The Climax of Prophecy: Studies on the Book of Revelation* (Edinburgh: T&T Clark, 1993), wherein he argues that the book presents itself as the summation of the whole biblical tradition of prophecy (especially chs. 5 and 9).

designating the Scriptures inherited from Israel. The adjective "old" is used in correlation with "new," for there would be no *Old* Testament without a *New* Testament to correspond to it (and vice versa). Such language embodies essentially Christian convictions about the Scriptures of Israel (and now also of the church) and promotes a covenantal reading of both Testaments that together record the history of God's dealings with his people and culminate in the coming of Jesus Christ to complete God's covenantal purposes.[62] For that reason, though open to misunderstanding, this way of speaking is not to be lightly discarded or replaced without due consideration of the hermeneutical convictions it embodies and expresses.

Testamentum, from which we get the English word "testament," is the rendering in the Latin Vulgate of the Greek word *diathēkē*, which in turn translates the Hebrew term *bərît*.[63] When this term is applied to the Old Testament, it is plain that the covenantal character of God's dealings with humanity as plotted in Scripture is in view. The application of the name "Old Testament" to the sacred writings of Israel is not strictly biblical, in that the reference in both Jeremiah 31 and 2 Corinthians 3 is to the Sinaitic covenant, but it is only a short step and a valid extension to apply this term to the Old Testament as a whole, in whose teachings the Sinai covenant plays a central role, though that step is nowhere taken in the New Testament itself.

The names assigned to persons and things (animate and inanimate) are never neutral, since they have connotations as well as denotations. The epithet "old" does not need to imply that the value of the teaching of the Old Testament has passed and that it has been replaced by the "new," for the Christian holds both Testaments as normative. The New Testament was not written to replace the Old Testament, and the correlative terms "old" and "new" can signify continuity as well as supplementation. One need not use the adjective "old" in the pejorative sense of antiquated and obsolete. Instead, it can be used in the affirming sense of venerable and treasured (see Matt 13:52; Luke 5:39).[64] Moreover, the application of the adjective "new" to the

---

62. For more, see Gregory Goswell, "The Two Testaments as Covenant Documents," *JETS* 62 (2019): 677–92.

63. The Vulgate text uses *pactum* (e.g., Jer 31:33), *foedus* (e.g., Exod 24:7, 8) and *testamentum* (e.g., 2 Cor 3:14; Heb 8:8) as translations for "covenant."

64. See, e.g., J. A. Loader, "Tenach and Old Testament—the Same Bible?," *TS* 58 (2002): 1415–30.

apostolic writings does not aim to elevate their importance to the detriment of the authority of the Old Testament. This way of talking does not impugn the Old Testament, seeing that the distinction is made in the Old Testament itself between the old covenant and the prospect of a new covenant.

CHAPTER 5 CONCLUSIONS

The aim is not merely to criticize the usually assigned book titles in the New Testament but to see how they may assist the understanding of the reader. The material assembled above demonstrates that a title implies an interpretation of the literary work it heads. A title may throw light on a work, or it may obscure its message. It is best to view the titles of the biblical books as valuable but fallible commentary on the text.

GUIDELINES FOR INTERPRETING THE TITLES
OF THE NEW TESTAMENT BOOKS

1. Make an effort to discover alternative titles that have been applied to the books of the New Testament. Commentaries often supply this information.

2. Do more than critique the traditional titles assigned to the New Testament books. Otherwise we would be guilty of what C. S. Lewis labels "chronological snobbery," the assumption that the ideas of earlier readers are discredited and inferior. Instead, consider whether the titles may supply an insight or present a viewpoint that may contribute to a deeper understanding of the work.

3. The basic and minimal function of a title is to identify a book and so differentiate it from other books, for example, the titles of the Pauline Epistles, Romans, Ephesians, and so on. Even here, however, the titles also amount to cross-references to accounts given in Acts about the different churches that have letters written to them, accounts that invite their use in providing important background information for the individual letters. In practice, no New Testament book title merely functions as an identification tag.

4. The second function is to indicate a book's general contents, a function that has obvious hermeneutical implications. A title such as the Acts of the Apostles is unfortunate, for it is in tension with the book's contents, for the book has a special interest in one apostle, Paul.

5. In the New Testament there is no third-function title (to highlight or recommend) in use in application to its books.

6. A fourth function is to indicate a book's genre, and titles such as Acts, the "Epistle of X," and Apocalypse (= Revelation) fall into this category. In each case they suggest a way of understanding the book so named. For example, "Acts," if a genre designation, misclassifies the book; the Petrine "letters" address problems in churches, but are really homiletical in character. Also, "Apocalypse" implies that the study of other (largely intertestamental) apocalyptic works is the key to its interpretation, whereas the book sees itself as standing in and culminating in the Old Testament prophetic tradition.

7. Properly understood, the names "Old Testament" and "New Testament" enshrine key Christian convictions about the relations of the two main parts of the Bible, in which salvation history culminates in the person and work of Jesus Christ, who is the answer to the hopes of Israel (Luke 24:27; Heb 1:1-2).

PART III

TEXTUAL
DIVISIONS

6

TEXTUAL DIVISIONS WITHIN OLD TESTAMENT BOOKS

INTRODUCTION

This and the following chapter examine a third feature of the paratext of
Scripture, the way in which the biblical text is subdivided into chapters,
paragraphs, and the like. This newer area of study is referred to as delimitation criticism.[1] It is not just a question of the significance and useful-
ness of the chapters and verses in the Bible with which we are familiar, for
there never was a time when the biblical text was not divided in some way.
In line with Semitic practice in general, Old Testament texts were always
written with spaces between words, unlike Greek manuscripts, which were
usually written in *scriptio continua*.[2] Division markers in the form of horizontal lines occur in Akkadian literature, a feature borrowed from earlier
Sumerian practice.[3] The Moabite Stone (Mesha Inscription) makes use of
a single point for word separation and of a vertical stroke for the purpose
of marking the end of verse-like sense units.[4] The use of dots to separate

---

1. The term was coined by Marjo C. A. Korpel, "Introduction to the Series Pericope," in
Delimitation Criticism: A New Tool in Biblical Scholarship, ed. Marjo C. A. Korpel and Josef M. Oesch,
Pericope 1 (Assen: Van Gorcum, 2000), 13.

2. A. R. Millard, "'Scriptio Continua' in Early Hebrew: Ancient Practice or Modern Surmise?,"
JSS 15 (1970): 2–15.

3. E.g., Code of Hammurabi in G. R. Driver, *Semitic Writing from Pictograph to Alphabet:
The Schweich Lectures of the British Academy 1944*, 3rd ed. (London: Published for the British
Academy, 1976), 43–45.

4. See J. Andrew Dearman, ed., *Studies in the Mesha Inscription and Moab*, ABS 2 (Atlanta:
Scholars Press, 1989), 307 fig. 1.

words is also found in Hebrew inscriptions (e.g., the Siloam Inscription).[5] Given such parallels, the presumption is that even the earliest Old Testament texts were marked and partitioned into sense divisions.[6]

TEXT DIVISIONS AND INTERPRETATION

The divisions within a biblical book suggest a literary structure that has significance for the interpretation of the contents of that book. Such divisions serve a number of related functions. The habits of readers suggest four possible functions of any given sense division. First, a division separates one section of a text from another section. This is the first and most obvious effect of a text division. For narrative, this serves to demarcate a different story, a separate episode, or a new scene. An example is the chapter breaks in Genesis 12–25, which reflect the episodic nature of the Abraham story. Divisions are often helpful, or sometimes not, since they may, at times, encourage interpretations of a text that ignore the wider literary context.

A correlative, second function of divisions is to join material. They demarcate a unit (longer or shorter), suggesting that the material joined is closely related in meaning. The literary portion is assumed by the reader to be a unit of meaning. The placement of the chapter division at Genesis 6:1, rather than at 6:9, where the Hebrew section is found, suggests that the obscure episode about "the sons of God" in 6:1–4 is related to the ensuing flood and perhaps favors an understanding of the wording in 6:3 ("his days shall be a hundred and twenty years") to mean that there will be 120 years till the flood comes to destroy humankind.[7]

A third function or effect of a division is to highlight certain material in a text, making it more prominent in the eyes of the reader. It may, for example, draw attention to a turning point in a narrative, which is the effect of the chapter division at Genesis 8:1, marking this as the pivotal point in the

---

5. J. Naveh, "Word Division in West Semitic Writing," *IEJ* 23 (1973): 206–8.

6. Marjo C. A. Korpel, "Unit Delimitation as a Guide to Interpretation: A Status Quaestionis," in *Les délimitations éditoriales des Écritures des bibles anciennes aux lectures modernes*, ed. Guillaume Bady and Marjo C. A. Korpel, Pericope 11 (Leuven: Peeters, 2020), 3–33.

7. Derek Kidner leaves the interpretation of the words open. See Kidner, *Genesis: An Introduction and Commentary*, TOTC (Leicester: Inter-Varsity, 1967), 85.

flood narrative ("But God remembered Noah"),[8] and from this juncture the flood waters begin to recede. God's intervention was decisive in saving Noah, and the break in the text highlights this fact. The reader's tendency is to see what is at the beginning as indicating what the section is about, and the end is scanned to discover how it all turned out.[9] In other words, what is read is understood in terms of the announced topic or theme at the beginning of the differentiated section.

The mirror image of the third function is the fourth function, to downplay or ignore certain textual features. It is not as easy for the reader to notice this effect on the reading process simply because of the character of the function itself. In Chronicles, the reigns of certain kings are downplayed, for example, that of Amon (2 Chr 33:21–25), whose accession notice does not coincide with a chapter division. The brevity of the description of his reign (only five verses) further suggests his relative unimportance in the thinking of the Chronicler.

When analyzed in this fashion, the status of breaks in the biblical text as commentary on the text is revealed, and also that divisions may lead (or mislead) the reader who seeks meaning in the text.

THE PHYSICAL DIVISIONS IN OLD TESTAMENT TEXTS

The Masoretes (AD 600–1000) supplied the traditional Hebrew text with several paratextual features that are part of the present organization of the biblical text:[10] the Hebrew open and closed paragraphs, and (of later origin) the *seder* reading lessons and the *parashah* reading lessons. In this discussion I will largely ignore versification. There are also the Christian chapter divisions with which we are familiar in our Bible.

The chapter divisions in Bibles are usually attributed to Stephen Langton (died 1228), a famous university teacher in Paris and later archbishop of Canterbury, who annotated the Vulgate.[11] Due to Langton's reputation as a

---

8. Gordon J. Wenham, "The Coherence of the Flood Narrative," *VT* 28 (1978): 338.

9. James Muilenburg states the same thing: "The delimitation of the passage is essential if we are to learn how its major motif, usually stated at the beginning, is resolved." See Muilenburg, "Form Criticism and Beyond," *JBL* 88 (1969): 9.

10. Israel Yeivin, *Introduction to the Tiberian Masorah*, trans. and ed. E. J. Revell, SBL MasS 5 (Missoula, MT: Scholars Press, 1980).

11. For details, see Joop H. A. van Banning, Studies in Judaism, "Reflections upon the Chapter Divisions of Stephan Langton," in *Method in Unit Delimitation*, ed. Marjo C. A. Korpel, Josef M.

biblical scholar, this system of reference became standard,[12] and the chapter divisions were taken over in the margins of the Bomberg Rabbinic Bibles (Venice) of 1516–1517, 1521, and 1525, and the Complutensian Polyglot (1517/22). Since then, they have been a feature of most Hebrew Bibles. The variant Hebrew chapter divisions (e.g., Deut 12:32 [Eng.] = 13:1 [Heb.]) first make their appearance in the Bomberg Second Rabbinic Bible (1525). These deviations in the placement of some chapter divisions are due to variations within the Latin (Vulgate) textual tradition, rather than being caused by misplacement or conscious adjustment when the Latin chapter divisions were transferred to Hebrew Bibles.[13]

The Hebrew paragraphs (*pisqot*) are marked by spaces in the text and are a feature of the oldest texts we possess.[14] There are two types: the open paragraph, which starts on a new line of text, and the closed paragraph, which continues on the same line after a space. According to Josef Oesch, the segmentation of biblical texts, seen already in the Dead Sea Scrolls, is part of a long reading tradition that included such divisions.[15] Oesch sees the likely origins of the divisions in the desire to protect the correct understanding of the biblical text by dividing it into sense units.[16] As stated by Emanuel Tov, the subdividing of the biblical text into sections "reflects exegesis on the extent of the content units."[17] The entire Hebrew Bible, except for the Psalms, is divided in this way. Evidence from Qumran lends credence to the

Oesch, and Stanley E. Porter, Pericope 6 (Leiden: Brill, 2007), 141-61.

12. Beryl Smalley, *The Study of the Bible in the Middle Ages* (Oxford: Basil Blackwell, 1952), 221-24. Berger provides information about earlier Latin divisions in the OT and NT (see *Histoire de la Vulgate*, 307-15).

13. See the margins of the RSV; and see Graham Davies, "Dividing Up the Pentateuch: Some Remarks on the Jewish Tradition," in *Leshon Limmudim: Essays on the Language and Literature of the Hebrew Bible in Honour of A. A. Macintosh*, ed. David A. Baer and Robert P. Gordon, LHBOTS 593 (London: Bloomsbury T&T Clark, 2013), 45-59.

14. John W. Olley sought to clarify the rationale underlying the locations of the literary divisions in the great Isaiah scroll found at Qumran. See Olley, "'Hear the Word of YHWH': The Structure of the Book of Isaiah in 1QIsaᵃ," VT 43 (1993): 19-49; Olley, "Texts Have Paragraphs Too—A Plea for Inclusion in Critical Editions," Textus 19 (1998): 111-25.

15. Josef M. Oesch, "Textgliederung im Alten Testament und in den Qumranhandschriften," *Hen* 5 (1983): 318.

16. Josef Oesch, *Petucha und Setuma: Untersuchungen zu einer überlieferten Gliederung im hebräischen Text des Alten Testaments*, OBO 27 (Freiburg: Universitätsverlag, 1979), 339.

17. Emanuel Tov, *Textual Criticism of the Hebrew Bible* (Minneapolis: Fortress, 1992), 51.

view that sense divisions of the Hebrew text are very old, even if not abso-
lutely settled and unchangeable.

As well as all this, the Hebrew Bible has been divided into 452 *seder* lessons
(plural *sedarim*), indicated by the large Hebrew letter *sāmek* in the margin.
These weekly liturgical readings are part of a three-year cycle associated with
the Palestinian tradition (154 or 156 in the Pentateuch). There are also longer
sections, marked in the margin by an abbreviation of the word *parashah*
(plural *parashiyyot*). These are associated with the Babylonian tradition and
appear only in the Pentateuch, providing fifty-four lessons for a one-year
lectionary cycle.[18] They are a feature of modern Jewish Bibles in English
(e.g., JPS).

These four schemes of division have separate origins but will be considered together, for they reflect alternative ways of reading the same text.
These diverse ways of dividing the biblical text suggest competing perspectives on a book. Nevertheless, the substantial overlap of schemes of totally
different origins also suggests that the divisions are neither arbitrary nor
without sense. In Genesis, for example, a number of *sedarim* coincide with
chapter divisions (e.g., 5:1; 8:1; 11:1; 12:1). On the other hand, that there are
different schemes that do not entirely coincide shows that they are interpretations of the text, providing alternative views of the meaning of the text.

The division into verses (*pěsûkîm*) was a later phenomenon than the division into paragraphs.[19] It seems, however, that the Old Testament was divided
into verses in Talmudic times, since there are *halakot* (legal findings) that
depend on this feature.[20] The Talmud (c. AD 600) tells us that the ancients
were called "scribes" (i.e., *sopherim* or counters) because they counted all
the letters in Scripture. These scribes identify Leviticus 13:33 as the middle
verse of the Pentateuch. The standard verse divisions were set by the Ben
Asher family (c. AD 900). In Hebrew Bibles, a large colon called *sôp pāsûq* (:)
signifies the end of a verse. The biblical verse is largely a liturgical unit. It

---

18. For further discussion of the Babylonian and Palestinian reading cycles, see Charles
Perrot, "The Reading of the Bible in the Ancient Synagogue," in *Mikra: Text, Translation, Reading
and Interpretation of the Hebrew Bible in Ancient Judaism and Early Christianity*, ed. Martin Jan
Mulder (Assen: Van Gorcum, 1990), 137–59.

19. For the possible origins of versification, see Ludwig Blau, "Massoretic Studies III and
IV," *JQR* 9 (1896–97): 122–44, 471–90. Blau suggests that a consideration of the logic by which the
division into verses is ruled "may be advantageous to Exegesis" (490).

20. Yeivin, *Tiberian Masorah*, 42.

varies greatly in length and may contain many clauses. It was meant to ensure correct recitation in the synagogue. It is not to be confused with the poetic verse (or line), which usually consists of two poetic half-lines (versets), each of which is a clause (usually about three Hebrew words in length). The verses of the New Testament, though modeled on Old Testament versification with regard to approximate length, are something different again in that they are not related to any system of recitation.[21]

PENTATEUCH

In what follows, due to limitations of space, I will only provide selected examples of how the different schemes of divisions might provide input into interpretation.

Genesis

The division at Genesis 2:1, at least at first sight, appears to place the account of the seventh day (2:1-3) in the wrong chapter. The creation week, though not the *work* of creation, continues in Genesis 2, and yet 2:1-3 is separated from what precedes by a chapter break, whereas the Masoretic *seder* division comes after 2:3, where we might have expected the break to come. Is the placement of Langton's division at 2:1 a blunder—breaking into the sequence of the seven days—or does it contain an insight? Its effect is to differentiate the seventh day from the preceding six, and indeed the seventh day of rest is quite different, and the idealistic picture in Genesis 2 fits quite well with it. According to Gordon Wenham, the "idyllic portrayal of the Garden of Eden in chapter 2 conveys the air of sabbatical bliss,"[22] and this observation may be used to justify the chapter division at 2:1.

The chapter divisions in Genesis take little account of the repeated genealogical formula that appears to unify and structure the entire book: "These are the generations of ..." This recurring *toledot* formula signals the start of the five major movements of the book into which the narrative movement is subdivided (2:4; 6:9; 11:27; 25:19; 37:2). The longer reading lessons (*parashiyyot*)

---

21. Moore, "Vulgate Chapters," 815-20; Jordan S. Penkower, "The Chapter Divisions in the 1525 Rabbinic Bible," VT 48 (1998): 350-74; Penkower, "Verse Divisions in the Hebrew Bible," VT 50 (2000): 379-93.

22. Gordon J. Wenham, *Story as Torah: Reading the Old Testament Ethically* (Edinburgh: T&T Clark, 2000), 27.

come at 6:9 and 12:1, and they produce a credible two-part division of the primeval history, given the crucial nature of the flood as the undoing of creation. By placing the chapter division at 12:1, instead of 11:27 with the *toledot* formula, this vital juncture where God makes promises to Abram is effectively highlighted. Both the Palestinian and Babylonian lessons also mark this point. The remaining chapters of Genesis record the stories of the patriarchs, which relate to one or other of the promises made to Abram in 12:1–3. Examination of the textual divisions in Genesis 1–12 shows that, though variable, they are not arbitrary. They show an understanding of the flow of the text. The modern reader does not have to agree with the traditional divisions and is free to discount them, but they should do so only after carefully considering them.

Exodus

The book of Exodus is divided into forty chapters by Langton, or alternatively into thirty-three *sedarim* and eleven *parashiyyot*. I will comment on the apparent significance of a number of these for the reading of Exodus. The sixth *seder* division at 7:8 is the beginning of the plague sequence proper, and 7:6–7 indicates a closure by noting the obedience of Moses and Aaron and giving their respective ages at this historical juncture. The final verse of the sixth *seder* (8:19) is in effect a punch line, with the admission of the Egyptian magicians: "This is the finger of God." The Palestinian and Babylonian lessons, starting at 10:1, highlight the divine speech of 10:1–2, which reveals the divine purpose behind the hardening of Pharaoh's heart. The chapter division and start of a *seder* at 11:1 mark the final break between Moses and Pharaoh.

Leviticus

In Leviticus many of the textual breaks are triggered by a speech attribution, often "The Lord said to Moses," with some seventeen out of the twenty-five *sedarim* (1:1; 4:1; 6:19; 8:1; etc.) and seven out of the ten *parashiyyot* (12:1; 14:1; 16:1; etc.) falling into this category. As well, a number of chapter divisions, when they do not coincide with the Palestinian and Babylonian lessons, are made on the same basis (6:1; 13:1; 20:1; 22:1; 23:1). This is the leading factor explaining both the Hebrew reading portions and the English chapter divisions and supports the Hebrew title of the book, *wayyiqrā'* ("And he called [to

Moses]").[23] The book of Leviticus largely consists of divine speeches to Moses, who is instructed to repeat God's instructions to the priests and/or the people.

Numbers

In the book of Numbers, as in Leviticus, text divisions are often linked to the commencement of divine speeches: the Palestinian (1:1; 2:1; 4:17; 5:11; etc.) and Babylonian lessons (4:21; 8:1; etc.) and the chapters of Langton (4:1; 9:1; 18:1; etc.).

Deuteronomy

The second *seder* division, at Deuteronomy 2:2, marks a turning point, with the divine command to "turn northward" toward the promised land (2:3). The third *seder* lesson encompasses the victories over Sihon and Og (2:31-3:22), together with the lesson to be drawn from their military success. The fourth *seder* lesson (3:23-4:24) is bounded by an inclusio of references to Moses's exclusion from the land as a salutary lesson for Israel (3:23-29; 4:21-22). In Deuteronomy 4 there is a focus on the danger of idolatry, but what sets 4:25 (the start of the fifth *seder*) apart from the earlier part of the chapter is the new concern over the danger of *future* idolatry ("When you beget children ..."). The contents of chapters 12-26 are structured according to the sequence of the Ten Words (what we tend to call the Ten Commandments),[24] so that the detailed instructions appear as specific applications of the Decalogue. For example, the fifth word, about honoring father and mother, is viewed as covering such authority figures as judges, the king, priests, and prophets (16:18-18:22), and the start of this section coincides with Hebrew divisions of the text in both the Palestinian (sixteenth *seder*) and Babylonian systems (fifth *parashah*).

---

23. C. J. Labuschagne argues that oracular formulae determine the structure of the Pentateuch. See Labuschagne, "The Literary and Theological Function of Divine Speech in the Pentateuch," in *Congress Volume: Salamanca 1983*, ed. J. A. Emerton, VTSup 36 (Leiden: Brill, 1985), 154-73.

24. Stephen A. Kaufman, "The Structure of the Deuteronomic Law," *Maarav* 1/2 (1978-1979): 105-58.

PROPHETS

Joshua

In the book of Joshua, the second *seder* begins with the divine declaration that God will begin to exalt Joshua in the sight of all Israel (3:7), and that is the divinely stated reason for the wonders God will perform. The fourth *seder* begins at 6:27 ("So the Lord was with Joshua, and his fame was in all the land" [ESV]), which amounts to a summary of what is achieved in the preceding six chapters, with the capture of Jericho as the crowning vindication of Joshua's leadership (ch. 6). Joshua 6:27 serves to confirm the promise made by God to Joshua (1:5).

Divisions at these junctures reinforce the theme of God's endorsement of Joshua's leadership, which dominates chapters 1-6. The chapter and *seder* divisions at 13:1 mark the transition from conquest (chs. 7-12) to distribution of land (chs. 13-22). Joshua is depicted as "old and advanced in years" (13:1 [2×]; cf. 23:1), seeing that (by definition) it is the aged patriarch who distributes inheritances, issues final warnings, and gives instructions about the future (cf. Gen 49; Deut 33).

Judges

In Judges, set phrases function as the introduction to major episodes and indicate the need for a judge: "And the people of Israel did what was evil in the sight of the Lord" (2:11 ESV; see 3:7, 12; 4:1; 6:1; 10:6; 13:1). A number of these coincide with chapter divisions. In the third *seder* (3:31-5:30) there are closed paragraphs marked after 4:3 and 4:12, which divide the content of this section into the Israelites' initial cry to God (4:1-3); the introduction of the key characters Deborah, Barak, and Heber (4:4-12); and the defeat of the enemy (4:13-24), with an open paragraph commencing after 4:24 and covering Judges 5, the victory song of Deborah and Barak.

Samuel

Langton's division at 1 Samuel 2:1 and the beginning of the second *seder* lesson at 2:10 each in its own way draws attention to the song of Hannah (2:1-10) that sets the theological tone of the book. The song as the overture prepares for all that follows, and the final note of the song is: "He [the Lord] will give strength to his king, and exalt the power of his anointed" (2:10 RSV). The chapter division at 11:1 suggests a lack of connection with what precedes and is in part responsible for the attractiveness of a lengthy addition to the Hebrew text found among the Dead Sea Scrolls in the eyes of some recent scholars (notably Tov).[25] Yet the suggested addition (giving the backstory about Nahash the Ammonite king) makes a lame introduction to the crisis, as well as failing to acknowledge that the section really begins at 10:26. The MT as we have it shows the sudden eruption of a crisis that is God's gift to Saul to demonstrate he can save Israel, with Saul's rescue of Jabesh-gilead answering the implied criticism in 10:27 ("How can this man save us?" [RSV]).

The death of Saul is a major juncture in the unified book of Samuel (2 Sam 1:1: "After the death of Saul ..."), but if the book is to be subdivided into two, the *seder* division after 2 Samuel 2:6 is another possible candidate, with David in 2:7 announcing the new post-Saul situation ("for Saul your lord is dead" [RSV]). This is close to the division suggested by J. P. Fokkelman, who says that the book of 1 Samuel should have ended with David's dirge in the second half of 2 Samuel 1 (only six verses away at 2:1).[26] Finally, the chapter division at 2 Samuel 12:1 highlights the statement of the Lord's displeasure at what David has done (11:27b), and the judgment pronounced by Nathan on David is given a climactic position at the close of the twenty-fifth *seder* lesson (12:10-12). Subsequent chapters in 2 Samuel show the outworking of the pronounced judgment.

Kings

The chapter division at 1 Kings 3:1 is triggered by the preceding summary statement: "So the kingdom was established in the hand of Solomon" (2:46 RSV). The chapter division in the Hebrew text at 5:1 (= 4:21 Eng.) enables a partition of the description of Solomon's reign over Israel (4:1-20) as a distinct unit from 5:1-32 (= 4:21–5:18 Eng.), which concerns this king's relations with the wider world, and 5:1 (= 4:21 Eng.) sketches the broad area of Solomonic

---

25. At 10:27b the LXX and 4QSamᵃ add a sizable paragraph whose originality Tov defends; (see *Textual Criticism*, 342-44). The 4QSamᵃ addition is no evidence of an older, more reliable text but is better viewed as a different *edition* of the story, which in my judgment is distinctly inferior in literary terms; see Terry L. Eves, "One Ammonite Invasion or Two? I Sam 10:27–11:2 in the Light of 4QSamᵃ," *WTJ* 44 (1982): 308-26. The addition is incorporated into the text of the NRSV (1989).

26. J. P. Fokkelman, *Reading Biblical Narrative: An Introductory Guide*, trans. Ineke Smit (Louisville: Westminster John Knox, 1999), 160.

influence. The fourth *seder* division is only one verse away at 4:20. First Kings 17:1 marks the dramatic appearance of Elijah and adds to the impression of his sudden arrival on the scene. The *seder* division starting at 2 Kings 20:8 brackets the account of Hezekiah's reception of the Babylonian envoys (20:12-19) with the account of Manasseh's reign (2 Kgs 21), which may imply that some readers saw fault with Hezekiah's action. The most that can be said is that the fate of the royal house of Judah is sealed from 20:16-18 onward, and its doom is only confirmed by Manasseh's evil reign (23:26-27).

Isaiah

In the prophecy of Isaiah, the fourth *seder* division at 9:7, the fifth *seder* at 11:1, and the seventh at 16:5 begin lessons with verses concerning a future Davidic figure, a significant theme in the early chapters of Isaiah. Some chapter divisions are explained by the formula beginning the oracles against the nations: "An oracle [*maśśā'*] concerning [name of nation]" (13:1; 15:1; 17:1; 19:1; 21:1; 22:1; 23:1), others by the eschatological phrase "on that day" (26:1; 27:1), and still others by the "woe" (*hôy*) formula (28:1; 29:1; 30:1; 31:1; 33:1). The chapter divisions draw the reader's attention to these structurally significant formulae.[27] W. H. Brownlee put forward the thesis that the book of Isaiah was edited and arranged as a two-volume work (chs. 1-33; 34-66), and he saw evidence for his thesis in a three-line gap between chapters 33 and 34 at the bottom of column XXVII in the Qumran scroll 1QIsaiah[a].[28] This thesis was an early example of the use of a paratextual feature for the purposes of literary analysis. Certainly, a number of the themes of chapters 34-35, placed by Brownlee in the second half of the book, anticipate those of Isaiah 40-66 (e.g., the way through the wilderness and the cry "Behold, your God").[29]

---

27. See Leon J. Liebreich, "The Compilation of the Book of Isaiah" *JQR* 46 (1956): 258-77.

28. W. H. Brownlee, *The Meaning of the Qumrân Scrolls for the Bible: With Special Attention to the Book of Isaiah* (New York: Oxford University Press, 1964), 247-59.

29. See Marvin Pope, "Isaiah 34 in Relation to Isaiah 35, 40-66," *JBL* 71 (1952): 235-43.

Jeremiah

Jeremiah 1 acts as prologue to this prophetic book, introducing its main themes: the prophet, the prophet and the nation (of Judah), and the prophet and the nations (see 1:5, 10).[30] Only in 2:1 does Jeremiah receive a word from the Lord that he is instructed to proclaim. The three alternative textual divisions at 8:22 (RSV paragraph), 9:1 (= 8:23 Heb.), and 9:2 (= 9:1 Heb.) are material to the interpretation of the passage, especially the issue of who is weeping in 9:1 (Eng.) ("O that my head were waters, and my eyes a fountain of tears" [RSV]). Is it the sorrow of Jeremiah, or of YHWH, or of both? The identification of YHWH as the speaker can be accepted only for 8:19b and 9:2-3 (Heb. 9:1-2), for the idiom of "the daughter of my people" (Eng. 8:19, 22; 9:1) seems to belong to the speech of the prophet,[31] and the chapter division at 9:1 (Heb. [= 9:2 Eng.]) helps to differentiate the divine wish to leave his people in 9:1-2 (Heb.) from the preceding speech (noting "says YHWH" in 9:2b). A number of the Hebrew divisions are explained by an apparent desire to begin *seder* lessons with a more hopeful saying of Jeremiah (e.g., 12:15; 17:7; 23:6; 24:2; 30:9; 31:33; 33:16; 39:18; 42:12), so that Jeremiah is shown not to be a one-sided prophet of doom.

Ezekiel

In Ezekiel, the division at 2:1 signals the point at which the Lord first speaks to Ezekiel ("And he said to me"). Most of the chapter divisions coincide with the "son of man" address to Ezekiel (4:1; 5:1) or the formula "The word of the LORD came to me" (6:1; 7:1; 12:1; etc.). A number of times the *sedarim* begin with the recognition formula: "and you/they shall know that I am the LORD" (22:16; 24:24; 29:21; 37:28; 39:22), highlighting its importance in the book. This formula (in slightly differing forms) occurs over sixty times in Ezekiel. God's action in judgment and mercy are designed to bring Israel and the nations to a recognition of who he is.

---

30. Harry P. Nasuti, "A Prophet to the Nations: Diachronic and Synchronic Readings of Jeremiah 1," *HAR* 10 (1987): 248-66.

31. Joseph M. Henderson, "Who Weeps in Jeremiah VIII 23 (IX 1)? Identifying Dramatic Speakers in the Poetry of Jeremiah," *VT* 52 (2002): 191-206.

The Book of the Twelve

The agricultural images at the end of Hosea (14:5-8) set the scene for the devastation brought by the army of locusts in the following prophecy of Joel. The *seder* lesson commencing at Hosea 14:5 extends into the prophecy of Joel and ends with the promise of the return of plentiful harvests (Joel 2:18-26). Almost all scholars agree that, in terms of structure, the prophecy of Joel has two halves, though there is not absolute agreement as to the point of bifurcation. There are three contenders for the main point of division of Joel (2:17/18; 2:27/28; 2:32/3:1), and each in its own way represents important insights gained by readers of this prophetic book. Even if the decision is not made to favor one break over the others, the exercise of considering alternatives and weighing arguments has not been without value.[32] Ronald Troxel argues that Joel 3 in the Hebrew Bible (= Eng. 2:28-32) is "a continuing of the story begun in chapters 1-2,"[33] and therefore he places the start of the second main division in Joel at 4:1 (= Eng. 3:1). In deciding the most viable halfway point in the prophecy, the varied views of readers to some extent come down to the criterion used in making this determination (content versus form).[34] In terms of the content of the prophet's message, the division may be best placed at 2:27/28,[35] the point at which the topic of the locust plague and its aftermath finally finishes, or else a little further down at 2:32/3:1, due to the different handling of the theme of the nations from that point onward. However, the main generic divide in the prophecy of Joel is between community lament and divine answer, and on that basis, the line of division is to be put at 2:17/18.[36]

---

32. For detailed discussion, see Gregory Goswell, "The Bifurcation of the Prophecy of Joel and Its Theology of Reversal," in Bady and Korpel, *Les délimitations éditoriales*, 85–105.

33. Ronald L. Troxel, *Joel: Scope, Genre(s), and Meaning*, CSHB 6 (Winona Lake, IN: Eisenbrauns, 2015), 58, 72–94.

34. As pointed out by James Nogalski, *Redactional Processes in the Book of the Twelve*, BZAW 218 (Berlin: de Gruyter, 1993), 2; cf. Mark LaRocca-Pitts, *The Day of Yahweh: The Use and Development of Yahweh's Motive on That Day as a Rhetorical Strategy by the Hebrew Prophets* (Saarbrücken: VDM Verlag, 2009), 261.

35. This break is supported by the Hebrew chapter division at 2:28 (= Heb. 3:1). There is also a "closed" paragraph break in L after 2:27, an "open" paragraph at the same juncture in the Aleppo Codex, and a vacant line is left after 2:27 in the Dead Sea Scroll Mur 88.

36. In regard to the Greek versions, in Vaticanus a break is found at Joel 2:18/19. In Sinaiticus, the textual divisions are placed at 2:18/19 and 2:28/3:1.

With regard to the theology of reversal on display in the book, each of the proposed points of division contributes to and clarifies that theology, but in a different way. A division at 2:17/18 alerts the reader that the reversal of fortunes is due to the divine response to the appeal of God's people. God himself says what he will do (2:18), and quoting God gives certainty to the promised outcome. The nations are a potential threat (2:17), and that possibility is actualized in Joel 4, and the heightened crisis of foreign oppression in that chapter requires a greater divine intervention to vindicate God's people. If the main break is placed at 2:27/28, the locust plague is the focus of the first half of the book, though this insect pest is dressed in apocalyptic garb (especially in 2:1-11), such that a thematic transition from an historical agricultural crisis to a future judgment of apocalyptic proportions in Joel 3 is facilitated. If the main break is put at 2:32/3:1, this helps to shape the interpretation of 2:28-32, for it suggests that the main connection of these five verses is with what precedes, the logic being that just as the fertility of the land will be restored, so also the people will be restored by the outpouring of God's spirit. On that reading, Joel 2:28-32 completes the picture of reversal in Joel 2, and the second half of the book (confined to Joel 3) focuses on the future judgment of the nations and the ultimate rescue of God's people.

In the prophecy of Amos, collections of oracles are loosely joined together by such rubrics as "Hear this word" (3:1; 4:1; 5:1) and the chapter divisions reflect the view that these mark the beginnings of sections.[37] As well, a series of woes ("Woe to those who ..." [5:18; 6:1, 4]) and the series of five visions (7:1, 4, 7; 8:1; 9:1) have influenced the placement of the chapter divisions. There are more compelling ways of subdividing the book,[38] but six of Langton's chapter breaks pick up either the hearing or seeing theme and thus support the basic division of the prophecy of Amos into oracles (chs. 1-6) and visions (chs. 7-9).[39] The *seder* division in Obadiah comes only just before verse 21, the final verse of the prophecy, so that almost the whole prophecy is placed with Amos 8-9. This is appropriate given the strategic mention of Edom in Amos

---

37. The expressions are a little different in Amos 7:16 and 8:4.

38. E.g., an inclusio of 1:2 and 3:8 ("roars") envelopes the first major subdivision of the book (1:2-3:8), a series of oracles against eight nations, which end in 3:3-8 with "a justifying speech" by Amos against criticism that his oracle against Israel may have called forth. See Paul R. Noble, "The Literary Structure of Amos: A Thematic Analysis," *JBL* 114 (1995): 209-26.

39. A. van der Wal, "The Structure of Amos," *JSOT* 26 (1983): 107-13.

9:12 as representative of "all the nations who are called by [YHWH's] name." The short prophecy of Obadiah that condemns Edom may be viewed as an appendix to the larger book and read in coordination with Amos.[40]

There is a slight difference in the chapter division between Jonah 1 and 2 in the English and Hebrew versions (Eng. 1:17 = Heb. 2:1). All mention of the fish is confined to chapter 2 in Hebrew form, which recounts the rescue of Jonah. As well, 1:17 and 2:10 (Eng.), the swallowing of Jonah and his being vomited up, respectively, provide an inclusio around the section taken up with Jonah's prayer.[41] On the other hand, notice of Jonah's three days and three nights in the belly of the fish (1:17b) could be read as a summary statement that achieves a partial closure of the action of Jonah 1.

Several of the chapter divisions in Micah relate to the hearing theme (1:2; 3:1; 6:1) and two are signaled by "woe" oracles (2:1; 7:1). The chapter division at 5:1, or alternatively 5:2 (= 5:1 Heb.), highlights the messianic prediction (5:2–4 Eng.), as also does the central placement of this oracle in the prophecy. According to Leslie Allen, 5:1–6 (Eng.) is the focal point of the book, which has a concentric structure.[42] The humiliation of Jerusalem's present king (5:1 Eng.) is contrasted with Israel's future ideal ruler in David's line (5:2–4 Eng.), with the progression from present troubles to future success displaying a pattern similar to adjacent units (4:9–10, 11–13), so that the messianic unit is best conceived as 5:1–6 (= 4:14–5:5 Heb.).

The twelfth *seder* of the Twelve commences at the last verse of Micah (7:20) and covers the Nahum section as well, so that the judgment on Nineveh that is the burden of Nahum becomes a demonstration of the covenant faithfulness of God announced in Micah 7:20. A similar pattern, where the lesson begins with the final verse of a book, is found in the fifteenth (Zeph 3:20), sixteenth (Hag 2:23), and twenty-first *sedarim* (Zech 14:21). The regularity of this arrangement shows that this method of division is a unifying move.

---

40. See Douglas Green, "Obadiah, Prophet of Retribution and Restoration," in *The Lion Has Roared: Theological Themes in the Prophetic Literature of the Old Testament*, ed. H. G. L. Peels and S. D. Snyman (Eugene, OR: Pickwick, 2012), 150: "the most obvious connection being that both books climax with the restoration of Jerusalem and Israel's possession of Edom (Amos 9:12; Obad 21)."

41. Supporting this way of dividing the text is the concentric structure that Rudolf Pesch discerns in Jonah 1:4–16, with the *Furchtmotiv* (fear motif) occurring at the beginning (vv. 4–5a), middle (vv. 9–10a) and end (vv. 15–16a). See Pesch, "Zur konzentrischen Strukur von Jona 1," *Bib* 47 (1966): 578.

42. Leslie C. Allen, *The Books of Joel, Obadiah, Jonah, and Micah*, NICOT (Grand Rapids: Eerdmans, 1976), 260.

The twelve books are not to be considered as totally separate. Zephaniah 3:20 anticipates the return of Judean exiles to their homeland, which is the context of the prophecy of Haggai that immediately follows. The person of Zerubbabel mentioned in Haggai 2:23 also features in the book of Zechariah that follows (see Zech 4:6-10). The theme of sacrifice in Zechariah 14:21 forges a credible link to Malachi with its religious themes (e.g., the critique of unworthy sacrifices in Mal 1). The prophecy of Haggai has two chapters, with the first of the four dated prophetic oracles (1:1; 1:15b-2:1; 2:10-20) occupying the whole of chapter 1, with the chapter break at this point (2:1) appropriately marking the significant change represented by the commencement of work on the house of YHWH (1:14-15). Langton's division at 2:1 gives a valuable exegetical clue, indicating that the message of the book of Haggai turns on the temple.

WRITINGS

Psalms

The numbering of the verses in most of the titled psalms is different between the Hebrew and the English texts, usually by one, seeing that the title is numbered in the Hebrew text. For example, the title of Psalm 3 ("A Psalm of David, when he fled from Absalom his son") is 3:1 in the Hebrew Bible. If the title is particularly long (e.g., the title of Ps 51), the numbering of the verses will be off by two. Despite considerable variation in the Psalter in the manuscript tradition, there is no evidence that the psalms ever lacked titles, and so the titles are to be viewed as *text* rather than as paratext.[43] The tendency in recent Bible versions is to put the psalm titles in smaller type (e.g., NASB, RSV, NIV), and this is unfortunate, for it gives the impression that they are (dispensable) appended notes. There is no justification for their wholesale removal by the NEB editors. The numbering of the titles in the Hebrew text reflects the view that the title is integral to the poetic piece.[44] If so, a title such as that at the head of Psalm 3 suggests that the psalm be read in the context of the life of David, especially as depicted in the book of Samuel.

---

43. *Pace* William Yarchin, "Is There an Authoritative Shape for the Book of Psalms? Profiling the Manuscripts of the Hebrew Psalter," *RB* 122 (2015): 355-70.

44. For more on psalm titles, see Roger T. Beckwith, "The Early History of the Psalter," *TynBul* 46 (1995): 1-27.

There is no system of Hebrew paragraphing in the Psalter because the individually demarcated psalms are, in effect, a paragraph. In the Leningrad Codex (L) there is a blank line or portion of a line between individual psalms, and in that space is placed the number of the psalm. In Sinaiticus usually no space is left between individual psalms, but a horizontal line shows where one psalm ends and another begins, and the psalms are numbered.[45] Such lines also frequently mark sections within psalms. In the LXX (and Vulgate) the canonical Psalms 9 and 10 are combined to become a single composition (9:1-21, 22-39 [Gk.]), while Psalm 147 is divided into two independent psalms: Psalm 146 (= 147:1-11 Eng.) and Psalm 147 (= 147:12-20 Eng.), with the result that the Psalter still contains 150 compositions. Also, Psalm 115 (Eng.) = 113:9-26 (Gk.); 116:1-9 (Eng.) = Psalm 114; and 116:10-19 (Eng.) = Psalm 115 (Gk.).[46] The LXX adds a Psalm 151, but there is the admission in the heading of this psalm that it is "outside the number" of the accepted collection. The joining of Psalms 9 and 10 is supported by the absence of a title to Psalm 10. Further evidence in favor of their joining is the presence of a fragmented acrostic, begun in Psalm 9 and completed in Psalm 10.[47] The division in the Hebrew can, however, be justified when the change of mood between the two psalms is observed.[48] There is no great difference in theme or form in Psalm 147:12-20 (Eng.) compared to earlier verses, so the division of Psalm 147 into two, such as happens in the Greek Bible, is not convincing.

Job

The chapters in Job are signaled by introductions to the various speeches, such as "Then Job answered" (12:1), but where the speeches by a character cover more than one chapter, there is no speech formula (e.g., 27:1; 29:1) and the divisions made to prevent extraordinarily long chapters are to some extent arbitrary. The speeches of suffering Job typically occupy the space of two chapters (e.g., Job 6-7; 9-10), or even more (Job 12-14), whereas those of

---

45. For examples, see Milne and Skeat, *Scribes and Correctors*, fig. 10.

46. For a discussion of the viability of dividing Ps 116 in this way, see M. L. Barré, "Psalm 116: Its Structure and Its Enigmas," *JBL* 109 (1990): 61-79.

47. For comments on the strophic structure of the combined composition Pss 9-10, see J. P. Fokkelman, *Reading Biblical Poetry: An Introductory Guide*, trans. Ineke Smit (Louisville: Westminster John Knox, 2001), 120-21.

48. As noted by Derek Kidner, *Psalms 1-72: An Introduction and Commentary on Books I and II of the Psalms*, TOTC (London: Inter-Varsity, 1973), 68-69.

his friends generally cover only a single chapter (e.g., Job 8; 11), but note the longer first speech of Eliphaz (chs. 4–5). This gives some force to the accusation by Job's friends that he is longwinded and verbose (8:2; 11:2–3; 15:2). The speeches of Job end at 31:40, and their final line reads: "The words of Job are ended." The chapter division at 28:1 in no way suggests that Job 28 is extraneous or self-contained material.[49] It could be read as a sarcastic comment on the preceding debate that has manifested little or no wisdom. It asserts that ultimate wisdom is not accessible to human beings; the only kind of wisdom that a human being can have is the kind that Job himself is described as having (28:28; see 1:1, 8; 2:3). According to Andrew Steinmann, this wisdom poem signals that Job has begun his journey back to the simple trust in God that he had before his suffering began.[50] Despite a lack of scholarly support, there is nothing to prevent this soliloquy being put in the mouth of Job.

Proverbs

In Proverbs a number of the chapter divisions are signaled by the "my son" mode of address (2:1; 3:1; 4:1 ["O sons"]; 5:1; 6:1; 7:1), which draws attention to the character of most of chapters 1–9 as speeches of a wise father to his son. This form of address can, however, also occur within chapters (1:8, 10, 15; 3:11, 21; 4:10, 20; 5:7 ["O sons"]; 6:20; 7:24 ["O sons"]; 8:32 ["my sons"]). The division at 8:1 is influenced by a change from fatherly advice to the call of Lady Wisdom, and 9:1 marks the close of the long address of Wisdom. The third *seder* division after 9:10 ("The fear of the LORD is the beginning of wisdom") draws attention to this verse as a punch line, and this verse together with 1:7 forms an inclusio around chapters 1–9. Then, two large collections of proverbs attributed to Solomon (either as author or collector) are marked by the start of new chapters at 10:1 and 25:1.[51] Proverbs 30:1 and 31:1 single out collections of wise sayings from Agur and Lemuel, respectively.

---

49. See Donald E. Gowan, "Reading Job as a 'Wisdom Script,'" *JSOT* 55 (1992): 85–96, who sees ch. 28 as an appropriate conclusion to the debate between Job and his friends (92).

50. Andrew E. Steinmann, "The Structure and Message of the Book of Job," *VT* 46 (1996): 85–100, esp. 98. Steinmann does not, however, suggest that it is Job who speaks in ch. 28.

51. We should discount 22:17 ("the words of the wise") and 24:23 ("These also are for the wise") as titles for sections. See Alex Luc, "The Titles and Structure of Proverbs," *ZAW* 112 (2000): 252–55. The poem about the "good wife" (31:10–31), though a separate unit (as indicated by the acrostic), is not differentiated from what precedes by means of a title of its own.

Ruth

The book of Ruth has four chapters that convincingly divide the book into four episodes.[52] A *seder* lesson division is found at 2:12,[53] thereby highlighting the statement by Boaz, who unknowingly forecasts Ruth's future, or alternatively, the *seder* follows 3:12, after Boaz's statement again commending Ruth and pledging to do all that she asks.[54] The *seder* division at this point has a cliffhanger effect, with Boaz revealing to Ruth (and the reader) that there is, however, a kinsman nearer than he (3:12). The only paragraph break (open) in Ruth in the Tiberian Masoretic tradition is at 4:17, before the genealogy of David (4:18-22).[55] It marks the boundary between story and genealogy and if anything highlights the genealogy as of special significance for the meaning of the preceding family history, linking it into God's wider purposes for Israel, which will be blessed through the house of David. The halfway point in the book is marked by the Masoretes at 2:21, immediately after Naomi tells Ruth of the connection Boaz has with the family. In other words, each division serves to accentuate a crucial stage in the plot of the book of Ruth.

The Hebrew divisions would seem to highlight what are in effect programmatic statements by Boaz (speaking about Ruth) and in this way foreground the part played by him and Ruth in the redemption of Naomi's family. The chapter divisions of Langton at 2:1 and 4:1 also put a focus on Boaz, with the first introducing the fact of his existence to the reader and the second narrating his decisive step of going up to the gate to "settle the matter" (3:18). On the other hand, Naomi has the last word in chapters 1, 2, and 3. As commentary on the text, only the chapter division at 3:1 underscores the role of Ruth. Different ways of dividing the text reflect ancient reading practices (in this case, who was perceived to be the main character of the book), and these breaks are significant for interpretation and frequently contain an exegetical insight.

---

52. This is supported by a chain of responsions (or refrains) between the final verses of the first three chapters; see Korpel, *Structure of the Book of Ruth*, 221-22.

53. This is not marked in the text of L, but it is indicated in the Masoretic list of L.

54. This is the beginning of the second *seder* lesson in L. John H. Sailhamer views the words of Boaz in 3:11 as the defining moment of the book, and the juxtapositioning of Ruth and the "woman of worth" in Prov 31 in the Hebrew canon also draws attention to the importance of this verse in the plot of the book of Ruth. See Sailhamer, *Introduction to Old Testament Theology: A Canonical Approach* (Grand Rapids: Zondervan, 1995), 213.

55. As noted by Korpel, several Hebrew manuscripts have an open or closed paragraph after 3:7, highlighting the key scene in 3:8-13. See Marjo C. A. Korpel, "Unit Division in the Book of Ruth: With Examples from Ruth 3," in Korpel and Oesch, *Delimitation Criticism*, 134.

Ecclesiastes

A number of the chapter divisions in Ecclesiastes are related to recurring themes and refrains, for example, 3:1 after the refrain, "This also is vanity [*hebel*] and a striving after wind" (RSV); 4:1 after a "nothing better" saying on the enjoyment theme; 5:1 after a vanity refrain (cf. 3:1);[56] 6:1 after the enjoyment theme; and 9:1 after the refrain-like expression "he cannot find out." The only value of the chapters is that they draw attention to recurring motifs.

The Song of Songs

The Song of Songs is subdivided into two *sedarim* (the second starting at 5:2). This scheme of division reads 5:1 as the poet's own concluding words of exclamation ("Eat, O friends, and drink: drink deeply, O lovers" [RSV]), which serve as the climax and center of the book.[57] Song of Songs 5:2 announces a new scene, with the young woman dreaming in her bed. The issue of the outline of the Song is a vexed one, with many alternative schemes being proposed but no scholarly consensus emerging. Most modern attempts to frame a credible outline of the Song make use of verses that may be identified as refrains, noting, for example, 2:7; 3:5; and 8:4, each of which adjures the daughters of Jerusalem "that you stir not up nor awaken love until it please" (5:8 is a further [but different] adjuration of the daughters of Jerusalem). These appear each time to mark a conclusion.

Lamentations

The five chapters of Lamentations coincide with the Hebrew open paragraphs. The first four poems are alphabetical acrostics, so that the chapter divisions coincide with the alphabetical structure. In chapters 1 and 2 each Hebrew stanza has three lines, and only the first word of each stanza begins with the appropriate letter of the Hebrew alphabet, which has twenty-two consonants (therefore, there are twenty-two verses in each chapter in our English Bibles). Chapter 4 shares the same basic pattern, but here the stanzas

---

56. "Vanity" (RSV *hebel*) is a key concept in Ecclesiastes, with the word used some thirty-eight times in the book. See Graham S. Ogden, "'Vanity' It Certainly Is Not," *BT* 38 (1987): 301-7. For the importance of the enjoyment theme in Ecclesiastes, see R. N. Whybray, "Qoheleth, Preacher of Joy," *JSOT* 23 (1982): 87-98.

57. Francis Landy, "The Song of Songs," in *The Literary Guide to the Bible*, ed. Robert Alter and Frank Kermode (Cambridge: Harvard University Press, 1987), 316.

only have two lines. Chapter 3 is more elaborate, with each line of each three-line stanza beginning with the respective letter of the alphabet (so this chapter in our English versions has sixty-six verses but is no longer than chapters 1 or 2). Chapter 5 is not an acrostic but has twenty-two lines and so conforms to the same general alphabetical pattern. The only *seder* division comes at 3:36. This approximately, but not exactly, divides the book in half, for the *masora* indicates 3:34 as the middle verse of the book. Either point of division can be seen as a turning point, coming as they do after the faith statements in 3:22–24, 25–27, and 31–33, which are thereby foregrounded, being near the close of the first *seder*. The climactic positioning of these remarkable testimonies just before the middle of the book suggests that the faith of the writer in the goodness and mercy of God is no passing phase.

Esther

The first *seder* lesson of the book of Esther closes with the removal of Queen Vashti, which creates a vacancy for Esther to fill (2:4). It is only after 2:4 that Mordecai and Esther (in that order) are introduced to the reader. The third *seder* division comes after 3:7, in which verse the fateful day for the destruction of the Jews is fixed by the casting of the lot (*pur*). The fourth *seder* division at 6:11 comes after the bombshell in 6:10 that it is Mordecai whom Ahasuerus wishes to honor in the way chosen by Haman, who thought he was the one whom the king wished to honor. This *seder* closes at 8:15 with Mordecai's triumphant departure from the king's presence. The *sedarim* appear to favor Mordecai's role over that of Esther. Esther 10 is a short chapter of only three verses that provides a summary of the reign of Ahasuerus and makes mention of Mordecai (there is also a Hebrew open paragraph at 10:1 in L), and this sectioning succeeds in excluding any reference to Esther from the final chapter (see 9:29–32) and could be understood as an attempt to make Mordecai the sole hero of the book.[58]

---

58. For more, see Gregory Goswell, "The Main Character of the Book of Esther: The Contribution of the Textual Divisions and the Assigned Titles of the Book of Esther to Uncovering its Protagonist," *JSOT* 46 (2021): 193–205.

Daniel

The second *seder* lesson in Daniel opens at 2:35, making the announced theme of the unit the establishment of the universal kingdom of God. The *seder* division separates the climax of the vision—the transformation of the stone into the mountain (2:35) and the interpretation of the vision (2:36-45)—from what precedes. This way of breaking up the text helps the reader to see chapter 3 as a continuation of the story about the vision of the image. There is no date formula in 3:1, unlike in 1:1 and 2:1 (though the LXX adds one),[59] implying the close connection of chapter 3 with what precedes. The lack of a preamble at the beginning of chapter 3 implies that the second image is a reaction of the Babylonian king to the first. The "image of gold" made by Nebuchadnezzar (3:1) recalls the description of this king as "the head of gold" in 2:38, for the king is duplicating, though with some variation, the "image" he had seen in his dream. There it was a head of gold, here a whole image of gold, with the king trying to overcome the perceived inadequacies of the earlier image. Nebuchadnezzar is attempting to prevent the replacement of his kingdom (as depicted in the vision of ch. 2) by enforcing universal homage to the image that is a symbol of his empire.[60]

With regard to whether Daniel 4:1-3 (Aramaic 3:31-33) refers forward or backward, despite the Aramaic numbering, the three verses properly belong to Daniel 4.[61] The words "Peace be multiplied to you!" (4:1) are part of a letter form (see 6:25) and make the whole of Daniel 4 an encyclical. The placement of the chapter division after 3:33 in the Hebrew Bible implies that the expression "the signs and wonders" in 3:32 refers to the miraculous deliverance from the fiery furnace described in Daniel 3 (see 6:27, which refers to Daniel's rescue from the lion's den using the same expression). The addition of the words "toward *me*" suggest, however, that the signs and wonders are events in which the king participated, when God humbled Nebuchadnezzar, such that his mind was turned to that of an animal (4:33). The order of the words "kingdom ... dominion" in 4:3 is reversed in 4:34, giving an inclusio of poetic

---

59. The LXX dating is not original, with "the eighteenth year" drawn from Jer 52:29, the date of Nebuchadnezzar's destruction of Jerusalem. This may suggest a certain understanding of the image, that the statue is erected to commemorate this notable victory. See André Lacocque, *The Book of Daniel* (London: SPCK, 1979), 56. A vacant line is left before 3:1 in 4QDanª.

60. For this interpretation of Nebuchadnezzar's actions, see Danna Nolan Fewell, *Circle of Sovereignty: A Story of the Stories in Daniel 1-6*, JSOTSup 72 (Sheffield: Almond, 1988), ch. 3.

61. These verses are missing in the Greek (except in Theodotion, who has them as 4:1-3), which begins at 4:4 (Eng.).

pieces at the beginning and near the end of the narrative, and this is another indication that 4:1–3 (Eng.) does indeed belong with Daniel 4.[62]

Ezra-Nehemiah

Chapter divisions in Ezra mark decisive turning points: the prophesying of Haggai and Zechariah (5:1) and the issuing of a decree by Darius (6:1). The double agency of divine decree and royal decree is summed up in 6:14. The joining of the last verse of the prayer of Nehemiah (Neh 1:11) with what follows as the start of the fifth *seder* lesson of this joint book reveals what Nehemiah thinks of his royal master (noting the pejorative expression "this man" in 1:11), whose permission he needs if he is to go to Jerusalem (2:1–8).

Chronicles

The Chronicler's interest in the temple is highlighted by the start of the eleventh (1 Chr 28:10) and twelfth *seder* lessons (2 Chr 2:4), which both concern Solomon's role as temple builder. The chapter division at 2 Chronicles 15:1 highlights the raising up of a seer, and the start of the eighteenth *seder* at 18:18 makes the speech of Micaiah the prophet the noted feature. However, most of the chapter divisions are connected to the accession of Judean kings. The work of prophets is by no means invisible in Chronicles, but the textual divisions on the whole fail to register their crucial involvement in events.

CHAPTER 6 CONCLUSIONS

A study of the physical breaks in the text of the Old Testament reveals that they are in effect a commentary on the text. It also uncovers that divisions may lead or mislead the reader who seeks meaning in the text.

---

62. William H. Shea, "Further Literary Structures in Daniel 2–7: An Analysis of Daniel 4," *AUSS* 23 (1985): 194. For more analysis of textual breaks in Daniel, see Gregory Goswell, "The Divisions of the Book of Daniel," in *The Impact of Unit Delimitation on Exegesis*, ed. Raymond de Hoop, Marjo C. A. Korpel, and Stanley E. Porter, Pericope 7 (Leiden: Brill, 2009), 89–114.

GUIDELINES FOR INTERPRETING THE DIVISIONS
IN OLD TESTAMENT BOOKS

1. The habits of readers in seeking meaning in texts suggest four possible functions of any given textual division, with textual breaks suggesting ways of interpreting the biblical text.

2. A division separates one section of a text from another section, demarcating a new story, episode, or scene. An example is the chapter divisions in Genesis 14–23, which reflect the episodic nature of the Abraham story, with a time gap sometimes specified or another chronological note present (e.g., 15:1; 16:16; 17:1; 22:1).

3. A correlative, second function of divisions is to join material, suggesting that the material joined is closely related in meaning. For example, the second *seder* lesson in Daniel opens at 2:35 and continues into chapter 3, helping the reader to see that the erection of the golden image is a reaction of Nebuchadnezzar to the earlier vision of an image whose head was gold.

4. A third function or effect of a division is to highlight certain material in a text, making it more prominent in the eyes of the reader. This is done by placing the features to be highlighted at the beginning or end of sections. For example, in the book of Joshua, the second *seder* begins with the divine declaration that God will begin to exalt Joshua in the sight of all Israel (3:7), and that is the divinely stated reason for the wonders God will perform, most notably, the capture of Jericho.

5. The mirror image of the third function is the fourth function, to downplay or ignore certain textual features, which is what happens when material is placed nowhere near section breaks. For example, in Chronicles, most of the divisions are triggered by the accession of kings, whereas both chapters and *sedarim* on the whole fail to register the involvement of prophets in the events narrated.

7

TEXTUAL DIVISIONS WITHIN NEW TESTAMENT BOOKS

INTRODUCTION

Most readers are unaware that all ancient Greek manuscripts of the New Testament have paragraphs and other forms of textual division that served as reader's aids.[1] The breaking up of a Greek text written in *scriptio continua* into paragraphs provided much-needed assistance to the reader, due to the challenges of making sense of a text that has no gaps between individual words.[2] The chapters with which we are familiar in modern Bibles (those of Langton) are also not without value, and the alternative schemes of internal division in ancient texts may each have a literary logic and justification, though that is not to suggest we can divide the biblical text into sections by whim.

THE PHYSICAL DIVISIONS IN NEW TESTAMENT TEXTS

For the New Testament, the oldest division into chapters that is known is that preserved in Codex Vaticanus (B) of the fourth century.[3] It seems clear that the division represents an evaluation of what are the sense units of the biblical passage. In terms of their dimension these *chapters* are more what we would call paragraphs; for example, Matthew has 170 chapters, Mark 62,

---

1. According to Larry W. Hurtado, *The Earliest Christian Artifacts: Manuscripts and Christian Origins* (Grand Rapids: Eerdmans, 2006), 77, these divisions reflect "a concern to guide and facilitate reading of the texts."

2. See M. B. Parkes, *Pause and Effect: An Introduction to the History of Punctuation in the West* (Aldershot: Scolar Press, 1992), 10: a text written in *scriptio continua* "required careful preparation before it could be read aloud with appropriate pronunciation and expression."

3. For this manuscript, see https://digi.vatlib.it/view/MSS_Vat.gr.1209.

Luke 152, John 80, and Acts 69. In the case of the Pauline Epistles,[4] the chapters are continuously numbered (with some disruption) as though the epistles were reckoned one larger book. This would add support to the suggestion of Robert Wall that, canonically, we should speak of the Pauline "Letter" (singular) rather than of separate letters.[5] There are 21 chapters in Romans, 21 in 1 Corinthians, 11 in 2 Corinthians, and so on. In the exemplar from which Vaticanus was copied, chapters 1–59 covered Romans, 1 and 2 Corinthians, and Galatians, but Ephesians, instead of beginning with section 60, begins with section 70, and it is Hebrews 1:1–9:14 that has sections 60–64 (there were presumably five more chapters covering the remaining portion of Hebrews). The ancestor of Vaticanus must have had Hebrews between Galatians and Ephesians. On average, the chapter divisions of Vaticanus are longer in the epistles than they are in the Gospels and Acts.[6]

There is much variation among the Greek codices, but the chapters (or paragraphs) of Sinaiticus and Alexandrinus are consistently much shorter than those in Vaticanus. The main types of markers used in the codices for the purposes of delimitation are enlarged capitals, open spaces, short horizontal lines (*paragraphoi*), and words protruding to the left of the column margin (*ekthesis*). As in Vaticanus, the textual breaks, *capitula* (Greek *kephalaia*) in Codex Alexandrinus (fifth century) represent scribal or editorial evaluation of what are the sense units.[7] One indication of this is that breaks are not regularly spaced. The length of sections varies over a wide range. Some sections are as short as 4 lines of text (Luke A66), 9 lines (Luke A40), and 10 lines (Mark A2, Luke A9); other sections are as long as 110 lines (Matt A68), 181 lines (Mark A46), 170 lines (Luke A78), and even 515 lines (John A17). The irregular placement of the breaks strongly implies that they are placed according to a perception of the flow of the narrative.

---

4. Vaticanus only preserves Romans through to Hebrews 9:14, with Hebrews coming after 2 Thessalonians.

5. Wall, "Multiple Letter Canon."

6. For more details, see Gregory Goswell, "An Early Commentary on the Pauline Corpus: The Capitulation of Codex Vaticanus," *JGRChJ* 8 (2011–2012): 51–82. In order to refer to the numbered chapters in Vaticanus, I will use the notation V1, V2, etc.

7. For a detailed discussion, see Gregory Goswell, "Early Readers of the Gospels: The *kephalaia* and *titloi* of Codex Alexandrinus," *JGRChJ* 6 (2009): 134–74. In order to refer to the *kephalaia* in Alexandrinus, I will use the notation A1, A2, etc. See W. Andrew Smith, *A Study of the Gospels in Codex Alexandrinus: Codicology, Palaeography, and Scribal Hands*, NTTSD 48 (Leiden: Brill, 2014), 156–81.

There are also twenty-seven *kephalion* in the form of running titles at the top of columns (*titloi*) present in Codex Sinaiticus (fourth century) for Acts.[8] There is no formal indication of where a *kephalion* might start in the text of Acts. The only physical link between running titles and text is their position at the head of columns. In Sinaiticus, almost invariably the *kephalion* describes a key person or significant event in the textual unit, for example, *ta peri kornēlion* ("The things concerning Cornelius"; K9). They serve to elevate certain persons and scenes in the eyes of the reader. The *kephalaia* are, then, a kind of "list of main contents" or narrative "highlights" at the head of the columns in Acts.[9] The first half of Acts in Sinaiticus is also subdivided into forty-two numbered chapters, with the last chapter division placed at Acts 15:40 (S42).[10]

In Alexandrinus titles are assigned to the demarcated sections in the Gospels, often, but not always, beginning with the Greek word *peri* ("about, concerning"). For example, the first such summary for Mark reads *peri tou diamonizomenou* ("Concerning the demon-possessed man"), indicating that the first major division (as reckoned in Alexandrinus) begins at Mark 1:23. The form of the titles is not an incipit, or quotation of the opening phrase of the section, but is in a form (*peri* followed by a genitive) that indicates the editor's evaluation of what a chapter is about.[11] These are found as a kind of kind of list of contents at the beginning of the Gospels of Mark, Luke, and John (but damage to the codex means that the list of *capitula* to Matthew is absent).[12]

Similarly worded *titloi* (singular *titlos*), or summary headings, briefly describing the contents are found at the head of the columns in the Gospels, though damage to the top margin of the codex has removed or mutilated many *titloi*. There are 68 *kephalaia* for Matthew (which we can reconstruct

---

8. For this text, see https://www.codexsinaiticus.org/en/.

9. For detailed discussion, see Gregory Goswell, "Ancient Patterns of Reading: The Subdivision of the Acts of the Apostles in Codex Sinaiticus," *JGRChJ* 7 (2010): 68–97. In order to refer to the *kephalaia* in Sinaiticus, I will use the notation K1, K2, etc.

10. In order to refer to one or other of these forty-two chapters in Sinaiticus, I will use the notation S1, S2, etc.

11. Both modes of titling were common for ancient Greek works. See Johannes Munck, "Evangelium Veritatis and Greek Usage as to Book Titles," *ST* 17 (1963): 133–38.

12. See http://www.bl.uk/manuscripts/FullDisplay.aspx?ref=Royal_MS_1_d_viii folios 5v, 19r, 19v, and 42r.

using later codices), 48 for Mark, 83 for Luke, and 18 for John. This translates
into a break on the average of every 76 lines for Matthew, 51 lines for Mark,
50 lines for Luke, and 170 lines for John.[13] The *kephalaia* and *titloi* are not
found in Vaticanus or Sinaiticus, except that Sinaiticus has *titloi* in Acts. The
first column of the text of Mark in Alexandrinus (there are two columns per
page) covers 1:1–15a, and the *titlos* at the head of the second column (covering
1:15b–30a) reads *peri tēs penthera Petrou* ("Concerning the mother-in-law of
Peter"), with that incident narrated in 1:29–31.

The first demarcated section is always after the opening of the Gospel,
for example, for Matthew in Alexandrinus it is at 2:1 (A1) and has the title
peri tōn magōn ("Concerning the Magi"). The *kephalaia* are earliest found in
Alexandrinus and had a strong influence on the Greek manuscript tradition,
so they appear as tables prefixed to several early codices, which enables us
to restore them for Matthew.[14]

The effect of the *capitula* (and *titloi*) is to elevate in the eyes of the reader
certain passages over others. The next number of passages in Mark so highlighted are healing various kinds of diseases (1:32–34), the leper (1:40–45), the
paralytic (2:1–12), Levi the tax collector (2:13–17), the man with the withered
hand (3:1–6), the choosing of the apostles (3:13–19), the parable of the sower
(4:1–9), the commanding of the wind and sea (4:35–41), the man called Legion
(5:1–20), and the daughter of the synagogue ruler (5:35–43). The material
that is downplayed is mostly the teachings of Jesus (e.g., 2:18–28; 3:20–35;
4:21–34), with the parable of the sower the lone exception in the early chapters of Mark.[15]

Modern Bible translations, and even critical editions of the Greek New
Testament, do not preserve and display the capitulation and paragraphing
of ancient Greek manuscripts, the exception being *The Greek New Testament*,

---

13. Or if John A9 (565 lines) is excluded (within which there are two missing leaves from
the codex), the average over the remaining seventeen *kephalaia* is still 147 lines. The average for
Matthew is calculated using the last nine *kephalaia* (A60–68).

14. See B. H. Cowper, *Codex Alexandrinus: Hē Kainē Diathēkē. Novum Testamentum Graece ex
antiquissimo codice Alexandrino a C .G. Woide olim descriptum* (London: David Nutt with Williams &
Norgate, 1860), which conveniently provides the *kephalaia* . It can be accessed at https://archive.
org/details/codexalexandrinuoowoid/page/n45/mode/2up.

15. See James R. Edwards, "The Hermeneutical Significance of Chapter Divisions in Ancient
Gospel Manuscripts," *NTS* 56 (2010): 413–26. Edwards suggests that the massive size of chapters
in John in Alexandrinus is due to the relative absence of miracles and parables in that Gospel
(426).

Produced at Tyndale House, Cambridge (2017). In this edition, following ancient Greek practice, paragraphs are demarcated by *ekthesis*, the opposite to indentation. Unfortunately, its editors do not see any system at work in the different codices and simply mark paragraphs where two or more significant manuscripts coincide,[16] and the editors do not specify which manuscripts support any particular break in the text. The net result is that this critical edition of the Greek New Testament is less useful than it might otherwise have been as a hermeneutical guide.[17]

Langton is held responsible for the New Testament chapter divisions familiar to us. It was the famous printer and publisher Robert Estienne, Latinized as Stephanus (1503–1559), who divided the New Testament into verses. Stephanus issued four editions of the Greek Testament, three in Paris (1546, 1549, 1550) and the last at Geneva (1551). His fourth edition is especially noteworthy because in it for the first time the biblical text is divided into numbered verses. It has often been stated that Stephanus marked the verse divisions while journeying "on horseback," and (so the story goes) some of the infelicitous divisions arose from the jogging of the horse that bumped his pen. The son of Stephanus says that his father did the work while on a journey (*inter equitandum*) from Paris to Lyons, but the most natural inference, according to Metzger, who seems intent on spoiling a good story, is that the task was performed while resting at inns along the way.[18] These verses usually coincide with a Greek sentence, and hence their substantial agreement with the divisions in Sinaiticus and Alexandrinus in many passages is no surprise. The first English version to contain verse numbers was the Geneva Version (1560). It would be unfair to accuse the chapter (and verse) divisions of being arbitrary, though more care may have been taken in some cases than others. In what follows, I will proceed, by way of example, book

---

16. Dirk Jongkind, *An Introduction to the Greek New Testament, Produced at Tyndale House, Cambridge* (Wheaton, IL: Crossway, 2019); but see Charles E. Hill, "Rightly Dividing the Word: Uncovering an Early Template for Textual Division in John's Gospel," in *Studies on the Text of the New Testament and Early Christianity: Essays in Honour of Michael W. Holmes*, ed. Daniel Grunter, Juan Hernández Jr., and Paul Foster, NTTSD 50 (Leiden: Brill, 2015), 238: "Christians were greatly concerned with the reading and interpreting of their sacred texts, and one of the ways this shows up is in the developing 'systems' of visual, textual delimitation."

17. For a sample of this edition (Gospel of Mark), see https://static.crossway.org/excerpt/the-greek- new-testament-mark.pdf.

18. Metzger, *Text of the New Testament*, 103–4. I acknowledge my substantial dependence on Metzger for this paragraph.

by book through the New Testament, comparing and contrasting some of
the different systems of text division, all with a view to seeing possible hermeneutical significance in the divisions made.[19]

GOSPELS

Matthew

Turning to some New Testament examples, Matthew has the structurally
significant formula "and when Jesus finished ..." (7:28[-29]; 11:1; 13:53; 19:1;
26:1),[20] and four out of the five instances have influenced the chapter divisions. This Gospel's most remarkable feature is the pentateuchal scheme of
five great discourses, which makes it appropriate for this book to stand at the
head of the New Testament, laying the foundation of the teaching of Jesus,
the second Moses. The mountain location of the teaching in 5:1-2 is more
than a mundane geographical description but has theological significance
for the author (see 4:8; 8:1; 17:1; 21:1; 24:3). Jesus is one who sits and teaches
like Moses (see 23:1) and indeed is greater than Moses.[21] A number of chapter
divisions accentuate this theme. The first division in Alexandrinus (A1, also
V7) shows that Matthew 1 is treated as a preface, the rationale perhaps being
that the birth of Jesus is not narrated until 2:1. The division at 2:1 commences
a chapter depicting the clash of kings, Herod versus the newborn "king of the
Jews." Also, 1:18-25, despite the fact that it contains the first of a series of five
Old Testament quotations using the fulfillment formula (1:21-22; see 2:5-6, 15,
17-18, 23), is put with the preceding genealogy as there is no "clash of kings"
theme in this paragraph.[22] Joseph, the legal father of Jesus, is addressed by
the angel as "Joseph, son of David" (1:20). The division at 2:1 suggests that

---

19. See John W. Olley, "Re-Versing Tradition: The Influence of Sense-Divisions in Reading
the Bible Then and Now," *ABR* 62 (2014): 43: "Sense delimitation and text layout are clues to
scribal intention and to public reading. They shape how texts are understood, then and now."

20. See B. W. Bacon, *Studies in Matthew* (New York: Holt, 1930), though few if any scholars
follow Bacon's exact scheme.

21. See Terence L. Donaldson, *Jesus on the Mountain: A Study in Matthean Theology*, JSNTSup
8 (Sheffield: JSOT, 1985).

22. The RSV editors read the text differently and placed a blank line after Matt 1:17.

1:18–25 amounts to an exposition of 1:16, confirming the Davidic lineage of the yet-to-be-born Jesus.[23]

The dimensions of Alexandrinus chapter 5 contain the whole of the Sermon on the Mount (5:1–7:29), but it is subdivided into twenty-five chapters in Vaticanus (V23–47). As the Matthean inaugural sermon of Jesus, it forms a logical unit, but the effect of placing it all in one section and under one heading ("Concerning the Beatitudes") is to obscure its diverse contents and downplay the teaching content of this Gospel. The concluding formula at 7:28 ("And when Jesus finished [these sayings]") brings the sermon to a close, and this formula is reused by Matthew at the end of each major discourse (11:1; 13:34; 19:1; 25:1).[24]

In striking contrast to the very long section A5, what follows in Alexandrinus are a number of shorter divisions, showing where the interest of the scribe responsible for the *kephalaia* lies, in the series of shorter miracle stories (8:1–4, 5–13, 14–15, 16–18, 23–27, 8:28–9:1; 9:2–8 [A6–9, 11–13]). Each miracle is allocated a section of its own. Confirming that this is the order of priorities, the return to longer sections in Alexandrinus coincides with the next body of dominical teaching at 10:1–11:1 (A19). This survey of the early part of Matthew's Gospel shows that the divisions made in the text are usually sensitive to the flow of the narrative and suggest ways of understanding its features.

Mark

Scholars disagree over the question of the extent of a prologue in Mark, with the main alternatives being that it ends at 1:8, 1:11, 1:13, or 1:15,[25] with the last two being the most favored. The dispute stories in 2:1–3:6 (there is a gap left after 3:6 in the RSV) appear to be interrupted by the chapter division at 3:1 (and the seventh chapter break in Alexandrinus), but it can also be argued that this serves to set apart the last story as the climax of the sequence in

---

23. See Warren Carter, *Matthew: Storyteller, Interpreter, Evangelist*, rev. ed. (Peabody, MA: Hendrickson, 2004), 109–11.

24. As noted by Davies and Allison, *Gospel according to Saint Matthew*, 1:725.

25. The Greek text of Westcott and Hort leaves a large space between 1:8 and 1:9. Supporters of the prologue ending at 1:11 include Wolfgang Feneberg, *Der Markusprolog: Studien zur Formbestimmung des Evangeliums*, SANT 36 (München: Kösel, 1974). Supporters of the prologue ending at 1:13 include R. T. France, "The Beginning of Mark," *RTR* 49 (1990): 11–19. Supporters of the prologue ending at 1:15 include Boring, "Mark 1:1–15."

which Jesus's enemies begin to plot his death (3:6), being an early intimation of his coming passion. Mark 4:1 commences a section of parabolic teaching that might have concluded at 4:34, as in Alexandrinus (A9; see V19), but 4:35 ("on that day") introduces the story about the sea crossing, Jesus taking leave of the crowds to whom he had been speaking in parables. Mark 6:1 draws attention to Jesus's visit to his hometown of Nazareth, and the brief account is brought to a close by a summary of his movements in 6:6b. The RSV makes this half-verse a separate paragraph, and Alexandrinus makes it the start of a new chapter (A14). The rejection of Jesus at Nazareth (6:1-6a) is not listed in the *kephalaia*,[26] but is joined with what precedes as part of the section (A13). This way of packaging the text brings out the contrast between the faith of Jairus and the woman with the flow of blood (5:34, 36) and the blind unbelief of those in Jesus's own country (6:6).[27]

The chapter division at 9:1 can be justified by the repeated speech attribution ("And he said to them"; see 8:34), but the RSV paragraph break at 9:2 (coinciding with V37 and A25) shows that the editors of these versions had another preference. Putting the division at 9:1 suggests a particular interpretation of this verse, implying that the transfiguration (9:2-8) fulfills (at least in part) the prediction that "some standing here ... will not taste death before they see the kingdom of God come with power" (9:1). This is a credible interpretation of the *crux interpretum*, and the precise time statement, "And after six days" (9:2a), also supports the connection with the preceding verse. This is the interpretation favored by C. E. B. Cranfield, who does not, however, make reference to Langton's chapter break as part of his argument.[28] It is generally the case that commentators have paid little or no attention to the chapter divisions as a commentary on the biblical text.

Luke

Luke 1 is largely devoted to the birth of John (the Baptist). The first division in Alexandrinus is at 2:1, where interest switches to the birth of Jesus, after the summary of John's maturation in 1:80, with Langton's chapter 2 closing

---

26. Though there is a division at 6:1 in Vaticanus (V22).

27. This is a connection pointed out by Robert H. Gundry, *Mark: A Commentary on His Apology for the Cross* (Grand Rapids: Eerdmans, 1993), 289.

28. C. E. B. Cranfield, *The Gospel according to St Mark*, CGTC (Cambridge: Cambridge University Press, 1959), 287-88.

with a similar verse about Jesus (2:52; see 2:40). The world context for these vital salvation-history developments is accentuated by the chapter divisions at 2:1 (A1) and 3:1 (A5), and the RSV editors leave a blank line before 3:1. Luke 6:1 (V40) breaks into a series of controversies with religious leaders (starting at 5:17), and a new section seems to begin at 6:12 (V42; the RSV editors leave a blank line before it). It is not necessary always to argue for the felicity of the traditional divisions. The division at 7:1 (A18) marks the end of the Sermon on the Plain.

A section is marked in Alexandrinus at 7:37 (A21) with the heading "Concerning the anointing of the Lord with ointment." Included within this section is a brief record of Jesus's female traveling companions whom he had healed (8:1-3), suggesting that, like the woman who anointed Jesus's feet, whose story is given in 7:37-50, their practical support of Jesus was a reflection of love and gratitude for what he had done for them.[29] The juxtaposing of the two accounts probably explains the early tradition that Mary Magdalene (8:2) was a prostitute, and she was identified by early readers with the women who was a "sinner" (7:37, 39). Luke 9:51 is the start of a significant new section, the central travel section as identified by Lukan scholars (9:51-19:46), and the RSV editors mark it with a blank line.[30] Langton's divisions on either side prefer to accentuate the mission of the Twelve (9:1) and the mission of the Seventy (10:1), which anticipate the mission spread of the gospel in Acts.

John

In the Fourth Gospel, John 1 is treated as a preface, with the main action beginning with the first recorded miracle (sign) of Jesus (2:1). The first section in Alexandrinus is marked at 2:1 (A1, V7) and has the heading "Concerning the wedding in Cana," so that, as in Mark (1:23), everything preceding the first miracle performed by Jesus is viewed in Alexandrinus as a prologue. The second section (A2), marked at 2:13, extends until 2:25 (like the later chapter division of Langton), for it is still Passover time in verses 23-25, and the motifs of seeing signs and of belief in these three verses pick up features in

---

29. Marshall, *Gospel of Luke*, 315. Luke 8:1-3 is a separate section in Vaticanus (V57).

30. Vaticanus has a chapter division (V73) at 9:51, with the divisions on either side at 9:44 and 57.

2:11, 18, and 22.[31] John 3:1 (A3) marks the beginning of Nicodemus's interview with Jesus (with the heading in Alexandrinus "Concerning Nicodemus"), but modern commentators tend to see the episode as building on 2:23-25, for Nicodemus, like others, has an inadequate faith in Jesus based on the impression made on him by Jesus's signs (3:2; see 2:23).[32]

ACTS

In Acts a series of brief progress reports divide the book into six main sections (6:7; 9:31; 12:24; 15:35; 19:20), none of which coincides with a chapter division, though 12:24 comes close if 12:25 is annexed to it. These summaries suggest that the triumphant progress of the gospel is due to the powerful word of God rather than Paul's abilities (see 1 Cor 2:1-5; Col 1:6; 1 Thess 1:5). As noted by Robert Tannehill, at Acts 2:42 the narrative shifts from events on a particular day (Pentecost) to a general description of church life.[33] By placing 2:42 with what follows (vv. 43-47; in contrast to the RSV paragraphing), the division in Sinaiticus (S7) suggests that verses 43-47 expand on the four community characteristics stated in summary form in verse 42. The division in Sinaiticus (2:42-47) encompasses a credible section describing the fledgling church in Jerusalem: the apostles' teaching (and the miracles that attested to its truth; vv. 42a, 43),[34] the fellowship of goods (vv. 42b, 44-45), the breaking of bread (vv. 42c, 46), and the prayers (vv. 42d, 47a).

Acts 3:1 (S8) coincides with the start of a new incident—what happened when Peter and John went up to the temple to pray—after the concluding summary at 2:47b ("And the Lord added to their number day by day those who were being saved" [ESV]). The division of the text at 3:1 coincides with the title of the first *kephalion* in Sinaiticus (K1; "The things concerning Peter and John and the man who was lame from birth"), and all of Acts 3-4 (excluding

---

31. See Josaphat C. Tam, "When Papyri and Codices Speak: Revisiting John 2:23-25," *Bib* 95 (2014): 570-88. She points out that ancient manuscripts mark the major break at 3:1 and present 2:23-25 as connected to the preceding context. She concludes, "It is hoped that the role of 2:23-25 in John 1-2 can be clarified by the interpretive insights embedded in the oldest available textual witnesses. These papyri and codices still speak today" (588).

32. Raymond E. Brown, *The Gospel according to John*, vol. 1, *I-XII*, AB 29 (London: Geoffrey Chapman, 1971), 126-30.

33. Robert C. Tannehill, *The Narrative Unity of Luke-Acts: A Literary Interpretation*, vol. 2, *The Acts of the Apostles* (Minneapolis: Fortress, 1990), 43.

34. Acts 3 goes on to show the correlation between teaching and "signs and wonders."

4:32-37) can be understood to concern the healing of the lame man and its aftermath in the persecution of Peter and John. Richard Longenecker sees Acts 1-2 as setting the scene for the ministry of the church that is illustrated from 3:1 onward by a series of snapshots.[35]

Identical with Langton's third chapter, S8 is a substantial unit that includes the miracle and subsequent sermon. A chapter division at 4:1 (S9) comes at the end of Peter's speech to the gathered crowd in the temple court, when the two apostles are arrested. It is perhaps best to view a new section beginning at 4:32, V5 demarcating a section covering 4:32-5:11, rather than six verses later at 5:1 (S13), because of the contrasting examples of the generosity of Barnabas (4:36-37) and the deception of Ananias and Sapphira (5:1-11), so it makes sense to have these two portraits in the same section.

LETTERS

Romans

The chapter divisions of Romans are often triggered either by a significant question (3:1; 4:1; 6:1; 7:1; 11:1) or "therefore" (*dio* or *oun*; 2:1; 5:1; 8:1; 12:1) or both. These divisions at least have the virtue of bringing to the fore the way in which the apostle is concerned rationally to set forth the faith, and of all his letters Romans is the most treatise-like. Almost all scholarly outlines of the structure and contents of Romans view the divisions at 5:1; 9:1; and 12:1 as major transitions, and 15:33 sounds like an ending, giving Romans 16 the character of an appendix.[36] The beginning of the second chapter of Romans in Vaticanus (V2) is placed at 1:18, which the editors of NA[27] (who place a blank line after 1:17) view as the start of the body of the book. The next chapter in Vaticanus commences at 2:12 (V3). This division has the effect of making the final statement of the preceding chapter a punch line (2:11: "For God shows no partiality" [RSV]). This way of dividing the text suggests that 2:11

---

35. Richard N. Longenecker, *Acts*, EBC (Grand Rapids: Zondervan, 1995), 29, 48. The view of chs. 1-2 as the overture to the book is argued more fully by Steve Walton, "Where Does the Beginning of Acts End?," in *The Unity of Luke-Acts*, ed. J. Verheyden, BETL 142 (Leuven: Peeters, 1999), 447-67.

36. See Thomas R. Schreiner, *Romans*, BECNT (Grand Rapids: Baker, 1998), 5-10, for a review and evaluation of whether Rom 16 was originally part of the letter. In Vaticanus the chapter divisions come at 15:30 and 16:17.

summarizes the opening argument of the letter.[37] As noted by Jouette Bassler, the statement about divine impartiality rounds off the argument, and 2:11 is a restatement and refinement of the thought in 2:6 ("For [God] will render to every man according to his works" [RSV]).[38] The viability of the demarcated section in Vaticanus is supported by the inclusio of the motif of divine wrath (1:18; 2:8-9),[39] with the section demonstrating that both Jew and Greek are subject to God's judgment and reward.

1 Corinthians

Several of the early chapters in Vaticanus coincide with Langton's divisions, 2:1 (V23); 3:1 (V24); and 6:1 (V27). Paul's instructions on spiritual gifts (chs. 12-14) are given a tripartite division, and the separate identity given to chapter 13 is in part responsible for the decontextualized understanding of it as the sentimental "chapter about love,"[40] rather than as highly critical of the unloving behavior of the Corinthians in their practice of the gifts. In Vaticanus, chapter 36 covers 12:1-14:4. Properly interpreted, 1 Corinthians 13 is a phase in a larger argument, as is clear from the summarizing command ("Make love your aim" [RSV]) and the resumptive imperative ("and earnestly desire the spiritual gifts" [RSV]) in 14:1 (see 12:31a), which show the nature of chapter 13 as a highly relevant digression in Paul's argument. His teaching about love is not a separate topic.

2 Corinthians

Langton's division at 2 Corinthians 2:1 is often viewed as an inept chapter division and placed in the midst of a paragraph, running through to 2:4 (e.g., RSV, GNT[4]), but Margaret Thrall exegetes 2:1-13 under the heading "The painful letter and its aftermath."[41] It is only in 2:1-4 that Paul makes mention of send-

---

37. Jouette M. Bassler, *Divine Impartiality: Paul and a Theological Axiom*, SBLDS 59 (Chico, CA: Scholars Press, 1982). She makes reference to the chapter division in Vaticanus (122), noting that the codex regards 1:18-2:11 "as a single thought unit" and that the *kephalaia* in Alexandrinus (A1 and A2) also begins at 1:18 and 2:12.

38. Bassler, *Divine Impartiality*, 126.

39. On indications of textual sections in Pauline letters, see J. A. Fischer, "Pauline Literary Forms and Thought Patterns," *CBQ* 39 (1977): 209-23.

40. Gordon D. Fee makes this complaint. See Fee, *The First Epistle to the Corinthians*, NICNT (Grand Rapids: Eerdmans, 1987), 626.

41. Margaret E. Thrall, *The Second Epistle to the Corinthians*, vol. 1, *Introduction and Commentary on II Corinthians I-VII*, ICC (Edinburgh: T&T Clark, 1994), 163.

ing a letter instead of visiting the Corinthians in person. A major new section of the letter begins at 2:14, but it is unmarked by a chapter division, though Vaticanus commences the second chapter of the letter at 2:12 (V44), apparently written in response to news brought by Titus (see 7:6). The description of Paul's anguished withdrawal from a promising evangelistic field in Troas (2:12-13) is taken up in the metaphor of Paul as a prisoner in a triumphal precession (2:14-17).[42] Scholars commonly view 2 Corinthians 2:14-7:4 as a self-contained defense of his apostolic ministry, though it is not necessary to view it as a separate letter,[43] but at 7:5 the apostle resumes the account about what happened in Macedonia, which was interrupted after 2:14b.

Galatians

In his analysis of the structure of Galatians, Walter Hansen understands it as a rebuke-request letter,[44] with 1:6-4:11 the rebuke section and 4:12-6:10 the request section. The long autobiographical section (1:13-2:21) serves the purpose of rebuking the Galatians for deserting the gospel, and Langton's chapter division at 2:1 draws attention to Paul's account of his second visit to Jerusalem, which is given extensive coverage (2:1-10). It is at this meeting with those "reputed to be pillars" (James, Cephas, and John) that the validity of his mission to the gentiles is acknowledged. There is the question of where Paul's rebuke and correction of Cephas (Peter) comes to an end and passes into his general exposition of the gospel principle at stake (the RSV confines it to 2:14), and 3:1 with its direct address to the erring Galatians ("O foolish Galatians") certainly marks its furthest possible limit.[45] At or near the end of the first three chapters of Galatians as subdivided in Vaticanus (V54-56) the same theme recurs, Paul's concern that his ministry to the Galatians (and to other gentiles) be not "in vain" (2:2-3; 3:4; 4:11), suggesting that the apostle wrote this letter in an attempt to ensure that his ministry among them was not in vain.

---

42. As noted by David R. Hall, *The Unity of the Corinthian Correspondence*, JSNTSup 251 (London: T&T Clark International, 2003), 122.

43. See Hall, *Unity of the Corinthian Correspondence*, 120-24, who rejects the theory that this section is an interpolation.

44. G. Walter Hansen, *Abraham in Galatians: Epistolary and Rhetorical Contexts*, JSNTSup 29 (Sheffield: JSOT, 1989), 53-54.

45. Hansen designates it a transitional use of the vocative (*Abraham in Galatians*, 53).

Ephesians

The breaking up of the one long Greek sentence in 1:3-14 into many verses is understandable, and English versions (e.g., NIV) divide it into several sentences. It is a matter of some dispute whether the phrase "in love" (*en agapē*) goes with the preceding verse (1:4: "that we should be holy and blameless before him *in love*") or with 1:5 ("He destined us *in love*").[46] This is an example of versification as commentary. Ephesians 2:1 comes at the end of a long Pauline thanksgiving and intercession. The alternative division in Vaticanus at 2:8 (V71) coincides with a new sentence,[47] and the close of the first chapter (2:7) echoes the theme with which the chapter commenced, the believer's heavenly blessings in Christ (1:3).

Philippians

Paul opens the body of the letter with a discussion of his present imprisonment (1:12-26),[48] and Vaticanus marks a chapter division at 2:12. The next major literary unit is indicated by the inclusio between 1:27 and 3:20-4:3. The church community was plagued by rivalries and disputes (1:27-30), and what follows is an exhortation to humility and self-abnegation. The apostle provides four examples of the selfless attitude that Paul wants the community to emulate—the examples of Jesus (2:1-11), Paul himself (2:12-18), Timothy (2:19-24), and Epaphroditus (2:25-30). Langton's division at 2:1 highlights the first (and supreme) example of Jesus himself, and these four positive examples are encompassed within chapter 2. Then, 3:1 signals the start of the next phase of the argument,[49] presenting the negative example of Jewish boasting. Vaticanus also places a chapter break at 3:1 (V78). Properly understood, the command in 3:2 (*blepete*) holds up the Jews for consideration as a cautionary example ("take note of [the dogs]"). Paul has abandoned his Jewish boasts and even as a Christian makes no claims to superiority (3:12-16). Paul comes to the culmination of his argument in 4:1-3, signaled by *hōste* ("Therefore")

---

46. For the arguments either way, see Ernest Best, *Ephesians*, ICC (Edinburgh: T&T Clark, 1998), 122-23.

47. Best, *Ephesians*, 225.

48. I depend on David E. Garland, "The Composition and Unity of Philippians: Some Neglected Literary Factors," *NovT* 27 (1985): 141-73.

49. Duane F. Watson views 3:1 as a transitional verse. See Watson, "A Rhetorical Analysis of Philippians and Its Implications for the Unity Question," *NovT* 30 (1988): 57-88, esp. 86.

in 4:1. All leads up to the entreaty to Syntyche and Euodia "to agree in the Lord." The final chapter division in Vaticanus at 4:4 (V79) is to be preferred to the one we are familiar with at 4:1.

Colossians

The first division in Colossians in Vaticanus is at 1:12 (V81), at the transition from intercession back to thanksgiving (1:12: "[with joy,] giving thanks ..."). A division at this juncture highlights what is in fact, for the Pauline Epistles, an unprecedented return to thanksgiving after intercession. In Colossians 2:6 Paul begins this direct interaction with the "philosophy" (*philosophia*) of the false teachers, and Vaticanus makes this verse the beginning of its third chapter division for Colossians (V82). In fact, 2:6-7 summarizes much of the argument up to this point and lays the foundation for the attack on the Colossian heresy that immediately follows. The editors of the RSV place a major division after 2:7 (leaving a line blank). The chapter division at 2:1 is triggered by Paul's direct address to his readers and the use of the disclosure formula "For I want you to know," but the theme of the apostle's "striving" (*agōnizomenos*) continues that in 1:29, so that 2:1 represents only a minor turn in the argument.

The fourth chapter division for Colossians in Vaticanus (V83) ends at 3:15 with the words "And be thankful," and the final chapter division in Vaticanus at 4:2 (V85) is better placed, as 4:2 ("with thanksgiving") recalls earlier appeals for the Colossians themselves to be thankful (see 1:12; 2:7; 3:15-17).[50] The perception of ancient readers represented by the divisions of Vaticanus draws attention to and highlights the theme of thanksgiving in the letter, and the significance of this theme is noted by Peter O'Brien ("Thanksgiving plays an important role in the Epistle to the Colossians").[51]

1 Thessalonians

In Vaticanus, the second chapter starts at 2:13 (V87), the commencement of Paul's second thanksgiving (2:13-16), a thanksgiving that repeats some of the themes of the first thanksgiving (e.g., their reception of the word in 2:12-13;

---

50. These connections are noted by Walter I. Wilson, *The Hope of Glory: Education and Exhortation in the Epistle to the Colossians*, NovTSup 88 (Leiden: Brill, 1997), 249, 251.

51. Peter T. O'Brien, *Introductory Thanksgivings in the Letters of Paul*, NovTSup 49 (Leiden: Brill, 1977), 62-67, esp. 62.

see 1:5-6). This division in Vaticanus shows a perception of the importance of the thanksgivings in the structuring of the first half of the letter (1:2-10; 2:13-16; 3:9-10).[52] The first break made by Langton at 2:1 coincides with the end of the Pauline thanksgiving (1:2-10).

2 Thessalonians

The chapter division in Vaticanus at 2:1 (V91) coincides with the announcement of the major topic dealt with in the short letter,[53] the timing and signs of "the coming of our Lord Jesus Christ and our assembling to meet him" (2:1 RSV), and what follows is a refutation of the heretical eschatology that threatens to trouble the Thessalonians (2:1-12). Vaticanus closes the chapter begun at 2:1 with verse 14. As noted by M. J. J. Menken, 2:13-14 takes up the topic announced at the beginning of the chapter (2:1), albeit using different terminology: God chose them, "so that [they] may obtain the glory [doxēs] of our Lord Jesus Christ" (RSV),[54] so 2:1-14 is a credible division (supported by this inclusio). In fact, the capitulation in Vaticanus highlights the "glory" theme that runs through the letter: At the end of the first chapter, Paul states that the aim of his prayer is the mutual glorification (endoxasthē) of the Lord Jesus and the Thessalonian believers (1:12); the close of the second chapter has already been noted (2:14); and at the opening of the fourth chapter in Vaticanus (V93), the aim of the prayer that Paul requests from his readers is that the word of the Lord may be "glorified" (RSV: "triumph" [doxazētai]; 3:1).

1 Timothy

In this letter the apostle entrusts the gospel and the teachings that flow from it to Timothy (1:18-20), and Langton's division at 2:1 marks the beginning of instructions relevant to proper conduct that Timothy is to faithfully deliver to the Ephesian church (2:1-3:16). These instructions cover the offering of prayer for all people (2:1-7) and the roles of men and women at prayer and in the church meeting (2:8-15). The chapter break at 3:1 helps to signal a

---

52. This insight is confirmed by Jan Lambrecht, "Thanksgivings in 1 Thessalonians 1-3," in *The Thessalonians Debate: Methodological Discord or Methodological Synthesis?*, ed. Karl P. Donfried and Johannes Beutler (Grand Rapids: Eerdmans, 2000), 135-62.

53. M. J. J. Menken, "The Structure of 2 Thessalonians," in *The Thessalonian Correspondence*, ed. Raymond F. Collins, BETL 87 (Leuven: Peeters, 1990), 373-82.

54. Menken, "Structure of 2 Thessalonians," 377.

transition to church *offices*, the overseer (3:1-7) and deacons (3:8-13), and the final verses of chapter 3 offer a context for the preceding instructions as specifying "how one ought to behave in the household of God" (3:15).

2 Timothy

Langton's division at 2:1 is triggered by the "my son" address. What follows is connected to examples, negative and positive, of cowardice and courage in 1:15-17, but it is only at 2:1 that the apostle makes specific application to Timothy himself ("You then, my son, …"). It may be better, however, to make a division after 2:7, which sounds like a conclusion ("Think over what I say, for the Lord will grant you understanding in everything" [RSV]), or even down as far as 2:13, for the theme of the suffering involved in faithful ministry is continued down to that verse. The point of this exercise is not to rush to the defense of the much-maligned chapter divisions with which we have become overfamiliar but to be alert to the implicit commentary they provide on the text.

Titus

Gordon Fee sees a chiastic structure in the letter to Titus that largely reflects the chapter divisions as we have them in our Bible:[55] warnings against false teachers, with their "false works" (1:10-16); specific "good works" for specific groups of believers, with the outsider in view, plus their theological basis (2:1-14); once again "good works" for outsiders, this time directed toward them, and again their theological basis (3:1-8); and final warning against false teachers and their "false works" (3:9-11). The opening sentence of chapter 2 (2:1) is a general instruction to Titus that acts as a heading for what follows, with the first words "But as for you" (*Su de*) setting Titus's role and responsibilities in contrast to the false teachers (see 1:10-16). The last verse of Titus 2 (2:15) points both backward and forward and is to be considered a transitional verse.[56] The RSV editors make this verse a paragraph on its own. A chapter division at 3:1 is justified in that chapter 3 consists of general exhortations that apply to all believers irrespective of the social grouping to which they belong, whereas the instructions of chapter 2 refer to specific groups.

---

55. Gordon D. Fee, *1 and 2 Timothy*, GNC (San Francisco: Harper & Row, 1984), 161.

56. E.g., William D. Mounce, *Pastoral Epistles*, WBC 46 (Nashville: Thomas Nelson, 2000), 421.

Philemon

There is no chapter division in Paul's letter to Philemon, as it was considered too short to require any (see 2–3 John, Jude). In Alexandrinus there are paragraph divisions beginning at verses 4, 7 (there is also a small break before v. 8), 19, 21, 23, and 25. In Sinaiticus there are numerous breaks in the text at the beginning of verses 4, 7, 8, 10, 12, 13, 15, 17, 18, 20, 21, 22, 23, and 25.[57]

Hebrews

Hebrews opens with an argument for the superiority of the Son to the angels (1:5–2:4), but 2:1 marks a transition from scriptural exposition to exhortation ("therefore" [*Dia touto*]). The warning in 2:1 builds on the preceding chapter (2:2: "if the message declared by angels" [RSV]), but the chapter division serves to accentuate these verses and the tone of exhortation in this homiletical piece (see 13:22). The first chapter break in Hebrews (V60) comes at 3:1, and this assists the reader in noticing that Hebrews 1–2 (= V59) is united by the theme of the status of Jesus relative to the angels: 1:5–14 (his superiority to the angels); 2:1–4 (an exhortation that builds on the preceding argument); and 2:5–18 (at the incarnation he was "made lower than the angels"). Next, 2:5–4:13 speak of Jesus as high priest, and again the chapter division (3:1) highlights a transition to exhortation (paraenesis), with a change to direct address in 3:1 ("holy brethren").[58]

A division at 4:1 might be viewed as disruptive, seeing that the theme of "rest" continues from Hebrews 3, but again the chapter division (4:1) signals the transition to exhortation ("therefore" [*oun*]; see 4:11). Hebrews 4:14 is a more credible starting point for the next section than the chapter division at 5:1 (three verses later) and coincides with a Vaticanus chapter break (V61), and the section runs through to the end of Hebrews 7. The chapter division at 6:1 ("Therefore") again accentuates the presence of exhortatory material in Hebrews, which can be viewed as consisting of alternating sections of doctrine and exhortation.[59]

The most important feature of the letter's literary structure is the interchange (and interrelation) of dogmatic and paraenetic sections. Doctrine is

---

57. Vaticanus is defective after Heb 9:14 and so gives no information about Philemon.

58. James Swetnam, "Form and Content in Hebrews 1–6," *Bib* 53 (1972): 368–85.

59. There have been many adaptations of the basic schema worked out by Albert Vanhoye, *La structure littéraire de l'Épitre aux Hébreux* (Paris: Desclée de Brouwer, 1963).

put to the service of exhortation, and the exhortation is rooted in the doctrine. Given the close relation of these two, Albert Vanhoye can perhaps be faulted in making too hard and fast a distinction between doctrine and paraenesis.[60] In an important sense the whole of the letter is exhortation (see 13:22), with its doctrinal arguments serving this end. The theme of Christ's high priesthood is highlighted by the placement of a number of chapter divisions in Hebrews in Vaticanus (3:1; 4:14; 9:11 [V60, V61, V64]), but other important themes are not highlighted (e.g., the new covenant), for there is no chapter division in Vaticanus at 8:1.

James

James 1:26-27 is best understood as a summary of the main themes in the first chapter, which itself has the character of an introductory survey of the main themes to be dealt with in the body of the letter.[61] The famous faith-works discussion in 2:14-26 is in the context of works *of mercy* (2:15; see 1:27) and the control of the tongue (1:26; 3:1-12), which is not the frame of thinking for the faith-works controversy reflected in the Pauline Epistles. Langton's division at 2:1 links the discussion with the law-breaking activity of showing partiality to the rich and despising the poor believer. The discourse on faith and works is in the context of the preceding exhortation to the impartial and merciful treatment of the poor (1:26-2:13).[62] This understanding is supported by the way in which the text of James is divided in the ancient codices, for the only two points in the letter where divisions in Vaticanus, Sinaiticus, and Alexandrinus coincide are before 1:26 (V3, S4, A9) and after 2:26 (V5, S7, V19), demarcating this extended section of text as a unit of meaning. Only Alexandrinus has a division at 2:1 (A10), but breaks in the text are much more frequent in Alexandrinus than in the other two codices, and on that basis this codex is not useful in determining what were viewed by scribes as major partitions in the text of the Catholic Epistles. The unit as a whole addresses the issue of the neglect of the destitute (esp. 1:27; 2:2-3, 15-16) and

---

60. Barnabas Lindars, "The Rhetorical Structure of Hebrews," *NTS* 35 (1989): 382-406, esp. 392 n. 2.

61. Bauckham, *James*, 63.

62. For the thematic connection of 1:26-27 with what follows, see Timothy B. Cargal, *Restoring the Diaspora: Discursive Structure and Purpose in the Epistle of James*, SBLDS 144 (Atlanta: Scholars Press, 1993), 93-136.

the related need to avoid the compromise involved in client relationships with the wealthy patrons.[63]

Langton's placement of the chapter breaks also warns against reading 2:14-26 in a decontextualized fashion, which is what seems to have led to the postulation that James is at loggerheads with Paul. The polarity of faith and works does not require a knowledge of Pauline idiom.[64] Its focus is not similar to Paul's concern with legalism. Nor does Paul tackle the problem of faith as mere intellectual assent (see Jas 2:19). There is nothing anti-Pauline here, with James calling for a faith that is demonstrated in acts of charity (2:13-14). James is not combating Paul, nor a radicalized and distorted Paulinism.[65]

1 Peter

Peter has a homiletical style with certain key themes, especially that of suffering,[66] which tie the letter together in a loose paraenetical fashion. The chapter division at 2:1 has little to commend it in that the theme of the word of God continues (1:22–2:3). The details of how to "maintain good conduct among the Gentiles" (2:12 RSV) follow, and these community regulations arise from who and what they are (2:9-10). Much later in the letter, elders are addressed (5:1-4), followed by a brief word to those younger (5:5a). The division at 3:1 breaks into the household regulations, yet it comes after and so gives prominence to instructions to servants that are given powerful theological grounding in the example of the suffering of Christ (1:18-25). Being addressed to the most socially vulnerable group in the church and given the importance of the suffering theme, this is an appropriate passage to highlight. This theme is picked up again in 3:9 and follows a meandering course through to the end of 1 Peter 4. The letter as a whole is loosely dependent on Psalm 34 (quoted in part in 1 Pet 3:10-12).

---

63. Alicia J. Batten, *Friendship and Benefaction in James*, ESEC 15 (Blandford Forum, UK: Deo, 2010), 122-144.

64. See Bauckham, *James*, 120-31, where he argues that James's discussion of faith and works is entirely intelligible against a (common) Jewish background, without reference to Paul.

65. Peter Davids, *The Epistle of James: A Commentary on the Greek Text*, NIGTC (Exeter: Paternoster, 1982), 19-21. For more details, see Goswell, "Early Readership," 146-48.

66. Floyd V. Filson, "Partakers with Christ: Suffering in First Peter," *Int* 9 (1955): 400-412.

2 Peter

The Second Letter of Peter is cast in the form of a farewell address, and in this respect it may be compared to Acts 20:17-38 and 2 Timothy. The genre, together with the statement at 2 Peter 3:1 about this being "the second letter," makes the position of this letter after 1 Peter appropriate. The soon-to-die Peter (2 Pet 1:13-14) writes with an eye to the situation of the church "after [his] departure" (1:15). The promise theme is sounded early in the letter (1:4), and it is the promise of the final coming of the Lord Jesus that is especially in mind (1:16; 3:4). In 2:1 the apostle turns to the threat posed by "false prophets," and a long negative portrayal of them occupies the whole of 2 Peter 2. The discussion is set in contrast to the apostles as true prophets (1:16-21). The application for the readers is to be steadfast in the apostolic teaching, with the chapter division at 3:1 signaling a change in the mode of speech to that of encouragement directed at the Christian readers ("beloved"; see Jude 17).[67] This is the only chapter division for 2 Peter in Vaticanus.

1 John

As with the letter of James, 1 John is characterized by a small number of recurring and interrelated themes, and this makes it difficult to determine the literary structure of 1 John in detail. The break at 1 John 2 is triggered by the address to the readers ("my little children"; 2:1), yet the broad theme of sin and obedience holds sway throughout 1:5-2:6. Vaticanus begins a new section at both 2:1 and 2:7 ("Beloved"). Langton's division at 3:1 is not wholly convincing, seeing that the discussion about believers as those "born of God" and as "the children of God" oversteps this boundary (2:28-3:10). The division in Vaticanus at 3:2 is partly supported by the address to readers as "beloved." Then, 4:1 helps to signal the change in theme from loving one another (3:11-24) to the true confession of Jesus as "come in the flesh" (4:1-6). A division at this point is further justified by the address to readers as "beloved" (4:1). Vaticanus places chapter divisions at both 4:1 and 4:7.

Langton's last division fails to carry conviction (5:1), for instructions and exhortations about loving one another appear to continue until 5:3. The final division in Vaticanus is at 5:13 (the editors of the RSV leave a blank line before

---

67. Michael Green, *The Second Epistle of Peter and the General Epistle of Jude: An Introduction and Commentary*, TNTC (Leicester: Inter-Varsity, 1968), 123.

this verse), with the writer at this point beginning his concluding remarks by reiterating his purpose in writing.[68] For a tightly integrated discussion such as in 1 John fault could be found with any scheme of capitulation.

Jude

There is no chapter division in Jude, though perhaps the letter is long enough for bifurcation (Vaticanus provides a division at v. 12). The letter is dominated by a large central section exposing the character of false teachers (vv. 5-16) but fails to go into the specifics of what the heretical teaching was. The lack of specificity assists the widest possible application of the letter. The corrupt errorists are described in stereotypical fashion, much like the polemic in 2 Peter and the Pastoral Epistles.[69] The letter warns believers that "scoffers" of "the last time" have arrived on the scene (v. 18). In the light of that present threat, warnings and instructions are given (vv. 17-23), so that a chapter division at verse 17 would not have been at all inappropriate ("But you ..."), and the RSV editors place a new paragraph at this point.

REVELATION

The letters to the seven churches are enclosed within Revelation 2-3, with seven being a significant number in the literary structuring of the book, but the chapter division at 2:1 perhaps obscures the connection of the letters to what precedes—the vision of the exalted Christ, who dictates to John the seven letters (1:4-20). It is possible to view the book of Revelation as a series of parallel visions. The seer goes through "an open door" (4:1) to the throne room of heaven. This scene occupies chapters 4 and 5, with the division at 5:1 justified by the new feature of the "scroll." Chapters 6-7 recount the seven seals, which are a series of judgments (6:1, 3, 5, 7, 9, 12; 8:1), and the vision climaxes with the mention of God's temple (7:15-17). In Revelation many of the chapter divisions coincide with a formula much like "Then I saw" (e.g., 18:1; 20:1; 21:1), which underscores the visionary character of the book (see 1:2, 11; 22:8).[70]

---

68. I. Howard Marshall, *The Epistles of John*, NICNT (Grand Rapids: Eerdmans, 1978), 242.

69. See Robert J. Karris, "The Background and Significance of the Polemic of the Pastoral Epistles," *JBL* 92 (1973): 549-64.

70. For a discussion of the structural conventions of apocalyptic literature, see Christopher R. Smith, "The Structure of the Book of Revelation in Light of Apocalyptic Literary Conventions," *NovT* 36 (1994): 373-93.

CHAPTER 7 CONCLUSIONS

There is the danger of allowing the chapter and verse divisions with which we are familiar to control our reading of Scripture, but this does not give us permission to exclude them from consideration. Readers should view the divisions within the New Testament books as commentary on the text that can, at times, be an insightful guide. Unfortunately, the usual pattern is that the chapter and verse divisions are only noted by students of Scripture when they are mocked and discounted as nonsensical. The modest aim of this chapter has been to encourage a reevaluation of the received divisions of the biblical text as an aid to interpretation.

GUIDELINES FOR INTERPRETING THE DIVISIONS IN NEW TESTAMENT BOOKS

1. The habits of readers in seeking sense in texts suggest four possible functions of any given textual division in the New Testament. Keep these functions in mind when evaluating the significance of textual breaks.

2. The first and most obvious effect is that a division separates one section of a text from another section. The chapter division at Matthew 2:1 places 1:18–25 with what precedes and suggests that these verses amount to an exposition of 1:16, confirming the Davidic lineage of the yet-to-be-born Jesus.

3. A correlative second function of divisions is to join material. Putting the chapter division at Mark 9:1, instead of at 9:2 (V36, A25), implies that the transfiguration (9:2–8) fulfills, at least in part, the prediction that "some standing here … will not taste death before they see that the kingdom of God has come with power" (9:1b RSV).

4. A third function of a textual division is to highlight certain material in a text, making it more prominent in the eyes of the reader. Acts 10:1 interrupts stories of Peter's travels (starting in 9:32) but also highlights his meeting with Cornelius, with this groundbreaking event subsequently rehearsed in Acts 11 and 15.

5. The mirror image of the third function is the fourth function, to downplay or ignore certain textual features. The familiar capitulation of James warns against reading the discussion in 2:14–26 in a decontextualized fashion, which is what seems to have led to the postulation that James is at loggerheads with Paul. In James, the opposition between faith and works is subordinated to a larger discussion of the necessity of works of charity (2:1–13).

CONCLUSIONS

In this volume I have sought to introduce readers to the biblical paratext and give training in detecting and evaluating the paratextual features of their Bibles. As we have seen, the three chief components of the paratext are the orders of the books, the different names assigned to the books, and the differing schemes of textual division within the books.

THE ORDER OF THE BIBLICAL BOOKS

The study commenced by reviewing and evaluating the order of the books in the Hebrew Bible, the Greek Old Testament, and the New Testament. The following are some principles of book order as inferred by the reader after an examination of the biblical material:

1. *Size of the book.* For example, the position of Romans at the head of the Pauline corpus is due to the mechanical principle of length, but its premier position makes eminent sense, for it is the most treatise-like of Paul's letters and less influenced by local church factors than Paul's other letters, and so appropriately functions as a theological introduction to the Pauline corpus.

2. *Chronological setting.* For example, Ruth 1:1 ("In the days when the judges ruled") would seem to explain the placement of this book in the Greek Bible following Judges, seeing that the story told is set in the same era of Israelite history as Judges.

3. *Common authorship.* This can be either stated or assumed— for example, the combination of Jeremiah-Lamentations in the LXX, though the text of Lamentations does not explicitly name Jeremiah as its author. Despite common authorship, Luke is not placed next to Acts in any Greek manuscript,

suggesting that the volumes have different contexts for their interpretation.

4. *Story line.* Examples are the Former Prophets (Joshua–Kings) and historical books (Joshua–Esther), with successive books narrating what happens next. Keep in mind, however, that it is the next *significant* thing that happens that is featured, not just the next thing per se, given the necessarily selective nature of biblical narrative.

5. *Genre.* Examples of this include the bringing together of different books into a prophetic corpus and the collecting of wisdom books (e.g., Proverbs–Ecclesiastes–Song of Solomon in Vaticanus), though a convincing definition of "wisdom" is notoriously difficult. Considerations of genre also resulted in the formation of the four-Gospel collection and of the corpora of Pauline and non-Pauline epistles.

6. *Thematic considerations.* However, any book is likely to have a number of major themes, so alternative placements are possible on this basis—for example, Proverbs followed by Ruth, with the figure of Ruth providing a real-life example of the "good wife" described in Proverbs 31:10-31.

7. *Literary linkages.* This can be by means of catchwords, such as used in the Book of the Twelve, explaining why Obadiah may follow Amos 9.

8. *No discernible principle of order.* There is a variety of canonical orders, even if some predominate, but probably the placement of no Bible book is fortuitous.

In terms of reading strategy, the assumption is that books placed in apposition are conversation partners (e.g., Proverbs and Ruth in the Hebrew Bible; or Acts and Catholic Epistles), such that the interaction of conjoined books takes priority over other possible intracanonical linkages (e.g., Ruth and Ezra-Nehemiah, or Luke and Acts). Book order is an interpretive frame that functions to present the books to later readers in a particular canonical setting. As a result, it provides prompts that guide the proper use of the books, leading readers to expect that neighboring books are related in significant ways and throw light on each other. The conjoining of books is an indication that ancient readers saw them as related in meaning, which can be uncovered by study of the resonances between adjacent books in the canon. The ancient practice of placing books in a certain order does not mandate what contemporary readers should do and think, but the judgment of earlier readers is one of several factors that need to be taken into consideration when exploring the coherence of the biblical books, with every new generation of readers likely to detect never-before-discerned links between adjacent books.

THE TITLES OF THE BIBLICAL BOOKS

Genette has provided a useful interpretive grid in analyzing the possible functions of any given book title. One function is to identify or designate the work, another to indicate its general contents or theme, a third to highlight it to the public, and a fourth to indicate its form or genre. Using these categories, I examined and evaluated some of the titles assigned to the books of the Old and New Testaments.

1. Identification is the first and most basic reason for naming a literary work, and a randomly chosen title is sufficient to achieve this end, though it is unlikely that any book in the Bible received an arbitrary title. To use the opening words of a book (incipit) as a title may, at first sight, appear an arbitrary procedure. However, authors usually think very carefully about how to commence a book. For example, the Hebrew title of Genesis, bərēšît ("In the beginning"), properly designates Genesis as a book of origins and so represents an exegetical insight that informs reading.

2. With regard to the second function, the relation between a title and the content of a literary work is extremely variable, and so, for example, the title "Proverbs" seems to highlight the collections of aphorisms found in Proverbs 10-31. The Hebrew title of Numbers, bəmidbar ("In the wilderness"), draws attention to the years of wilderness testing occupying the central section of the book (Num 11-21). In regard to subject matter or theme, book titles inevitably simplify and are highly selective,

and a title may easily mislead readers as to what a text is about (e.g., Ezra-Nehemiah).

3. The title "The Song of Songs" (= The Greatest Song) is a recommendation to the potential reader, but unfortunately this has not prevented this book from being largely neglected in teaching and preaching, perhaps because it is viewed as too hot to handle in a congregational setting.

4. A fourth function of a title is to indicate and assert a work's form, for example, Psalms, Proverbs, Lamentations, and Chronicles. The Hebrew title of Psalms, *təhillîm* ("Praises"), emphasizes the feature of praise that is found in almost all the psalms, even the psalms of lament (e.g., 3:3; 7:11), and the Psalter ends with five psalms that are all praise (Pss 146–50). A book via its title may be given an inappropriate genre designation (e.g., Acts, Revelation). Acts does not conform well to the ancient literary genre described as "Acts" (*praxeis*), for typically the mighty deeds of only one hero are narrated, not those of several heroes (Stephen, Philip, Peter), and the noble death of the figure is described, whereas the narrative of Acts closes before the martyrdom of Paul. With regard to Revelation, John is not describing his composition as belonging to the literary type called "apocalypse," but sees his book as a work of prophecy.

The aim of my survey was not merely to criticize the usually assigned book titles in the Old and New Testaments but to see how they may assist the understanding of the reader, for they imply an interpretation of the literary works they head. A title may throw light on a work or it may obscure its message. It is best to view the titles of the books as valuable but fallible commentary on the text.

THE DIVISIONS WITHIN THE BIBLICAL BOOKS

The textual breaks within a book suggest a literary structure that has significance for the interpretation of its contents. Such divisions serve a number of related functions. The habits of readers in seeking meaning in texts suggest four possible functions of any given sense division:

1. A textual division separates one section of a text from another section, making a break in the flow of the text. For example, Esther 10 is a short chapter of only three verses that provides a summary of the reign of Ahasuerus and makes much of Mordecai, but excludes any mention of Esther from the last chapter of the book (see 9:32).[1] This way of partitioning the text could be understood as an attempt to make Mordecai the sole hero of the book.

2. A correlative, second function of divisions is to join material. They demarcate a unit (longer or shorter), suggesting that the material joined is closely related in meaning. An example is the parabolic material grouped together in Luke 15: the parable of the lost sheep (15:3–7), the parable of the lost coin (15:8–10), and the parable of the lost son (15:11–32), with the grouping of the three parables in the one chapter suggesting such an interpretation of the third parable (see 15:32: "he was lost ...").

3. A third function or effect of a division is to highlight certain material in a text, making it more prominent in the eyes of the reader. For example, the chapter divisions at Ruth 2:1 and 4:1 put the focus on Boaz, with the first bringing his existence to the knowledge of the reader and the second narrating his decisive step of going up to the gate to "settle the matter" (3:18). On the other hand, the importance of Naomi in the story is underlined by giving her the last word in chapters 1, 2, and 3.

---

1. See David Marcus, "Alternate Chapter Divisions in the Pentateuch in the Light of the Masoretic Sections," *HS* 44 (2003): 128: "By starting the chapter division at a different place the parameters of the text are then changed and so a different hermeneutic may be produced."

4. The mirror image of the third function is the fourth function, to downplay or ignore certain textual features. No chapter break signals the major transition at Matthew 16:21 ("From that time Jesus began to ..."), with the break at 17:1 triggered by the chronological note "After six days." The progress reports about the spread of "the word of God" in Acts are not reflected in the chapter divisions (6:7; 9:31; 12:24; 16:5; 19:20), unfortunately implying that these notices are not to be viewed as structurally important in dividing the book into six major sections.

When analyzed in this fashion, the status of such textual breaks in the biblical text as commentary on the text is revealed, and also that divisions may lead (or mislead) the reader who seeks meaning in the text.

NEW HERMENEUTICAL TOOLS
AVAILABLE TO THE READER

A helpful way to view the perspectives and procedures for detecting and evaluating the biblical paratext presented in this book is that they provide readers with new *tools* to use in seeking to understand and apply the text of Scripture. In terms of ways of studying the Bible, scholars have tended to speak of different types of biblical criticism, and thus one of the interpretive tools has been named by one of its pioneers "delimitation criticism," wherein different ways of dividing texts is explored." While in common parlance "criticism" has a negative connotation, and indeed its practice has often been questionable, it does not need to be detrimental for interpretation.[2] We can compare critical approaches with the work of the art or music "critic," who may show an appreciation of the aesthetic value of the work placed under their critical gaze. However, a more neutral and so more useful way of speaking may be that of interpretive *tools*, and in this book I have given multiple examples of the use of three tools. Using these tools requires readers to ask

---

2. For Adele Berlin's survey of what she views as scholarly *avoidance* of interpretation by means of biblical criticism, see "A Search for a New Biblical Hermeneutics: Preliminary Observations," in *The Study of the Ancient Near East in the Twenty-First Century: The William Foxwell Albright Centennial Conference*, ed. Jerrold S. Cooper and Glenn M. Schwartz (Winona Lake, IN: Eisenbrauns, 1996), 195–99.

the right questions, discern alternative viewpoints, and be open to new ways of looking at familiar texts.

In terms of asking the right questions, here are some examples: Why are these two books placed next to each other? Why is this collection of books placed in this particular order? Why was this name and not another chosen for the book? Is there a leading theme or key character in the book that is ignored or downplayed by the usually assigned title? Why might a chapter break have been placed at this point? Is the demarcated section of text a coherent unit of meaning?

In regard to discerning alternative viewpoints, we have seen that the paratext of Scripture encodes the evaluations of early readers. The act of placing books side-by-side implies that the conjoined books are related in meaning in some way, but it is left to the modern reader to work out what that link is—common themes, similar genre, or story line thread? The imposition of a title on a book reflects a deliberate choice by those responsible, and the relation between a title and a book's content is extremely variable, for most books have more than one theme, and more than one genre classification may also be possible. In regard to internal divisions in books, deciding major or minor breaks is an act of discernment. The choices of ancient readers do not have to be followed blindly; rather, their value is that they provide the modern reader with interpretive possibilities to consider. When the same book is placed in more than one canonical location, this assists readers to notice certain features of the book that might otherwise be overlooked or underplayed, and in this way it assists in refining interpretation. The various arrangements of books, the different names assigned to them, and the alternative ways of dividing a text are best viewed as options now offered to present-day readers for their pondering.

With respect to developing an openness to new ways of looking at familiar texts, the biblical paratext puts the modern reader in touch with earlier generations of readers, who read the same text we do but did not necessarily understand it in the same way. No two persons think exactly alike, and being exposed to the ideas of others assists us to improve our own reading of Scripture. Since the paratextual features of the Bible come from another time and place, it is almost inevitable that they will expose us to new ways of looking at the Bible, some of which may be better than the views we currently hold. Are we humble enough to consider that possibility and, when needed, refine our ideas?

Tools can be used well, and they can be used badly. As a child I followed my father around as he did maintenance work on our house on weekends, and I can remember him telling me to always use a tool in the way in which it was designed to be used. In line with this advice, I have insisted on the distinction between text and paratext. The sacred text is not to be tampered with or resisted. The paratext, on the other hand, though deserving of respect, is not supposed to be treated as sacrosanct. For example, neither the Hebrew nor the Greek way of ordering the books of the Old Testament should have absolute priority over the other, and neither organization should be made the exclusive basis for a theological appreciation of the Old Testament. In terms of method, the contemporary reader is not required to decide which sequence of books is to have precedence as a frame for interpretation. The title assigned to a Bible book may represent an insight; on the other hand, it may mislead the reader, and I have suggested that the title of Ezra-Nehemiah does mislead and that the Acts of the Apostles may not be entirely helpful as a title for a book that centers primarily on Paul. Likewise, the chapter divisions with which we are familiar are not to have a stranglehold on interpretation, for there have been other ways of dividing the text in the history of interpretation, and it is important that alternative ways of dividing a text be considered. We misuse the biblical paratext if it is never questioned or subjected to evaluation.

THE IMPORTANCE OF THE BIBLICAL
PARATEXT IN THE DIGITAL AGE

We live in a time of sound bites, tweets, posts, and the Bible on the smartphone, whose screen only shows several verses at a time. These technologies have contributed to and accelerated the fragmentation of biblical knowledge, and Christian wisdom is being drowned in a sea of information. More and more, at the present time, passages of Scripture are being presented to readers without a context for their interpretation.[3] Meaning depends heavily

---

3. See Jeffrey S. Siker, *Liquid Scripture: The Bible in a Digital World* (Minneapolis: Fortress, 2017), 69: "The unbound Bible on a screen does not lend itself to an immediate awareness of any particular shape of the Bible, canonical or otherwise. From this perspective skimming the Bible on screens would necessarily seem to undermine understanding the Bible in its canonical frame."

on *context*, and freed from any context, the possible meaning of Bible passages becomes highly fluid. Since this is our situation, it is more important than ever to assist the ordinary believer to become familiar with the story line of Scripture and—as is the focus of the present volume—to grasp the paratextual structuring of the canon.[4]

There is a story line running through the Bible, as reflected in passages such as Nehemiah 9; Psalm 78; Daniel 9; Acts 7 and 13. Likewise, in terms of the structuring of the canon, the Former Prophets (Hebrew canon) and historical books (Greek canon) play a central macro-structural role in the Old Testament canon. These books continue the story of salvation begun in the Pentateuch, and they form the narrative framework for the prophetic books and wisdom books that follow.[5] The book of Acts plays a similar organizational role in the canon of the New Testament, for it continues the narration of salvation history begun in the Gospels and provides an historical and theological frame for reading the letters of Peter, John, James, and Paul.[6] These narratival works play a role in assisting to mold the variegated contents of the Old and New Testaments into a coordinated canonical structure. There is no need to play the biblical story line off against the canonical framing of the books, for both frameworks are vital for a proper reading of Scripture. The first feature can be put under the title of metanarrative, and the second that of metastructure.

The structuring of the canon places a limit on the possible interpretations of a text, and relations with *neighboring* books are especially significant for interpretation and an important factor to be taken into consideration in seeking to read and apply any book and any passage within any book. Otherwise, there is the danger of turning the Bible into a *collage* of moveable pieces, with every would-be interpreter coming up with a different picture of what the Bible is about. Such a procedure too quickly dismisses the ordering of the

---

4. For the first, see, e.g., Craig G. Bartholomew and Michael W. Goheen, *The Drama of Scripture: Finding Our Place in the Biblical Story* (Grand Rapids: Baker Academic, 2004).

5. Gregory Goswell, "The Macro-Structural Role of the Former Prophets and the Historical Books in Old Testament Canons," *JETS* 63 (2020): 455–71. Cf. Richard Bauckham, "Reading Scripture as a Coherent Story," in *The Art of Reading Scripture*, ed. Ellen F. Davis and Richard B. Hays (Grand Rapids: Eerdmans, 2003), 39: "Some books have no narrative material at all, but it is not difficult to see that the canon implicitly gives some nonnarrative books (e.g., Psalms, Lamentations) a narrative setting within the story told by the narrative books."

6. Walter Vogels, "La Structure symétrique de la Bible chrétienne," in *The Biblical Canons*, ed. J.-M. Auwers and H. J. de Jonge, BETL 163 (Leuven: Peeters, 2003), 298, 300.

books (e.g., Jeremiah-Lamentations, Acts-Catholic Epistles) and the grouping of books (e.g., Pentateuch, the Twelve, the four Gospels) in ancient Bibles and canon lists, features that reflect the judgments of early scribes and the believing communities they served. Book order is a nascent form of biblical theology, for it shows how different Bible books relate to one another.[7]

On the same basis, the names assigned to the books provide valuable interpretive prompts, for example, the titles Joshua, Judges, Samuel, and Kings suggest that the Former Prophets provides a story of leadership in Israel, with no category of leader entirely free from blame for the eventual exile of the Northern and Southern kingdoms. So too, the titles that were assigned to the four Gospels (e.g., "The Gospel according to Matthew") prevent an idiosyncratic reading of any of the four in isolation from the perspectives of the other three on the life and ministry of Jesus. Likewise, textual divisions within books suggest how their contents are to be packaged into units of meaning.

In one of his essays Umberto Ecco asks and seeks to answer the question, "What's the point of having a teacher?"[8] After all, students of today have access to a vast repository of knowledge on the internet and are no longer dependent on the school curriculum to discover what is happening in the world. But, as Ecco points out, "The internet tells us almost everything apart from how to search, filter, select, accept, or reject that information."[9] In other words, teachers are still needed to train students how to adjudicate between counterclaims, how to weigh competing options, and how to arrange apparently disparate facts in a coherent pattern. Paratext plays similar educational roles. As for an analogy for the internet, it is as if a library exploded and millions of pages are floating down from the sky or lie scattered on the ground in the immediate vicinity, with passers-by picking up random sheets of paper and trying to make sense of what they read. Applying this picture of the current

---

7. See Darian Lockett, "Limitations of a Purely Salvation-Historical Approach to Biblical Theology," *HBT* 39 (2017): 222: "Christian Scripture has a canonical shape and order that should not be dismissed as a late or anachronistic arrangement of texts in favor of an historically reconstructed salvation-historical framework." Also see Jeremy M. Kimble and Ched Spellman, *Invitation to Biblical Theology: Exploring the Shape, Storyline, and Themes of the Bible*, ITS (Grand Rapids: Kregel, 2020), 58: "An important initial step to understanding the Bible as whole is to see it as a collection of carefully connected collections."

8. Umberto Ecco, *Chronicles of a Liquid Society*, trans. Richard Dixon (London: Vintage, 2018), 62–64.

9. Ecco, *Chronicles of a Liquid Society*, 64.

atomization of knowledge to what we have been studying in this volume, the biblical paratext provides a much-needed frame of reference for the contents of the Bible, suggesting how books relate to each other, labeling the books, and packaging the material supplied in the books into coherent units of thought.[10]

WHERE TO NOW?

As for suggestions of next steps and further study, noting that I have only provided selected examples of how the paratext can assist and enrich one's reading of Scripture, it is a case of *go and do thou likewise.* The attached bibliography provides helpful resources for assisting readers in this venture. Really, it is a never-ending task, for who can claim to perfectly understand everything in the Bible or to have fully applied its teachings to home, church, society, and self? The study and use of the biblical paratext enables us to continue our journey of discovery and discipleship in fellowship with ancient believers, who had the same ambition of understanding and applying the Scriptures.

---

10. See Ched Spellman, "The Canon after Google: Implications of a Digitized and Destabilized Codex," *HTR* 16 (2010): 42: "The development of this type of canon-consciousness can be an effective way to salvage a 'whole Bible' interpretive framework in a context that values serendipity over stability."

GLOSSARY OF KEY WORDS

apocalyptic: a literary genre and worldview that provides a visionary depiction of world history and its culmination, whose name derives from the title of the book of Revelation in Greek (*Apokalypsis*)

Ashkenazic: pertaining to the Jewish diaspora population in Europe around the end of the first millennium

canon: the collection of sacred books intended by God to provide authoritative guidance to the people of God in doctrine and ethics

capitulation: the system of chapters in a manuscript

codex (codices): ancient manuscripts bound together in book form rather than as a scroll

eschatology: ideas and teaching pertaining to the course of history that culminates with the "last things"

ekthesis: letters protruding to the left of the column margin

Epiphanius: the bishop of Salamis, Cyprus, at the end of the fourth century

Eusebius: Eusebius of Caesarea, an historian of Christianity (died AD 339)

genre (adj. generic): a known category of literary composition characterized by a particular style, form, and function

gospel: the Greek word "gospel" (*euangelion*) means news or proclamation, and this becomes the name of a literary genre depicting the life of Jesus Christ

incipit: the opening words of a literary work, which in ancient times where often used to generate a title for the work

Josephus: the late first-century Jewish historian

law: the Hebrew word (*torah*) is better rendered "instruction," such that it does not imply or encourage any kind of legalism

Maimonides: also known by the acronym Rambam; a medieval Sephardic Jewish philosopher (died AD 1204)

Masoretes: families of Jewish scribes and scholars who worked in the period AD 600–1000 and produced model Hebrew Bibles; they were based primarily in Tiberias and Babylonia

Masoretic Text (MT): the traditional Hebrew text of the Jewish Bible, complete with vowel points and a system of accents, produced by the Masoretes (AD 600–1000)

Melito: the bishop of Sardis (died AD 180)

Moabite Stone (Mesha Inscription): a basalt stele dated around 840 BC, containing an inscription in the name of King Mesha of Moab; it is now housed in the Louvre

Muratorian Fragment: a fragment of a Latin list (c. AD 200) of New Testament writings then regarded by Christians as canonical

Octateuch: the group of eight books (Genesis–Ruth) that begins the Greek Old Testament

Origen: Alexandrian church father and biblical scholar (died AD 254)

paragraph: a section of text physically delimited by means of drawn lines or spaces

parashah **(***parashiyyot***):** a Torah portion in the annual cycle of fifty-four weekly lessons read during Jewish prayer services in the Babylonian tradition

paratext: an interpretive literary frame that encloses a text

Pentateuch: the title given to the first five books of the Old Testament as a corpus, derived from the Greek *hē pentateuchos* (*biblos*), meaning "the five-roll [book]"

Praxapostolos: the combination of the Acts of the Apostles and Catholic Epistles as a canonical corpus

Qumran: the most important of the Dead Sea sites where ancient scrolls were discovered in caves in the 1940s and 1950s, with the manuscripts dated from the third century BC to the first century AD

scriptio continua: a pattern of writing without spaces or other marks between the words or sentences of a text

seder **(***sedarim***):** a portion of a biblical book, consisting of 452 weekly liturgical readings (154 or 156 in the Torah) in a three-year cycle in the Palestinian tradition

Sephardic: pertaining to Hispanic Jews, who established communities in Spain and Portugal

Septuagint (LXX): the Greek Old Testament primarily translated for the Jewish community in Egypt and then used by the Greek-speaking early church

Siloam Inscription: an inscription (c. 700 BC) found in the water tunnel that links the Gihon Spring to the Pool of Siloam, in the city of David; it is now housed in the Istanbul Archaeology Museums

Sirach: the book of Sirach, also called the Wisdom of Sirach or Ecclesiasticus, written by Jewish scribe Ben Sira (200–175 BC)

subscription: the conclusion or postscript of a literary work

superscription: the opening or heading of a literary work

Talmud: the revered text of rabbinic Judaism, consisting of the Mishnah (c. AD 200) and the Gemara (c. AD 500); it is the primary source of Jewish law and theology

Theodotion: Jewish scholar who translated the Hebrew Bible into Greek (c. AD 150)

title: a description or summary of a work that is graphically distinct from the main text

titloi: running titles at the top of columns of text

Vulgate: the Latin Bible sanctioned by the Roman Catholic Church and primarily translated by Jerome; its order of books was influenced by the Greek canonical tradition

wisdom: true wisdom in the Old Testament is godliness rather than cleverness, and its foundation is the fear of the Lord (Prov 1:7)

APPENDIX

APPENDIX A: ORDER OF OLD TESTAMENT BOOKS [1]

HEBREW (TANAK)[2]	SEPTUAGINT[3]	VULGATE[4]	ENGLISH
Torah	**Law**	**Law**	**Law**
Genesis	Genesis	Genesis	Genesis
Exodus	Exodus	Exodus	Exodus
Leviticus	Leviticus	Leviticus	Leviticus
Numbers	Numbers	Numbers	Numbers
Deuteronomy	Deuteronomy	Deuteronomy	Deuteronomy
Prophets	**Histories**	**Histories**	**Histories**
Former Prophets	Joshua	Joshua	Joshua
Joshua	Judges	Judges	Judges
Judges	Ruth	Ruth	Ruth
Samuel	1 Kingdoms (= 1 Samuel)	1 Kings	1 Samuel
Kings	2 Kingdoms (= 2 Samuel)	2 Kings	2 Samuel
Latter Prophets	3 Kingdoms (= 1 Kings)	3 Kings	1 Kings
Isaiah	4 Kingdoms (= 2 Kings)	4 Kings	2 Kings
Jeremiah	1 Chronicles	1 Chronicles	1 Chronicles
Ezekiel	2 Chronicles	2 Chronicles	2 Chronicles
The Twelve (= Minor Prophets)	Ezra	Ezra	Ezra
	Nehemiah	Nehemiah[5]	Nehemiah
	Esther	Esther	Esther

---

1. Adapted from Paul D. Wegner, *The Journey from Texts to Translations: The Origin and Development of the Bible* (Grand Rapids: Baker, 1999), 43.
2. This is the order in printed Hebrew Bibles (e.g., BHS).
3. This is the order in Rahlfs, ed., *Septuaginta*, leaving out the deuterocanonical books.
4. Leaving out the apocryphal books; see the next four footnotes for these books.
5. Plus Tobit and Judith.

HEBREW (TANAK)	SEPTUAGINT	VULGATE	ENGLISH
Writings	**Poetry**	**Poetry**	**Poetry**
Psalms	Psalms	Job	Job
Job	Proverbs	Psalms	Psalms
Proverbs	Ecclesiastes	Proverbs	Proverbs
	Song of Songs	Ecclesiastes	Ecclesiastes
Megilloth	Job	Song of Solomon[6]	Song of Solomon
Ruth			
Song of Songs	**Prophets**	**Prophets**	**Prophets**
Ecclesiastes	Hosea	Isaiah	Isaiah
Lamentations	Amos	Jeremiah	Jeremiah
Esther	Micah	Lamentations[7]	Lamentations
	Joel	Ezekiel	Ezekiel
Daniel	Obadiah	Daniel	Daniel
Ezra-Nehemiah	Jonah	Hosea	Hosea
Chronicles	Nahum	Joel	Joel
	Habakkuk	Amos	Amos
	Zephaniah	Obadiah	Obadiah
	Haggai	Jonah	Jonah
	Zechariah	Micah	Micah
	Malachi	Nahum	Nahum
	Isaiah	Habakkuk	Habakkuk
	Jeremiah	Zephaniah	Zephaniah
	Lamentations	Haggai	Haggai
	Ezekiel	Zechariah	Zechariah
	Daniel	Malachi[8]	Malachi

---

6. Plus Wisdom and Ecclesiasticus.

7. Plus Baruch.

8. Plus 1–2 Maccabees.

APPENDIX B: DIFFERENT HEBREW ORDERS OF BOOKS[9]

ALEPPO/ LENINGRAD	BHS	SNAITH[10]	TALMUD (BABA BATRA)
Torah	**Torah**	**Torah**	**Torah**
Genesis	Genesis	Genesis	[Genesis]
Exodus	Exodus	Exodus	[Exodus]
Leviticus	Leviticus	Leviticus	[Leviticus]
Numbers	Numbers	Numbers	[Numbers]
Deuteronomy	Deuteronomy	Deuteronomy	[Deuteronomy]
Prophets	**Prophets**	**Prophets**	**Prophets**
Joshua	Joshua	Joshua	Joshua
Judges	Judges	Judges	Judges
Samuel	Samuel	Samuel	Samuel
Kings	Kings	Kings	Kings
Isaiah	Isaiah	Isaiah	Jeremiah
Jeremiah	Jeremiah	Jeremiah	Ezekiel
Ezekiel	Ezekiel	Ezekiel	Isaiah
The Twelve	The Twelve	The Twelve	The Twelve
Writings	**Writings**	**Writings**	**Writings**
Chronicles	Psalms	Psalms	Ruth
Psalms	Job	Proverbs	Psalms
Job	Proverbs	Job	Job
Proverbs	Ruth	Song of Songs	Proverbs
Ruth	Song of Songs	Ruth	Ecclesiastes
Song of Songs	Ecclesiastes	Lamentations	Song of Songs
Ecclesiastes	Lamentations	Ecclesiastes	Lamentations
Lamentations	Esther	Esther	Daniel
Esther	Daniel	Daniel	Esther
Daniel	Ezra-Nehemiah	Ezra-Nehemiah	Ezra-Nehemiah
Ezra-Nehemiah	Chronicles	Chronicles	Chronicles

---

9. For a much more extensive listing of alternative orders of the Prophets and Writings in Jewish tradition, see Beckwith, *Old Testament Canon*, appendix 2. Square brackets indicate that the book is absent from the list.

10. Snaith, *Sefer Torah, Nevi'im uKetuvim*.

APPENDIX C: ORDER OF BOOKS IN
MAJOR SEPTUAGINT MANUSCRIPTS [11]

CODEX VATICANUS (B)	CODEX SINAITICUS (ℵ)	CODEX ALEXANDRINUS (A)
Pentateuch	**Pentateuch**	**Pentateuch**
Genesis	Genesis	Genesis
Exodus	[Exodus]	Exodus
Leviticus	[Leviticus]	Leviticus
Numbers	Numbers	Numbers
Deuteronomy	[Deuteronomy]	Deuteronomy
History	**History**	**History**
Joshua	[Joshua]	Joshua
Judges + Ruth	[Judges + Ruth]	Judges + Ruth
1, 2 Kingdoms	[1, 2 Kingdoms]	1, 2 Kingdoms
3, 4 Kingdoms	[3, 4 Kingdoms]	3, 4 Kingdoms
1, 2 Paraleipomena	1, [2] Paraleipomena	1, 2 Paraleipomena
1 Esdras*	[Ezra]-Nehemiah	
Ezra-Nehemiah	Esther + Tobit*	**Prophets**
	Judith*	The Book of the Twelve[#]
Poetry	1, 4 Maccabees*	Isaiah
Psalms		Jeremiah + Baruch*
Proverbs	**Prophets**	Lamentations + Epistle of Jeremiah
Ecclesiastes	Isaiah	
Song of Solomon	Jeremiah	Ezekiel
Job + Wisdom*	Lamentations	Daniel + Susanna*
Sirach*	[Epistle of Jeremiah]	Bel and the Dragon*
	[Ezekiel]	
More History?	[Daniel + Susanna]	**More History**
Esther + Judith*	[Bel and the Dragon]	Esther + Tobit*
Tobit*	The Book of the Twelve[#]	Judith*
	[Hosea-Micah missing]	1 Esdras*
		Ezra-Nehemiah
		1-4 Maccabees*

---

11. Adapted from Wegner, *Journey from Texts to Translations*, 48.

CODEX VATICANUS (B)	CODEX SINAITICUS (ℵ)	CODEX ALEXANDRINUS (A)
Prophets	**Poetry**	**Poetry**
The Book of the Twelve#	Psalms + Psalm 151*	Psalms + Psalm 151* + Odes*
Isaiah	Proverbs	Job
Jeremiah + Baruch*	Ecclesiastes	Proverbs
Lamentations + Epistle of Jeremiah*	Song of Solomon + Wisdom*	Ecclesiastes
Ezekiel	Sirach*	Song of Solomon + Wisdom*
Daniel + Susanna*	Job	Sirach*
Bel and the Dragon*		Psalms of Solomon*

[ ] = defective or missing

* noncanonical work(s)

order: Hosea, Amos, Micah, Joel ...

APPENDIX D: ORDER OF NEW TESTAMENT BOOKS [12]

VATICANUS (B)	SINAITICUS (ℵ)	ALEXANDRINUS (A)	VULGATE
Gospels	**Gospels**	**Gospels**	**Gospels**
Matthew	Matthew	Matthew (defective)	Matthew
Mark	Mark	Mark	Mark
Luke	Luke	Luke	Luke
John	John	John (defective)	John
Acts	**Pauline Epistles**	Acts	Acts
	Romans		
Catholic Epistles	1 Corinthians	**Catholic Epistles**	**Pauline Epistles**
James	2 Corinthians	James	Romans
1 Peter	Galatians	1 Peter	1 Corinthians
2 Peter	Ephesians	2 Peter	2 Corinthians
1 John	Philippians	1 John	Galatians
2 John	Colossians	2 John	Ephesians
3 John	1 Thessalonians	3 John	Philippians
Jude	2 Thessalonians	Jude	Colossians
	Hebrews		1 Thessalonians
Pauline Epistles	1 Timothy	**Pauline Epistles**	2 Thessalonians
Romans	2 Timothy	Romans	1 Timothy
1 Corinthians	Titus	1 Corinthians	2 Timothy
2 Corinthians	Philemon	2 Corinthians (defective)	Titus
Galatians		Galatians	Philemon
Ephesians	Acts	Ephesians	Hebrews
Philippians		Philippians	
Colossians	**Catholic Epistles**	Colossians	**Catholic Epistles**
1 Thessalonians	James	1 Thessalonians	James
2 Thessalonians	1 Peter	2 Thessalonians	1 Peter
Hebrews (–9:14)	2 Peter	Hebrews	2 Peter
1 Timothy (missing)	1 John	1 Timothy	1 John
2 Timothy (missing)	2 John	2 Timothy	2 John
Titus (missing)	3 John	Titus	3 John
Philemon (missing)	Jude	Philemon	Jude

---

12. Adapted from Wegner, *Journey from Texts to Translations*, 58.

VATICANUS (B)	SINAITICUS (ℵ)	ALEXANDRINUS (A)	VULGATE
Revelation (missing)	Revelation Epistle of Barnabas Shepherd of Hermas (defective)	Revelation 1 Clement (defective) 2 Clement (defective) Psalms of Solomon (missing)	Revelation

STUDY QUESTIONS FOR FURTHER EXPLORATION

CHAPTER 1

1. How credible is the division of the Pentateuch (Torah) into five books?

2. How does the canonical position of Deuteronomy assist the reader in appreciating this book's contribution to the theology of the Old Testament?

3. Why might the Hebrew Bible place narrative books such as Samuel and Kings in the same canonical section (Prophets) as books of prophetic oracles such as Isaiah and Jeremiah?

4. How do the four books that make up the Former Prophets interact with one another and together present an overall theology for this canonical unit?

5. What does the placement of the Psalter in the Hebrew Bible suggest about how it should be classified?

6. What possible significance can be found in the differing order of prophetic books in the Hebrew Bible and the Talmudic listing?

7. What does the bringing together of the prophetic books as a collection suggest about their continued relevance?

8. Is the Book of the Twelve (= Minor Prophets) one book or twelve? Evaluate recent arguments for both viewpoints.

9. Scholars are not agreed about the message of the book of Jonah. If its position in the Twelve is significant for interpretation, how does the canonical context assist our understanding of this small book?

CHAPTER 2

1. Is it right to view the arrangement of the Greek Bible as presenting a Christian reading of the Old Testament? Why or why not?

2. How might the different canonical positions of Ruth assist its interpretation? Is any one of these positions better than the others?

3. How might the alternate positions of the book of Daniel in Writings (Hebrew Bible) and Prophets (Greek Old Testament) influence its interpretation?

4. How might the consideration of the three alternative positions of Chronicles in different canons throw light on its contents and use?

5. If the Song of Songs is a wisdom book with lessons for readers, what might those lessons be?

6. What is the last book of the Old Testament in the different canons? How might the alternative endings influence our understanding of the relationship between the two testaments?

7. Is the issue of Jew-gentile relations the leading theme of the books Joshua–Esther in the Greek canon? If not, what is?

8. The placement of Chronicles after Kings in the Greek order makes it look like an addendum and supplement to Kings. Is that all Chronicles does?

9. Proverbs, Ecclesiastes, and Job are always found near or next to each other in biblical canons. What does that suggest about their interpretation?

CHAPTER 3

1. How does the canonical presentation in which the four Gospels are placed side by side influence the reading of the individual Gospels?

2. How does John's Gospel as the climax of the four Gospels provide a link with the rest of the New Testament books?

3. What difference does it make to the book of Acts when it plays the role of a preface to the Catholic Epistles or the Pauline Epistles?

4. Romans is given special prominence by being placed in premier position in the Pauline corpus. How might a reading of Romans influence the interpretation of the epistles that follow it in canonical order?

5. In what ways does the Letter to the Hebrews help to unify the epistolary material of the New Testament?

6. How does the collection known as the Catholic Epistles influence the reading of the seven individual letters that are brought together in this way?

7. How does the book of Revelation provide an effective conclusion to the witness of the New Testament to Jesus Christ?

CHAPTER 4

1. The titles assigned to the five books of the Pentateuch are quite different in the Hebrew and Greek canonical traditions. What alternative insights are provided to readers via these titles?

2. What is the best name for the book of Samuel, in which several characters vie for dominance?

3. Is the book of Kings well-named? Does the title mean to downplay the important role of prophets in its stories?

4. The different prophetic books are labeled according to the prophetic mouthpieces whose oracles they preserve. What is the value of these titles for readers? Are the titles open to being misinterpreted?

5. Is the title Ezra-Nehemiah appropriate for the joint book it labels? Give reasons for your answer.

6. Two Old Testament books are named after women (Ruth, Esther). Why are these titles appropriate?

7. Study the different titles assigned to the book of Psalms. What is the value of each as a guide to the reader?

8. What do the titles "The Song of Songs" and "The Song of Solomon" suggest about the meaning and message of this unique biblical book?

9. Consider the various names given to the book of Chronicles. What name is to be preferred?

CHAPTER 5

1. What do the titles assigned to the four Gospels ("The Gospel according to X") suggest about how they should be used and interpreted?

2. Is "Acts of the Apostles" a fitting title for the book it heads? What does it suggest about the book's contents and message?

3. Each of the letters of Paul is labeled according to the church to which it was addressed and sent. What is revealed and what is concealed by this method of naming and differentiating the apostle's letters?

4. Why was the Letter to the Hebrews given this name? Is the title appropriate?

5. Why was the collection of Catholic Epistles given this title? How might or should the bringing together of the seven letters influence the interpretation of the individual letters?

6. The title "Revelation" as an incipit drawn from Revelation 1:1 is appropriate enough, but how might it be misunderstood?

CHAPTER 6

1. The fourth Babylonian lesson (*parashah*) commences at Genesis 18:1 and, with the fifth *parashah* at 23:1, gives a credible two-part division of the first cycle of Abraham stories (chs. 12–17; 18–22). Why might chapter 18 be seen as a key turning point in the account about Abraham?

2. Judges 9:1 comes at the point where Abimelech is introduced into the narrative, and Judges 9 covers the account of his misrule. An alternative reading is provided by the *seder* division at 9:7 that comes immediately after Abimelech's installation in office (9:6). By linking 9:1–6 with Judges 8, what is implied? Is Gideon in any way to blame for Abimelech's disastrous experimentation with kingship?

3. As the chapter division stands, 1 Samuel 4:1 ("And the word of Samuel came to all Israel") is linked to what follows, but the RSV editors put 4:1a with the preceding material. What different understandings of this text are in play?

4. The chapter divisions of Kings sometimes highlight the coming of God's word to a prophet (1 Kgs 13:1; 16:1; 17:1; 2 Kgs 2:1; 7:1; 9:1). Why is this appropriate in a book whose common title is "Kings"? What does it suggest about the theology and message of the book?

5. The chapter division at Isaiah 37:1 serves to highlight Hezekiah's hearing and his response to the Assyrian threat, and a closed Hebrew paragraph also comes at this point. His reaction to the message is thereby highlighted. How important is Hezekiah in this narrative? The *seder* division occurs just before 37:20. What does this suggest is the main theological point the narrative wishes to make?

6. A number of times the *seder* divisions in Ezekiel are related to the "recognition formula," "and you/they shall know that I am the LORD" (22:16; 24:24; 29:21; 37:28; 39:22). Why is this highlighted?

7. The twelfth *seder* of the Twelve commences at the last verse of Micah (7:20) and covers the Nahum section. A similar pattern, with the lesson commencing with the final verse of a book, is found in the fifteenth (Zeph 3:20), sixteenth (Hag 2:23), and twenty-first *sedarim* (Zech 14:21). What does this regular arrangement imply? Are the twelve books of the Minor Prophets to be considered totally separate?

8. The speeches of Job end at 31:40, and its final line reads, "The words of Job are ended." What does the chapter division at 28:1 suggest about the content of chapter 28? Why was a break placed at this point? Does anything prevent this soliloquy being put in the mouth of Job?

9. Daniel 5:31 [= Aramaic 6:1] is the first mention of Darius and so is appropriate at the start of the Aramaic chapter. The Masoretic open paragraph coincides with the Aramaic chapter division. To which chapter does this pivotal verse belong? How might its significance change, depending on the chapter to which it belongs?

10. The Chronicler's special interest in the temple is highlighted by the start of the eleventh (1 Chr 28:10) and twelfth *sedarim* (2 Chr 2:4), which both concern Solomon's role as temple

builder. How do the chapter divisions at 2 Chronicles 2:1; 3:1; 5:1; and 8:1 support such a reading of Solomon's reign?

CHAPTER 7

1. The parables discourse in Matthew 13 finishes at 13:52, as indicated by the "when Jesus finished" formula in 13:53 (V92), rather than six verses later at 14:1 (A25, V93). What value might there being in placing 13:53-58 and 14:1-12 together? Do they share a common theme?

2. In the passion narrative of Mark's Gospel, Langton's chapter divisions at 14:1; 15:1; and 16:1 foreground certain episodes. What is their logic? What alternate logic do you see in the breaks in Vaticanus at 15:16 (V58), 15:24 (V59), and 15:38 (V60)?

3. The division at Luke 11:1 (A38, V81) may be justified by the introduction of the new topic of prayer (11:1-13), but how may the twin themes of love for God and love for neighbor, introduced by the lawyer's question (10:25-28), continue into chapter 11? Where is the best place to put a break?

4. John 9:1 (A10) marks the beginning of another "sign" narrative, the healing of the man born blind, as does the chapter division at 11:1 (A11), the raising of Lazarus. The division at 10:1 draws attention to the change in imagery to that of shepherd and sheep (10:1-18), but Alexandrinus combines chapters 9-10. What exegetical insight is suggested by Alexandrinus?

5. Should Acts 8:1a ("And Saul was consenting to his death") be put with Acts 7, in line with the RSV editors, who depart from the usual versification and place a paragraph break after this half-verse? Or 8:1-3 might have been joined with it as the immediate aftermath of Stephen's death (the start of V8 does not come till 8:4). Where is the break best placed?

6. At 1 Corinthians 7:1 Paul turns to matters about which the Corinthians wrote to him, so that the "Now concerning [topic]"

(*Peri de*) formula is found at 7:1 (V28), 25 (V29); 8:1 (V30); 12:1 (V36); and 16:1 (V42) and has influenced the chapter divisions of Langton and Vaticanus. The editors of the RSV view the break at 11:1 as unfortunate and place this verse with what precedes (V34 also starts at 11:2). Where is this break best placed and why?

7. Ephesians 5:21 may be a credible point of division ("Be subject to one another out of reverence for Christ"), providing a heading for the *Haustafel* that follows, hence the RSV paragraph break. A new section is signaled at 6:10 by the adverbial Greek phrase *tou loipou* ("finally"; V75) and the change in subject to that of "the whole armor of God." Is there any logic to Langton's breaks at 5:1 and 6:1?

BIBLIOGRAPHY

Aageson, James W. "The Pastoral Epistles, Apostolic Authority, and the Development of the Pauline Scriptures." In *The Pauline Canon*, edited by Stanley E. Porter, 5–26. PAST 1. Leiden: Brill, 2004.

Ackroyd, P. R. "A Judgment Narrative between Kings and Chronicles? An Approach to Amos 7:9–17." In *Canon and Authority: Essays in Old Testament Religion and Theology*, edited by George W. Coats and Burke O. Long, 71–87. Philadelphia: Fortress, 1977.

Aland, Barbara et al., eds. *The Greek New Testament*. 4th rev. ed. Stuttgart: Deutsche Bibelgesellschaft, 2001.

Alexander, T. Desmond. *From Paradise to the Promised Land: An Introduction to the Main Themes of the Pentateuch*. Carlisle: Paternoster, 1995.

Allegro, John M. *Qumrân Cave 4.1 (4Q158–4Q186)*. DJD 5. Oxford: Clarendon, 1968.

Allen, Garrick V. "Paratexts and the Reception History of the Apocalypse." *JTS* 70 (2019): 600–632.

Allen, Garrick V., and Kelsie G. Rodenbiker. "Titles of the New Testament (TiNT): A New Approach to Manuscripts and the History of Interpretation." *EC* 11 (2020): 265–80.

Allen, Leslie C. *The Books of Joel, Obadiah, Jonah, and Micah*. NICOT. Grand Rapids: Eerdmans, 1976.

Andersen, Francis I. "Yahweh, the Kind and Sensitive God." In *God Who Is Rich in Mercy: Essays Presented to Dr. D. B. Knox*, edited by Peter T. O'Brien and David G. Peterson, 41–88. Homebush West, NSW: Lancer Books, 1986.

Andrist, Peter. "Toward a Definition of Paratexts and Paratextuality: The Case of Ancient Greek Manuscripts." In *Bible as Notepad: Tracing Annotations and Annotation Practices in Late Antique and Medieval Biblical Manuscripts*, edited by Liv Ingeborg Lied and Marilena Maniaci, 130–49. MB 3. Berlin: de Gruyter, 2018.

Audet, J.-P. "A Hebrew-Aramaic List of the Books of the Old Testament in Greek Transcription." *JTS* 1 (1950): 135–54.

Auld, A. Graeme. *Kings without Privilege: David and Moses in the Story of the Bible's Kings*. Edinburgh: T&T Clark, 1994.

Aune, David E. *Prophecy in Early Christianity and the Ancient Mediterranean World*. Grand Rapids: Eerdmans, 1983.

———. *Revelation 1–5*. WBC 52a. Dallas: Word, 1997.

Bacon, B. W. *Studies in Matthew*. New York: Holt, 1930.

Balla, Peter. "Evidence for an Early Christian Canon (Second and Third Century)." In *The Canon Debate*, edited by L. M. McDonald and J. A. Sanders, 372–85. Peabody, MA: Hendrickson, 2002.

Banning, Joop H. A. van, SJ. "Reflections upon the Chapter Divisions of Stephan Langton." In *Method in Unit Delimitation*, edited by Marjo C. A. Korpel, Josef M. Oesch, and Stanley E. Porter, 141–61. Pericope 6. Leiden: Brill, 2007.

Barker, Paul A. "The Theology of Deuteronomy 27." *TynBul* 49 (1998): 277–303.

Barnes, W. E. *An Apparatus Criticus to Chronicles in the Peshitta Version with a Discussion of the Value of Codex Ambrosianus*. Cambridge: Cambridge University Press, 1897.

Barré, M. L. "Psalm 116: Its Structure and Its Enigmas." *JBL* 109 (1990): 61–79.

Barrett, C. K. *The Acts of the Apostles*. Vol. 1. ICC. Edinburgh: T&T Clark, 1994.

———. *The Second Epistle to the Corinthians*. 2nd ed. BNTC. London: Black, 1973.

Bartholomew, Craig G., and Michael W. Goheen. *The Drama of Scripture: Finding Our Place in the Biblical Story*. Grand Rapids: Baker Academic, 2004.

Barton, John. "'The Law and the Prophets': Who Are the Prophets?" In *The Old Testament: Canon, Literature and Theology: Collected Essays of John Barton*, 5–18. Aldershot: Ashgate, 2007.

———. *Oracles of God: Perceptions of Ancient Prophecy in Israel after the Exile*. London: Darton, Longman & Todd, 1986.

Bassler, Jouette M. *Divine Impartiality: Paul and a Theological Axiom*. SBLDS 59. Chico, CA: Scholars Press, 1982.

Basson, Alec. *Divine Metaphors in Selected Hebrew Psalms of Lamentation*. FAT 2/15. Tübingen: Mohr Siebeck, 2006.

Batten, Alicia J. *Friendship and Benefaction in James*. ESEC 15. Blandford Forum, UK: Deo, 2010.

Bauckham, Richard. *The Climax of Prophecy: Studies on the Book of Revelation*. Edinburgh: T&T Clark, 1993.

———. "The Gospel of Mark: Origins and Eyewitnesses." In *Earliest Christian History: History, Literature, and Theology: Essays from the Tyndale Fellowship in Honor of Martin Hengel*, edited by Michael F. Bird and Jason Maston, 145–69. WUNT 2/320. Tübingen: Mohr Siebeck, 2012.

———. *The Gospels for All Christians: Rethinking the Gospel Audiences*. Edinburgh: T&T Clark, 1998.

———. *James: Wisdom of James, Disciple of Jesus the Sage*. NTR. London: Routledge, 1999.

———. "Reading Scripture as a Coherent Story." In *The Art of Reading Scripture*, edited by Ellen F. Davis and Richard B. Hays, 38–53. Grand Rapids: Eerdmans, 2003.

———. *The Theology of the Book of Revelation*. Cambridge: Cambridge University Press, 1993.

Baum, Armin D. "The Original Epilogue (John 20:30–31), the Secondary Appendix (21:1– 23), and the Editorial Epilogues (21:24–25) of John's Gospel: Observations against the Background of Ancient Literary Conventions." In *Earliest Christian History: History, Literature, and Theology: Essays from the Tyndale Fellowship in Honor of Martin Hengel*, edited by Michael F. Bird and Jason Maston, 227–70. WUNT 2/320. Tübingen: Mohr Siebeck, 2012.

Bayard, Pierre. *How to Talk about Books You Haven't Read*. Translated by Jeffrey Mehlman. London: Granta Books, 2007.

Beale, G. K. *The Book of Revelation: A Commentary on the Greek Text*. NIGTC. Grand Rapids: Eerdmans, 1999.

———. *John's Use of the Old Testament in Revelation*. JSNTSup 166. Sheffield: Sheffield Academic, 1998.

Beckwith, Roger T. "The Early History of the Psalter." *TynBul* 46 (1995): 1–27.

———. *The Old Testament Canon of the New Testament Church and Its Background in Early Judaism*. London: SPCK, 1985.

Ben Zvi, Ehud. "Is the Twelve Hypothesis Likely from an Ancient Readers' Perspective?" In *Two Sides of a Coin: Juxtaposing Views on Interpreting the Book of the Twelve/the Twelve Prophetic Books*, edited by Ehud Ben Zvi and James D. Nogalski, 47–96. AG 201. Piscataway, NJ: Gorgias, 2009.

Berg, Sandra Beth. *The Book of Esther: Motifs, Themes and Structure*. SBLDS 44. Missoula, MT: Scholars Press, 1979.

Berger, Samuel. *Histoire de la Vulgate: Pendant les premiers siècles du moyen âge*. Hildesheim: Olms, 1976.

Berlin, Adele. *Poetics and Interpretation of Biblical Narrative.* BLS 9. Sheffield: Almond, 1983.

——. "A Search for a New Biblical Hermeneutics: Preliminary Observations." In *The Study of the Ancient Near East in the Twenty-First Century: The William Foxwell Albright Centennial Conference,* edited by Jerrold S. Cooper and Glenn M. Schwartz, 195–207. Winona Lake, IN: Eisenbrauns, 1996.

Best, Ernest. *Ephesians.* ICC. Edinburgh: T&T Clark, 1998.

——. "Ephesians i.1." In *Text and Interpretation: Studies in the New Testament Presented to Matthew Black,* edited by Ernest Best and R. McL. Wilson, 29–41. Cambridge: Cambridge University Press, 1979.

Birch, Bruce C., Walter Brueggemann, Terence E. Fretheim, and David L. Petersen. *A Theological Introduction to the Old Testament.* 2nd ed. Nashville: Abingdon, 2005.

Bird, Michael F. "The Unity of Luke-Acts in Recent Discussion." *JSNT* 29 (2007): 425–48.

Black, C. Clifton. *Mark: Images of an Apostolic Interpreter.* Columbia: University of South Carolina Press, 1994.

Blau, Ludwig. "Massoretic Studies III and IV." *JQR* 9 (1896–1897): 122–44, 471–90.

Blenkinsopp, Joseph. "Wisdom in the Chronicler's Work." In *In Search of Wisdom: Essays in Memory of John G. Gammie,* edited by Leo G. Perdue, Bernard Brandon Scott, and William Johnston Wiseman, 19–30. Louisville: Westminster John Knox, 1993.

Blomberg, Craig L. *The Historical Reliability of the Gospels.* 2nd ed. Downers Grove, IL: IVP Academic, 2007.

——. *The Historical Reliability of John's Gospel.* Leicester: Apollos, 2001.

Bogaert, Pierre-Maurice. "Ordres anciens des évangiles et tétraévangile en un seul codex." *RTL* 30 (1999): 297–314.

Boring, M. Eugene. "Mark 1:1–15 and the Beginning of the Gospel." *Semeia* 52 (1990): 43–81.

Botte, B., and Pierre-Maurice Bogaert. "Septante et versions grecques." In *Supplément au Dictionnaire de la Bible,* edited by L. Pirot and A. Roberts, 12:541–43. Paris: Letouzey & Ané, 1996.

Bovell, Carlos. "Symmetry, Ruth and Canon." *JSOT* 28 (2003): 175–91.

Brandt, Peter. *Endgestalten des Kanons: Das Arrangement der Schriften Israels in der jüdischen und christlichen Bibel.* BBB 131. Berlin: Philo, 2001.

Brenner, Athalya. "Women Poets and Authors." In *The Feminist Companion to the Song of Songs*, edited by Athalya Brenner, 86–97. Sheffield: JSOT, 1993.

Brown, Raymond E. *The Gospel according to John*. Vol. 1, *I–XII*. AB 29. London: Chapman, 1971.

———. *An Introduction to the Gospel of John*. Edited and updated by Francis J. Moloney. New York: Doubleday, 2003.

Brownlee, W. H. *The Meaning of the Qumrân Scrolls for the Bible: With Special Attention to the Book of Isaiah*. New York: Oxford University Press, 1964.

Bruce, F. F. *Commentary on the Book of the Acts: The English Text with Introduction, Exposition and Notes*. NICNT. Grand Rapids: Eerdmans, 1954.

Brueggemann, Walter. "Bounded by Obedience and Praise: The Psalms as Canon." *JSOT* 50 (1991): 63–92.

———. *The Creative Word: Canon as a Model for Biblical Education*. 2nd ed., rev. Amy Erickson. Minneapolis: Fortress, 2015.

Burridge, Richard A. *What Are the Gospels? A Comparison with Graeco-Roman Biography*. 2nd ed. Grand Rapids: Eerdmans, 2004.

Callan, Terrance. "Use of the Letter of Jude by the Second Letter of Peter." *Bib* 85 (2004): 42–64.

Campbell, A. F. *1 Samuel*. FOTL 7. Grand Rapids: Eerdmans, 2003.

———. *Of Prophets and Kings: A Late Ninth Century Document (1 Samuel 1–2 Kings 10)*. CBQMS 17. Washington, DC: Catholic Biblical Association of America, 1986.

Campbell, E. F. *Ruth*. AB 7. Garden City, NY: Doubleday, 1975.

Cargal, Timothy B. *Restoring the Diaspora: Discursive Structure and Purpose in the Epistle of James*. SBLDS 144. Atlanta: Scholars Press, 1993.

Carter, Warren. *Matthew: Storyteller, Interpreter, Evangelist*. Rev. ed. Peabody, MA: Hendrickson, 2004.

Childs, Brevard S. *Biblical Theology of the Old and New Testaments: Theological Reflection on the Christian Bible*. London: SCM, 1992.

———. *The Church's Guide for Reading Paul: The Canonical Shaping of the Pauline Corpus*. Grand Rapids: Eerdmans, 2008.

———. *Introduction to the Old Testament as Scripture*. London: SCM, 1979.

———. *The New Testament as Canon: An Introduction*. London: SCM, 1984.

Christianson, Eric S. *A Time to Tell: Narrative Strategies in Ecclesiastes*. JSOTSup 280. Sheffield: Sheffield Academic, 1998.

Clarke, Kent D. "Canonical Criticism: An Integrated Reading of Biblical Texts for the Community of Faith." In *Approaches to New Testament Study*, edited by Stanley E. Porter and David Tombs, 170–221. JSNTSup 120. Sheffield: Sheffield Academic, 1995.

Clements, R. E. "The Purpose of the Book of Jonah." In *Congress Volume: Edinburgh 1974*, edited by J. A. Emerton et al., 16–28. VTSup 28. Leiden: Brill, 1975.

Cole, Graham A. "Why a Book? Why This Book? Why the Particular Order within This Book? Some Theological Reflections on the Canon." In *The Enduring Authority of the Christian Scriptures*, edited by D. A. Carson, 456–76. Grand Rapids: Eerdmans, 2016.

Conrad, Edgar W. "The End of Prophecy and the Appearance of Angels/ Messengers in the Book of the Twelve." *JSOT* 73 (1997): 65–79.

———. *Reading the Latter Prophets: Toward a New Canonical Criticism*. JSOTSup 376. London: T&T Clark International, 2003.

Cooper, Alan. "In Praise of Divine Caprice: The Significance of the Book of Jonah." In *Among the Prophets: Language, Image, and Structure in the Prophetic Writings*, edited by Philip R. Davies and David J. A. Clines, 144–63. JSOTSup 144. Sheffield: Sheffield Academic, 1993.

Cowper, B. H. *Codex Alexandrinus: Hē Kainē Diathēkē. Novum Testamentum Graece ex antiquissimo codice Alexandrino a C .G. Woide olim descriptum*. London: David Nutt with Williams & Norgate, 1860.

Craigie, Peter C. *The Book of Deuteronomy*. NICOT. London: Hodder and Stoughton, 1976.

Cranfield, C. E. B. *The Gospel according to St Mark*. CGTC. Cambridge: Cambridge University Press, 1959.

Creach, Jerome F. D. *Yahweh as Refuge and the Editing of the Hebrew Psalter*. JSOTSup 217. Sheffield: Sheffield Academic, 1996.

Cullmann, Oscar. "The Plurality of the Gospels as a Theological Problem in Antiquity." In *The Early Church: Studies in Early Christian History and Theology*, edited by A. J. B. Higgins, 39–54. London: SCM, 1956.

Curtis, Byron G. "The Zion-Daughter Oracles: Evidence on the Identity and Ideology of the Late Redactors of the Book of the Twelve." In *Reading and Hearing the Book of the Twelve*, edited by James D. Nogalski and Marvin A. Sweeney, 166–84. SymS 15. Atlanta: Society of Biblical Literature, 2000.

Dahl, N. A. "The Particularity of the Pauline Epistles as a Problem in the Ancient Church." In *Neotestamentica et Patristica: Eine Freundesgabe, Herrn Professor Dr. Oscar Cullmann zu seinem 60. Geburtstag überreicht*, edited by W. C. van Unnik, 261–71. VTSup 6. Leiden: Brill, 1962.

Daise, Michael A. *Feasts in John: Jewish Festivals and Jesus' "Hour" in the Fourth Gospel.* WUNT 2/229. Tübingen: Mohr Siebeck, 2007.

Darnton, Robert. *The Case for Books, Past, Present, and Future.* New York: PublicAffairs, 2009.

———. "First Steps towards a History of Reading." *AJFS* 22 (1986): 5–30.

Davids, Peter. *The Epistle of James: A Commentary on the Greek Text.* NIGTC. Exeter: Paternoster, 1982.

Davies, Graham. "Dividing up the Pentateuch: Some Remarks on the Jewish Tradition." In *Leshon Limmudim: Essays on the Language and Literature of the Hebrew Bible in Honour of A. A. Macintosh*, edited by David A. Baer and Robert P. Gordon, 45–59. LHBOTS 593. London: Bloomsbury T&T Clark, 2013.

———. "The Theology of Exodus." In *In Search of True Wisdom: Essays in Old Testament Interpretation in Honour of Ronald E. Clements*, edited by Edward Ball, 137–52. JSOTSup 300. Sheffield: Sheffield Academic, 1999.

Davies, W. D., and Dale C. Allison Jr. *The Gospel according to Saint Matthew.* Vol. 1. ICC. Edinburgh: T&T Clark, 1988.

Dearman, J. Andrew, ed. *Studies in the Mesha Inscription and Moab.* ABS 2. Atlanta: Scholars Press, 1989.

Deines, Roland. "The Term and Concept of Scripture." In *What Is Bible?*, edited by Karin Finsterbusch and Armin Lange, 235–81. CBET 67. Leuven: Peeters, 2012.

Dekker, John T., and Anthony H. Dekker. "Centrality in the Book of Ruth." *VT* 68 (2018): 41–50.

Delling, G. "archō." *TDNT* 1:478–89.

Dempster, Stephen G. *Dominion and Dynasty: A Biblical Theology of the Hebrew Bible.* NSBT 15. Leicester: Apollos, 2003.

Denaux, Adelbert. "The Q-Logion Mt 11,27 / Luke 10,22 and the Gospel of John." In *John and the Synoptics*, edited by Adelbert Denaux, 163–99. BETL 101. Leuven: Peeters, 1992.

Dillard, Raymond B. "Reward and Punishment in Chronicles: The Theology of Immediate Retribution." *WTJ* 46 (1984): 164–72.

Donaldson, Terence L. *Jesus on the Mountain: A Study in Matthean Theology.* JSNTSup 8. Sheffield: JSOT, 1985.

Driver, G. R. *Semitic Writing from Pictograph to Alphabet: The Schweich Lectures of the British Academy 1944.* 3rd ed. London: Published for the British Academy, 1976.

Dukan, Michèle. *La Bible hébraïque: Les codices copiés en Orient et dans la zone séfarade avant 1280.* Bibliologia 22. Turnhout: Brepols, 2006.

Dumbrell, William J. "'In Those Days There Was No King in Israel; Every Man Did What Was Right in His Own Eyes': The Purpose of the Book of Judges Reconsidered." *JSOT* 25 (1983): 23–33.

———. "Malachi and the Ezra-Nehemiah Reforms." *RTR* 35 (1976): 42–52.

Dunnill, John. *Covenant and Sacrifice in the Letter to the Hebrews.* SNTSMS 75. Cambridge: Cambridge University Press, 1992.

Dyck, Elmer. "Jonah among the Prophets: A Study in Canonical Context." *JETS* 33 (1990): 63–73.

Ecco, Umberto. *Chronicles of a Liquid Society.* Translated by Richard Dixon. London: Vintage, 2018.

Edelman, Diana Vikander. *King Saul in the Historiography of Judah.* JSOTSup 121. Sheffield: Sheffield Academic, 1991.

Edwards, James R. "The Hermeneutical Significance of Chapter Divisions in Ancient Gospel Manuscripts." *NTS* 56 (2010): 413–26.

Ellington, John. "Translating Old Testament Book Titles." *BT* 34 (1983): 225–31.

Elliot, Mark W. "Ethics and Aesthetics in the Song of Songs." *TynBul* 45 (1994): 137–52.

Elliott, J. K. "Manuscripts, the Codex and the Canon." *JSNT* 63 (1996): 105–23.

Epstein, I., ed. *Baba Bathra.* Hebrew-English Edition of the Babylonian Talmud. New ed. Vol. 1. London: Soncino, 1976.

Eskenazi, Tamara Cohn. "The Chronicler and the Composition of 1 Esdras." *CBQ* 48 (1986): 39–61.

———. *In an Age of Prose: A Literary Approach to Ezra-Nehemiah.* SBLMS 36. Atlanta: Scholars Press, 1988.

Eves, Terry L. "One Ammonite Invasion or Two? I Sam 10:27–11:2 in the Light of 4QSam^a." *WTJ* 44 (1982): 308–26.

Farkasfalvy, Denis. "The Apostolic Gospels in the Early Church: The Concept of Canon and the Formation of the Four-Gospel Canon." In *Canon and Biblical Interpretation,* edited by Craig Bartholomew et al., 111–22. SHS 7. Milton Keynes: Paternoster, 2006.

Fee, Gordon D. *1 and 2 Timothy.* GNC. San Francisco: Harper & Row, 1984.

———. *The First Epistle to the Corinthians.* NICNT. Grand Rapids: Eerdmans, 1987.

Feneberg, Wolfgang. *Der Markusprolog: Studien zur Formbestimmung des Evangeliums.* SANT 36. München: Kösel, 1974.

Fewell, Danna Nolan. *Circle of Sovereignty: A Story of the Stories in Daniel 1–6.*

JSOTSup 72. Sheffield: Almond, 1988.

Filson, Floyd V. "Partakers with Christ: Suffering in First Peter." *Int* 9 (1955): 400–412.

Finegan, Jack. "The Original Form of the Pauline Collection." *HTR* 49 (1956): 85–103.

Fischer, J. A. "Pauline Literary Forms and Thought Patterns." *CBQ* 39 (1977): 209–23.

Fokkelman, J. P. *Reading Biblical Narrative: An Introductory Guide.* Translated by Ineke Smit. Louisville: Westminster John Knox, 1999.

———. *Reading Biblical Poetry: An Introductory Guide.* Translated by Ineke Smit. Louisville: Westminster John Knox, 2001.

France, R. T. "The Beginning of Mark." *RTR* 49 (1990): 11–19.

———. *Matthew: Evangelist and Teacher.* Exeter: Paternoster, 1989.

Francis, Fred O. "The Form and Function of the Opening and Closing Paragraphs of James and 1 John." *ZNW* 61 (1970): 110–26.

Freedman, David Noel. "The Symmetry of the Hebrew Bible." *ST* 46 (1992): 83–108.

———. *The Unity of the Hebrew Bible.* Ann Arbor: University of Michigan Press, 1991.

Friedländer, M., ed. and trans. *The Guide for the Perplexed.* 2nd rev. ed. New York: Dover, 1956.

Frye, Northrop. *The Great Code: The Bible and Literature.* London: Routledge & Kegan Paul, 1983.

Funk, Robert W. "The Form and Structure of II and III John." *JBL* 86 (1967): 424–30.

Gallagher, Edmon L., and John D. Meade. *The Biblical Canon Lists from Early Christianity: Texts and Analysis.* Oxford: Oxford University Press, 2017.

Garland, David E. "The Composition and Unity of Philippians: Some Neglected Literary Factors." *NovT* 27 (1985): 141–73.

Gathercole, Simon J. "The Titles of the Gospels in the Earliest New Testament Manuscripts." *ZNW* 104 (2013): 33–76.

Genette, Gérard. "Introduction to the Paratext." *NLH* 22 (1991): 261–72.

———. *Paratexts: Thresholds of Interpretation.* Translated by Jane E. Lewin. Cambridge: Cambridge University Press, 1997.

———. "Structure and Functions of the Title in Literature." *CI* 14 (1988): 692–720.

Ginsburg, Christian D. Introduction to the Massoretico-Critical Edition of the Hebrew Bible. New York: Ktav, 1966.

Ginzberg, Louis. *The Legends of the Jews.* Translated by Henrietta Szold. 7 vols. Philadelphia: Jewish Publication Society of America, 1911.

Goswell, Gregory. "Ancient Patterns of Reading: The Subdivision of the Acts of the Apostles in Codex Sinaiticus." *JGRChJ* 7 (2010): 68–97.

———. "Assigning the Book of Lamentations a Place in the Canon." *JESOT* 4 (2015): 1–19.

———. "The Attitude to Kingship in the Book of Judges." *TJ* 40 (2019): 3–18.

———. "Authorship and Anonymity in the New Testament Writings." *JETS* 60 (2017): 733–49.

———. "The Bifurcation of the Prophecy of Joel and Its Theology of Reversal." In *Les délimitations éditoriales des Écritures des bibles anciennes aux lectures modernes*, edited by Guillaume Bady and Marjo C. A. Korpel, 85–105. Pericope 11. Leuven: Peeters, 2020.

———. "The Book of Ruth and the House of David." *EvQ* 86 (2014): 116–29.

———. "The Canonical Position(s) of the Book of Daniel." *ResQ* 59 (2017): 129–40.

———. "The Divisions of the Book of Daniel." In *The Impact of Unit Delimitation on Exegesis*, edited by Raymond de Hoop, Marjo C. A. Korpel, and Stanley E. Porter, 89–114. Pericope 7. Leiden: Brill, 2009.

———. "An Early Commentary on the Pauline Corpus: The Capitulation of Codex Vaticanus." *JGRChJ* 8 (2011–2012): 51–82.

———. "Early Readers of the Gospels: The *kephalaia* and *titloi* of Codex Alexandrinus." *JGRChJ* 6 (2009): 134–74.

———. "The Early Readership of the Catholic Epistles." *JGRChJ* 13 (2018): 129–51.

———. "Finding a Home for the Letter to the Hebrews." *JETS* 59 (2016): 747–60.

———. "Having the Last Say: The End of the OT." *JETS* 58 (2015): 15–30.

———. "Is Ruth Also among the Wise?" In *Exploring Old Testament Wisdom: Literature and Themes*, edited by David G. Firth and Lindsay Wilson, 115–33. London: Apollos, 2016.

———. "The Johannine Corpus and the Unity of the New Testament Canon." *JETS* 61 (2018): 717–33.

———. "Jonah among the Twelve Prophets." *JBL* 135 (2016): 283–99.

———. "Keeping God Out of the Book of Esther." *EvQ* 82 (2010): 99–110.

———. "King and Cultus: The Image of David in the Book of Kings." *JESOT* 5.2 (2016–2017): 167–86.

———. "The Macro-Structural Role of the Former Prophets and the Historical Books in Old Testament Canons." *JETS* 63 (2020): 455–71.

———. "The Main Character of the Book of Esther: The Contribution of the Textual Divisions and the Assigned Titles of the Book of Esther to Uncovering its Protagonist" *JSOT* 60 (2021): 193–205.

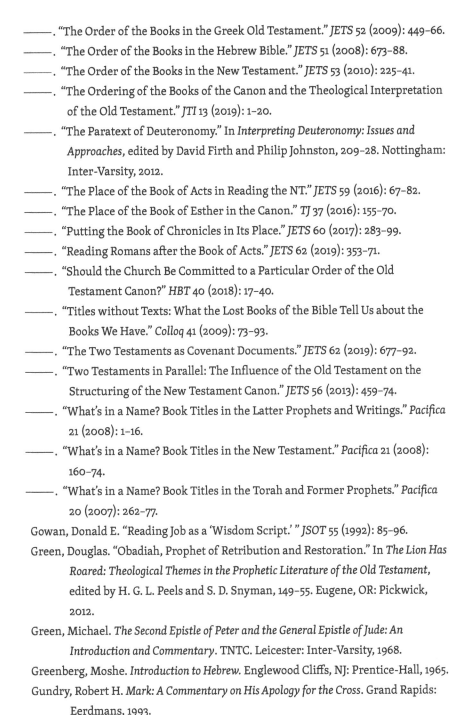

———. "The Order of the Books in the Greek Old Testament." *JETS* 52 (2009): 449–66.

———. "The Order of the Books in the Hebrew Bible." *JETS* 51 (2008): 673–88.

———. "The Order of the Books in the New Testament." *JETS* 53 (2010): 225–41.

———. "The Ordering of the Books of the Canon and the Theological Interpretation of the Old Testament." *JTI* 13 (2019): 1–20.

———. "The Paratext of Deuteronomy." In *Interpreting Deuteronomy: Issues and Approaches*, edited by David Firth and Philip Johnston, 209–28. Nottingham: Inter-Varsity, 2012.

———. "The Place of the Book of Acts in Reading the NT." *JETS* 59 (2016): 67–82.

———. "The Place of the Book of Esther in the Canon." *TJ* 37 (2016): 155–70.

———. "Putting the Book of Chronicles in Its Place." *JETS* 60 (2017): 283–99.

———. "Reading Romans after the Book of Acts." *JETS* 62 (2019): 353–71.

———. "Should the Church Be Committed to a Particular Order of the Old Testament Canon?" *HBT* 40 (2018): 17–40.

———. "Titles without Texts: What the Lost Books of the Bible Tell Us about the Books We Have." *Colloq* 41 (2009): 73–93.

———. "The Two Testaments as Covenant Documents." *JETS* 62 (2019): 677–92.

———. "Two Testaments in Parallel: The Influence of the Old Testament on the Structuring of the New Testament Canon." *JETS* 56 (2013): 459–74.

———. "What's in a Name? Book Titles in the Latter Prophets and Writings." *Pacifica* 21 (2008): 1–16.

———. "What's in a Name? Book Titles in the New Testament." *Pacifica* 21 (2008): 160–74.

———. "What's in a Name? Book Titles in the Torah and Former Prophets." *Pacifica* 20 (2007): 262–77.

Gowan, Donald E. "Reading Job as a 'Wisdom Script.'" *JSOT* 55 (1992): 85–96.

Green, Douglas. "Obadiah, Prophet of Retribution and Restoration." In *The Lion Has Roared: Theological Themes in the Prophetic Literature of the Old Testament*, edited by H. G. L. Peels and S. D. Snyman, 149–55. Eugene, OR: Pickwick, 2012.

Green, Michael. *The Second Epistle of Peter and the General Epistle of Jude: An Introduction and Commentary*. TNTC. Leicester: Inter-Varsity, 1968.

Greenberg, Moshe. *Introduction to Hebrew*. Englewood Cliffs, NJ: Prentice-Hall, 1965.

Gundry, Robert H. *Mark: A Commentary on His Apology for the Cross*. Grand Rapids: Eerdmans, 1993.

Haglund, Erik. *Historical Motifs in the Psalms.* ConBOT 23. Uppsala: Gleerup, 1984.

Hall, David R. *The Unity of the Corinthian Correspondence.* JSNTSup 251. London: T&T Clark International, 2003.

Hansen, G. Walter. *Abraham in Galatians: Epistolary and Rhetorical Contexts.* JSNTSup 29. Sheffield: JSOT, 1989.

Harris, Murray J. *The Second Epistle to the Corinthians: A Commentary on the Greek Text.* NIGTC. Grand Rapids: Eerdmans, 2005.

Hatch, W. H. P. "The Position of Hebrews in the Canon of the New Testament." *HTR* 29 (1936): 133–52.

Hellerman, Joseph H. *Reconstructing Honor in Roman Philippi: Carmen Christi as Cursus Pudorum.* SNTSMS 132. Cambridge: Cambridge University Press, 2005.

Henderson, Joseph M. "Who Weeps in Jeremiah VIII 23 (IX 1)? Identifying Dramatic Speakers in the Poetry of Jeremiah." *VT* 52 (2002): 191–206.

Hengel, Martin. *Studies in the Gospel of Mark.* London: SCM, 1985.

Hennecke, E., and W. Schneemelcher. *New Testament Apocrypha.* English translation edited by R. McL. Wilson. 2 vols. Philadelphia: Westminster, 1964.

Hieke, Thomas. "Jedem Ende wohnt ein Zauber inne … Schlussverse jüdischer und christlicher Kanonausprägungen." In *Formen des Kanons: Studien zu Ausprägungen des biblischen Kanons von der Antike bis zum 19. Jahrhundert*, edited by Thomas Hieke, 225–52. SBS 228. Stuttgart: Katholisches Bibelwerk, 2013.

Hill, Charles E. "Rightly Dividing the Word: Uncovering an Early Template for Textual Division in John's Gospel." In *Studies on the Text of the New Testament and Early Christianity: Essays in Honour of Michael W. Holmes*, edited by Daniel Grunter, Juan Hernández Jr., and Paul Foster, 221–42. NTTSD 50. Leiden: Brill, 2015.

Hobbs, T. R. "2 Kings 1 and 2: Their Unity and Purpose." *SR* 13 (1984): 327–34.

Holmes, Stephen R. *Listening to the Past: The Place of Tradition in Theology.* Grand Rapids: Baker Academic, 2002.

House, Paul R. *Old Testament Theology.* Downers Grove, IL: InterVarsity, 1998.

———. *The Unity of the Twelve.* JSOTSup 97. Sheffield: Almond, 1990.

Humphreys, W. L. "A Life-Style for Diaspora: A Study of the Tales of Esther and Daniel." *JBL* 92 (1973): 211–23.

Hurtado, Larry W. *The Earliest Christian Artifacts: Manuscripts and Christian Origins*. Grand Rapids: Eerdmans, 2006.

Jackson, Kevin. *Invisible Forms: A Guide to Literary Curiosities*. New York: Thomas Dunne Books, 1999.

Jacobs, Louis. *Structure and Form in the Babylonian Talmud*. Cambridge: Cambridge University Press, 1991.

Japhet, Sara. *I and II Chronicles: A Commentary*. OTL. London: SCM, 1993.

Jerome. *Praefationes Sancti Hieronymi in Liber Paralipomenon*. In *Biblia Sacra, Iuxta Latinam Vulgatam Versionem*, vol. 7, *Verba Dierum*. Rome: Typis Polyglottis Vaticanis, 1948.

Johnstone, William. "Guilt and Atonement: The Theme of 1 and 2 Chronicles." In *A Word in Season: Essays in Honour of William McKane*, edited by J. D. Martin and P. R. Davies, 113–38. JSOTSup 42. Sheffield: Sheffield Academic, 1986.

———. "Hope of Jubilee: The Last Word in the Hebrew Bible." *EvQ* 72 (2000): 307–14.

Jones, Bruce W. "More about the Apocalypse as Apocalyptic." *JBL* 87 (1968): 325–27.

———. "Two Misconceptions about the Book of Esther." *CBQ* 39 (1977): 171–81.

Jongkind, Dirk. *An Introduction to the Greek New Testament, Produced at Tyndale House, Cambridge*. Wheaton, IL: Crossway, 2019.

Jongkind, Dirk, et al., eds. *The Greek New Testament, Produced at Tyndale House, Cambridge*. Wheaton, IL: Crossway, 2017.

Kalimi, Isaac. *The Retelling of Chronicles in Jewish Tradition and Literature: A Historical Journey*. Winona Lake, IN: Eisenbrauns, 2009.

Karrer, M. *Die Johannesoffenbarung als Brief: Studien zu ihrem literarischen, historischen und theologischen Ort*. FRLANT 140. Göttingen: Vandenhoeck & Ruprecht, 1986.

Karris, Robert J. "The Background and Significance of the Polemic of the Pastoral Epistles." *JBL* 92 (1973): 549–64.

Kaufman, Stephen A. "The Structure of the Deuteronomic Law." *Maarav* 1/2 (1978–1979): 105–58.

Keil, C. F. *The Minor Prophets*. Translated by J. Martin. COT 10. Reprint, Grand Rapids: Eerdmans, 1980.

Kenyon, Frederic G., ed. *The Chester Beatty Biblical Papyri Descriptions and Texts of Twelve Manuscripts on Papyrus of the Greek Bible: Fasciclus III Supplement Pauline Epistles*. London: Emery Walker, 1936.

———. *The Codex Alexandrinus (Royal MS. 1 D V-VIII) in Reduced Photographic Facsimile: Old Testament Part III Hosea–Judith.* British Museum. London: Longmans, 1936.

Kidner, Derek. *Genesis: An Introduction and Commentary.* TOTC. Leicester: Inter-Varsity, 1967.

———. *Psalms 1–72: An Introduction and Commentary on Books I and II of the Psalms.* TOTC. London: Inter-Varsity, 1973.

Kimble, Jeremy M., and Ched Spellman. *Invitation to Biblical Theology: Exploring the Shape, Storyline, and Themes of the Bible.* ITS. Grand Rapids: Kregel, 2020.

Kingsbury, J. D. "The Gospel in Four Editions." *Int* 33 (1979): 363–75.

Klein, Ralph W. *First Samuel.* WBC 10. Waco, TX: Word Books, 1983.

Klein, William W., Craig L. Blomberg, and Robert L. Hubbard Jr. *Introduction to Biblical Interpretation.* 3rd ed. Grand Rapids: Zondervan, 2017.

Knobel, Peter S. *The Targum of Qohelet: Translated, with a Critical Introduction, Apparatus, and Notes.* ArBib 15. Collegeville, MN: Liturgical Press, 1991.

Knoppers, Gary N., and Paul B. Harvey Jr. "Omitted and Remaining Matters: On the Names Given to the Book of Chronicles in Antiquity." *JBL* 121 (2002): 227–43.

Koester, Helmut. "From the Kerygma-Gospel to Written Gospels." *NTS* 35 (1989): 361–81.

Koorevaar, Hendrik J. "Chronicles as the Intended Conclusion to the Old Testament Canon." In *The Shape of the Writings*, edited by Julius Steinberg and Timothy J. Stone, 207–36. Siphrut 16. Winona Lake, IN: Eisenbrauns, 2015.

———. "The Torah Model as Original Macrostructure of the Hebrew Canon: A Critical Evaluation." *ZAW* 122 (2010): 64–80.

Korpel, Marjo C. A. "Introduction to the Series Pericope." In *Delimitation Criticism: A New Tool in Biblical Scholarship*, edited by Marjo C. A. Korpel and Josef M. Oesch, 1–50. Pericope 1. Assen: Van Gorcum, 2000.

———. *The Structure of the Book of Ruth.* Pericope 2. Assen: Van Gorcum, 2001.

———. "Unit Delimitation as a Guide to Interpretation: A Status Quaestionis." In *Les délimitations éditoriales des Écritures des bibles anciennes aux lectures modernes*, edited by Guillaume Bady and Marjo C. A. Korpel, 3–33. Pericope 11. Leuven: Peeters, 2020.

———. "Unit Division in the Book of Ruth: With Examples from Ruth 3." In *Delimitation Criticism: A New Tool in Biblical Scholarship*, edited by Marjo C. A. Korpel and Josef M. Oesch, 131–39. Pericope 1. Assen: Van Gorcum, 2000.

Köstenberger, Andreas J. *The Jesus of the Gospels: An Introduction.* Grand Rapids: Kregel, 2020.

———. "John's Transposition Theology: Retelling the Story of Jesus in a Different
Key." In *Earliest Christian History: History, Literature, and Theology: Essays
from the Tyndale Fellowship in Honor of Martin Hengel*, edited by Michael F.
Bird and Jason Maston, 191–26. WUNT 2/320. Tübingen: Mohr Siebeck, 2012.

———. "The Seventh Johannine Sign: A Study in John's Christology." *BBR* 5 (1995):
87–103.

———. *A Theology of John's Gospel and Letters: The Word, the Christ, the Son of God.*
BTNT. Grand Rapids: Zondervan, 2009.

Kruger, Michael J. "The Authenticity of 2 Peter." *JETS* 42 (1999): 645–71.

———. *The Question of Canon: Challenging the Status Quo in the New Testament Debate.*
Nottingham: Apollos, 2013.

Kümmel, W. G. *Introduction to the New Testament.* Rev. ed. Translated by Howard
Clark Kee. London: SCM, 1975.

Kutsko, John F. *Between Heaven and Earth: Divine Presence and Absence in the Book of
Ezekiel.* BJSUCSD 7. Winona Lake, IN: Eisenbrauns, 2000.

Kwakkel, Gert. "Under Yahweh's Wings." In *Metaphors in the Psalms*, edited by Antje
Labahn and Pierre Van Hecke, 141–65. BETL 231. Leuven: Peeters, 2010.

Labuschagne, C. J. "The Literary and Theological Function of Divine Speech in the
Pentateuch." In *Congress Volume: Salamanca 1983*, edited by J. A. Emerton,
154–73. VTSup 36. Leiden: Brill, 1985.

Lacocque, André. *The Book of Daniel.* London: SPCK, 1979.

Lambert, W. G., and A. R. Millard. *Atra-hasis: The Babylonian Story of the Flood.*
Oxford: Clarendon, 1969.

Lambrecht, Jan. "Thanksgivings in 1 Thessalonians 1–3." In *The Thessalonians
Debate: Methodological Discord or Methodological Synthesis?*, edited by Karl P.
Donfried and Johannes Beutler, 135–62. Grand Rapids: Eerdmans, 2000.

Landy, Francis. "The Song of Songs." In *The Literary Guide to the Bible*, edited
by Robert Alter and Frank Kermode, 305–19. Cambridge, MA: Harvard
University Press, 1987.

LaRocca-Pitts, Mark. *The Day of Yahweh: The Use and Development of Yahweh's Motive
on That Day as a Rhetorical Strategy by the Hebrew Prophets.* Saarbrücken:
VDM Verlag, 2009.

Lau, Peter H. W., and Gregory Goswell. *Unceasing Kindness: A Biblical Theology of
Ruth.* NSBT 41. London: Apollos, 2016.

Lee, Dorothy A. *The Symbolic Narratives of the Fourth Gospel: The Interplay of Form
and Meaning.* JSNTSup 95. Sheffield: Sheffield Academic, 1994.

Liebreich, Leon J. "The Compilation of the Book of Isaiah." *JQR* 46 (1956): 258–77.

Lindars, Barnabas. "The Rhetorical Structure of Hebrews." *NTS* 35 (1989): 382–406.

———. "Torah in Deuteronomy." In *Words and Meanings: Essays Presented to David Winton Thomas*, edited by P. R. Ackroyd, 117–36. Cambridge: Cambridge University Press, 1968.

Loader, J. A. "Tenach and Old Testament—the Same Bible?" *TS* 58 (2002): 1415–30.

Lockett, Darian. *Letters from the Pillar Apostles: The Formation of the Catholic Epistles as a Canonical Collection*. Eugene, OR: Pickwick, 2017.

———. "Limitations of a Purely Salvation-Historical Approach to Biblical Theology." *HBT* 39 (2017): 211–31.

Longenecker, Richard N. *Acts*. EBC. Grand Rapids: Zondervan, 1995.

Longman, Tremper, III. *Song of Songs*. NICOT. Grand Rapids: Eerdmans, 2001.

Luc, Alex. "The Titles and Structure of Proverbs." *ZAW* 112 (2000): 252–55.

Lührmann, Dieter. "Gal 2 9 und die katholischen Briefe: Bemerkungen zum Kanon und zur regula fidei." *ZNW* 72 (1981): 65–87.

Maclean, Marie. "Pretexts and Paratexts: The Art of the Peripheral." *NLH* 22 (1991): 273–79.

MacRae, Allan A. "The Book Called 'Numbers.' " *BSac* 111 (1954): 47–53.

Malamat, A. "Charismatic Leadership in the Book of Judges." In *Magnalia Dei: The Mighty Acts of God; Essays on the Bible and Archeology in Memory of G. Ernest Wright*, edited by F. M. Cross et al., 152–68. Garden City, NY: Doubleday, 1976.

Mandolfo, Carleen R. *Daughter Zion Talks Back to the Prophets: A Dialogic Theology of the Book of Lamentations*. SemeiaSt 58. Atlanta: Society of Biblical Literature, 2007.

Marcus, David. "Alternate Chapter Divisions in the Pentateuch in the Light of the Masoretic Sections." *HS* 44 (2003): 119–28.

Margolis, Max L. *The Hebrew Scriptures in the Making*. Philadelphia: Jewish Publication Society of America, 1922.

Marshall, I. Howard. *The Epistles of John*. NICNT. Grand Rapids: Eerdmans, 1978.

———. *The Gospel of Luke: A Commentary on the Greek Text*. NIGTC. Exeter: Paternoster, 1978.

Matthews, Victor H. "Kings of Israel: A Question of Crime and Punishment." In *SBL 1988 Seminar Papers*, edited by David J. Hull, 517–26. Atlanta: Scholars Press, 1988.

Mattill, A. J., Jr. "The Jesus-Paul Parallels and the Purpose of Luke-Acts." *NovT* 17 (1975): 15–46.

McCarthy, Dennis J. "The Theology of Leadership in Joshua 1–9." *Bib* 52 (1971): 165–75.

McDonald, Lee Martin. *The Biblical Canon: Its Origin, Transmission, and Authority.* Peabody: MA: Hendrickson, 2007.

———. *The Formation of the Biblical Canon. Vol. 1, The Old Testament: Its Authority and Canonicity.* London: Bloomsbury T&T Clark, 2017.

Menken, M. J. J. "The Structure of 2 Thessalonians." In *The Thessalonian Correspondence*, edited by Raymond F. Collins, 373–82. BETL 87. Leuven: Peeters, 1990.

Metzger, Bruce M. *The Canon of the New Testament: Its Origin, Development, and Significance.* Oxford: Clarendon, 1987.

———. *The Text of the New Testament: Its Transmission, Corruption and Restoration.* 2nd ed. Oxford: Clarendon, 1968.

———. *A Textual Commentary on the Greek New Testament.* 2nd ed. Stuttgart: Bibelgesellschaft, 1994.

Miles, Jack. *God: A Biography.* New York: Knopf, 1995.

Millar, J. Gary. *Now Choose Life: Theology and Ethics in Deuteronomy.* NSBT 6. Leicester: Apollos, 1998.

Millard, A. R. "'Scriptio Continua' in Early Hebrew: Ancient Practice or Modern Surmise?" *JSS* 15 (1970): 2–15.

Milne, H. J. M., and T. C. Skeat. *Scribes and Correctors of the Codex Sinaiticus.* London: British Museum, 1938.

Moessner, David P. "'The Christ Must Suffer': New Light on the Jesus-Peter, Stephen, Paul Parallels in Luke-Acts." *NovT* 28 (1986): 220–56.

Moo, Douglas J. *The Letter of James.* PNTC. Grand Rapids: Eerdmans, 2000.

Moore, G. F. "The Vulgate Chapters and Numbered Verses in the Hebrew Bible." In *The Canon and Masorah of the Hebrew Bible: An Introductory Reader*, edited by Sid Z. Leiman, 815–20. New York: Ktav, 1974.

Morgan, Robert. "Which Was the Fourth Gospel? The Order of the Gospels and the Unity of Scripture." *JSNT* 54 (1994): 3–28.

Morris, Leon L. *Jesus Is the Christ: Studies in the Theology of John.* Grand Rapids: Eerdmans, 1989.

Mounce, William D. *Pastoral Epistles.* WBC 46. Nashville: Thomas Nelson, 2000.

Muilenburg, James. "Form Criticism and Beyond." *JBL* 88 (1969): 1–18.

Munck, Johannes. "Evangelium Veritatis and Greek Usage as to Book Titles." *ST* 17 (1963): 133–38.

Murphy, Roland E. "The Classification 'Wisdom Psalms.' " In *Congress Volume Bonn 1962*, edited by G. W. Anderson et al., 156–67. VTSup 9. Leiden: Brill, 1963.

Murphy-O'Connor, Jerome. *Paul the Letter-Writer: His World, His Options, His Skills.* GNS 41. Collegeville, MN: Liturgical Press, 1995.

Nasuti, Harry P. *Defining the Sacred Songs: Genre, Tradition and the Post-critical Interpretation of the Psalms.* JSOTSup 218. Sheffield: Sheffield Academic, 1999.

———. "A Prophet to the Nations: Diachronic and Synchronic Readings of Jeremiah 1." *HAR* 10 (1987): 248–66.

Naveh, J. "Word Division in West Semitic Writing." *IEJ* 23 (1973): 206–8.

Neusner, Jacob, trans. *The Talmud of Babylonia: An American Translation, XXII.A: Tractate Baba Batra, Chapters 1–2.* BJS 239. Atlanta: Scholars Press, 1992.

Nicklas, Tobias. "The Apocalypse in the Framework of the Canon." In *Revelation and the Politics of Apocalyptic Interpretation*, edited by Richard B. Hays and Stefan Alkier, 143–53. Waco, TX: Baylor University Press, 2012.

Niebuhr, Karl-Wilhelm. "Der Jakobusbrief im Licht frühjüdischer Diasporabriefe." *NTS* 44 (1998): 420–43.

Noble, Paul R. "The Literary Structure of Amos: A Thematic Analysis." *JBL* 114 (1995): 209–26.

Nogalski, James. *Redactional Processes in the Book of the Twelve.* BZAW 218. Berlin: de Gruyter, 1993.

Noth, Martin. *The Deuteronomistic History.* JSOTSup 15. Sheffield: JSOT, 1981.

O'Brien, Mark A. "The 'Deuteronomistic History' as a Story of Israel's Leaders." *ABR* 37 (1989): 14–34.

O'Brien, Peter T. *Introductory Thanksgivings in the Letters of Paul.* NovTSup 49. Leiden: Brill, 1977.

Oesch, Josef M. *Petucha und Setuma: Untersuchungen zu einer überlieferten Gliederung im hebräischen Text des Alten Testaments.* OBO 27. Freiburg: Universitätsverlag, 1979.

———. "Textgliederung im Alten Testament und in den Qumranhandschriften." *Hen* 5 (1983): 289–321.

Ogden, Graham S. "'Vanity' It Certainly Is Not." *BT* 38 (1987): 301–7.

Olley, John W. "'Hear the Word of YHWH': The Structure of the Book of Isaiah in 1QIsaᵃ." *VT* 43 (1993): 19–49.

———. "Re-Versing Tradition: The Influence of Sense-Divisions in Reading the Bible Then and Now." *ABR* 62 (2014): 31–43.

———. "Texts Have Paragraphs Too—A Plea for Inclusion in Critical Editions." *Textus* 19 (1998): 111–25.

Olsen, Dennis T. *The Death of the Old and the Birth of the New: The Framework of Numbers and the Pentateuch.* BJS 71. Chico, CA: Scholars Press, 1985.

Orlinsky, Harry M. "Prolegomenon: The Masoretic Text: A Critical Evaluation." In *Introduction to the Massoretico-Critical Edition of the Hebrew Bible,* by C. D. Ginsburg, i–xlv. New York: Ktav, 1966.

Parker, David C. *An Introduction to the New Testament Manuscripts and Their Texts.* Cambridge: Cambridge University Press, 2008.

Parkes, M. B. *Pause and Effect: An Introduction to the History of Punctuation in the West.* Aldershot: Scolar Press, 1992.

Parris, David P. *Reading the Bible with Giants: How 2000 Years of Biblical Interpretation Can Shed Light on Old Texts.* Milton Keynes: Paternoster, 2006.

Payne, Robin. "The Prophet Jonah: Reluctant Messenger and Intercessor." *ExpTim* 100 (1989): 131–34.

Penkower, Jordan S. "The Chapter Divisions in the 1525 Rabbinic Bible." VT 48 (1998): 350–74.

———. "Verse Divisions in the Hebrew Bible." VT 50 (2000): 379–93.

Perrot, Charles. "The Reading of the Bible in the Ancient Synagogue." In *Mikra: Text, Translation, Reading and Interpretation of the Hebrew Bible in Ancient Judaism and Early Christianity,* edited by Martin Jan Mulder, 137–59. Assen: Van Gorcum, 1990.

Pervo, Richard I. *Dating Acts: Between the Evangelists and the Apologists.* Santa Rosa, CA: Polebridge, 2006.

Pesch, Rudolf. "Zur konzentrischen Strukur von Jona 1." *Bib* 47 (1966): 577–81.

Peterlin, Davorin. *Paul's Letter to the Philippians in the Light of Disunity in the Church.* NovTSup 79. Leiden: Brill, 1995.

Petersen, David L. "Portraits of David: Canonical and Otherwise." *Int* 40 (1986): 130–42.

Pope, Marvin H. "Isaiah 34 in Relation to Isaiah 35, 40–66." *JBL* 71 (1952): 235–43.

———. *Song of Songs.* AB 7C. Garden City, NY: Doubleday, 1977.

Porter, Stanley E. *The Paul of Acts: Essays in Literary Criticism, Rhetoric, and Theology.* WUNT 115. Tübingen: Mohr Siebeck, 1999.

———. "When and How Was the Pauline Canon Compiled? An Assessment of Theories." In *The Pauline Canon,* edited by Stanley E. Porter, 95–127. PAST 1. Leiden: Brill, 2004.

Praeder, Susan Marie. "Jesus-Paul, Peter-Paul, and Jesus-Peter Parallelisms in
    Luke-Acts: A History of Reader Response." In *SBL 1982 Seminar Papers*,
    edited by Kent Harold Richards, 23–39. Chico, CA: Scholars Press, 1984.

Prior, Michael. *Paul the Letter-Writer and the Second Letter to Timothy*. JSNTSup 23.
    Sheffield: JSOT, 1989.

Provan, Iain W. "Reading Texts against a Historical Background: The Case of
    Lamentations 1." *SJOT* 1 (1990): 130–43.

Qimron, E., and J. Strugnell. *Qumrân Cave 4.V: Miqsat Ma'ase ha-Torah*. DJD 10.
    Oxford: Clarendon, 1984.

Quinn, Jerome D. "𝔓⁴⁶: The Pauline Canon?" *CBQ* 36 (1974): 379–85.

Rahlfs, A., ed. *Septuaginta*. 2 vols. Stuttgart: Deutsche Bibelstiftung, 1935.

Rendtorff, Rolf. *The Canonical Hebrew Bible: A Theology of the Old Testament*.
    Translated by David E. Orton. TBS 7. Leiden: Deo, 2005.

———. *The Old Testament: An Introduction*. Translated by John Bowden. London: SCM,
    1985.

Richards, E. Randolph. "The Codex and the Early Collection of Paul's Letters." *BBR*
    8 (1998): 151–66.

———. *The Secretary in the Letters of Paul*. WUNT 2/42. Tübingen: Mohr Siebeck, 1991.

———. "Silvanus Was Not Peter's Secretary: Theological Bias in Interpreting *dia
    Silouanou ... egrapsa* in 1 Peter 5:12." *JETS* 43 (2000): 417–32.

Riley, William. *King and Cultus in Chronicles: Worship and the Reinterpretation of
    History*. JSOTSup 160. Sheffield: Sheffield Academic, 1993.

Robinson, John A. T. *The Priority of John*. Edited by J. F. Coakley. London: SCM, 1985.

Ryle, H. E. *Philo and Holy Scripture*. London: Macmillan, 1895.

Sailhamer, John H. "Biblical Theology and the Composition of the Hebrew Bible."
    In *Biblical Theology: Retrospect and Prospect*, edited by Scott J. Hafemann,
    25–37. Downers Grove, IL: InterVarsity, 2002.

———. *Introduction to Old Testament Theology: A Canonical Approach*. Grand Rapids:
    Zondervan, 1995.

———. *The Meaning of the Pentateuch: Revelation, Composition and Interpretation*.
    Downers Grove, IL: InterVarsity, 2009.

Sarna, Nahum. "The Authority and Interpretation of Scripture in Jewish Tradition."
    In *Understanding Scripture: Explorations of Jewish and Christian Traditions of
    Interpretation*, edited by Clemens Thoma and Michael Wyschogrod, 9–20.
    New York: Paulist, 1987.

Sawyer, John F. A. "A Change of Emphasis in the Study of the Prophets." In *Israel's*

Prophetic Heritage: Essays in Honour of Peter R. Ackroyd, edited by Richard Coggins, 233–49. Cambridge: Cambridge University Press, 1982.

Schmid, Hansjörg. "How to Read the First Epistle of John Non-Polemically." *Bib* 85 (2004): 24–41.

Schnackenburg, Rudolf. *The Gospel according to John*. Vol. 3, *Commentary on Chapters 13–21*. Tunbridge Wells: Burns & Oates, 1982.

Schreiner, Thomas R. *Romans*. BECNT. Grand Rapids: Baker, 1998.

Scott, R. B. Y. *The Way of Wisdom in the Old Testament*. New York: Macmillan, 1971.

Seitz, Christopher R. *The Goodly Fellowship of the Prophets: The Achievement of Association in Canon Formation*. Grand Rapids: Baker Academic, 2009.

———. *Prophecy and Hermeneutics: Toward a New Introduction to the Prophets*. STI. Grand Rapids: Baker Academic, 2007.

Seow, C. L. "Qohelet's Autobiography." In *Fortunate the Eyes That See: Essays in Honor of David Noel Freedman in Celebration of His Seventieth Birthday*, edited by Astrid B. Beck et al., 275–87. Grand Rapids: Eerdmans, 1995.

Shea, William H. "Further Literary Structures in Daniel 2–7: An Analysis of Daniel 4." *AUSS* 23 (1985): 193–202.

Siker, Jeffrey S. *Liquid Scripture: The Bible in a Digital World*. Minneapolis: Fortress, 2017.

Skeat, T. C. "The Codex Sinaiticus, the Codex Vaticanus and Constantine." *JTS* 50 (1999): 583–625.

Smalley, Beryl. *The Study of the Bible in the Middle Ages*. Oxford: Basil Blackwell, 1952.

Smith, Christopher R. "The Structure of the Book of Revelation in Light of Apocalyptic Literary Conventions." *NovT* 36 (1994): 373–93.

Smith, D. Moody. "John, the Synoptics, and the Canonical Approach to Exegesis." In *Tradition and Interpretation in the New Testament: Essays in Honor of E. Earle Ellis*, edited by Gerald F. Hawthorne with Otto Betz, 166–80. Grand Rapids: Eerdmans, 1987.

Smith, David E. *The Canonical Function of Acts: A Comparative Analysis*. Collegeville, MN: Liturgical Press, 2002.

Smith, W. Andrew. *A Study of the Gospels in Codex Alexandrinus: Codicology, Palaeography, and Scribal Hands*. NTTSD 48. Leiden: Brill, 2014.

Snaith, Norman H. *Sefer Torah, Nevi'im uKetuvim*. London: British and Foreign Bible Society, 1958.

Soden, H. F. von. *Die Schriften des Neuen Testaments I. Teil Untersuchungen I. Abteilung die Textzeugen*. Berlin: Arthur Glaue, 1902.

Souter, A. *The Text and Canon of the New Testament*. London: Duckworth, 1912.

Spellman, Ched. "The Canon after Google: Implications of a Digitized and Destabilized Codex." *HTR* 16 (2010): 39–42.

———. *Toward a Canon-Conscious Reading of the Bible: Exploring the History and Hermeneutics of the Canon*. NTM 34. Sheffield: Sheffield Phoenix, 2014.

Stanton, Graham N. "The Early Reception of Matthew's Gospel: New Evidence from Papyri?" In *The Gospel of Matthew in Current Study: Studies in Memory of William G. Thompson S.J.*, edited by David E. Aune, 42–61. Grand Rapids: Eerdmans, 2011.

———. "The Fourfold Gospel." *NTS* 43 (1997): 317–46.

Steinmann, Andrew E. "The Structure and Message of the Book of Job." *VT* 46 (1996): 85–100.

Stendahl, Krister. "The Apocalypse of John and the Epistles of Paul in the Muratorian Fragment." In *Current Issues in New Testament Interpretation: Essays in Honor of Otto A. Piper*, edited by William Klassen and Graydon F. Snyder, 239–45. London: SCM, 1962.

Stevens, Chris S. *History of the Pauline Corpus in Texts, Transmissions and Trajectories: A Textual Analysis of Manuscripts from the Second to the Fifth Century*. TENTS 14. Leiden: Brill, 2020.

Stone, Timothy H. *The Compilational History of the Megilloth: Canon, Contoured Intertextuality and Meaning in the Writings*. FAT 2/59. Tübingen: Mohr Siebeck, 2013.

Sweeney, Marvin A. "Sequence and Interpretation in the Book of the Twelve." In *Reading and Hearing the Book of the Twelve*, edited by James D. Nogalski and Marvin A. Sweeney, 49–64. SymS 15. Atlanta: Society for Biblical Literature, 2000.

———. "Tanak versus Old Testament: Concerning the Foundation for a Jewish Theology of the Bible." In *Problems in Biblical Theology: Essays in Honor of Rolf Knierim*, edited by Henry T. C. Sun and Keith L. Eades with James M. Robinson and Garth I. Moller, 353–72. Grand Rapids: Eerdmans, 1997.

———. *The Twelve Prophets*. Vol. 1, *Hosea, Joel, Amos, Obadiah, Jonah*. BO. Collegeville, MN: Liturgical Press, 2000.

Swete, H. B. *The Apocalypse of St John*. 3rd ed. London: Macmillan, 1909.

Swetnam, James. "Form and Content in Hebrews 1–6." *Bib* 53 (1972): 368–85.

———. "On the Literary Genre of the 'Epistle' to the Hebrews." *NovT* 11 (1969): 261–69.

Tam, Josaphat C. "When Papyri and Codices Speak: Revisiting John 2:23–25." *Bib* 95

(2014): 570–88.

Tannehill, Robert C. *The Narrative Unity of Luke-Acts: A Literary Interpretation.* Vol. 2, *The Acts of the Apostles.* Minneapolis: Fortress, 1990.

Thomas, John C. *The Spirit of the New Testament.* Leiderdorp: Deo, 2005.

Thrall, Margaret E. *The Second Epistle to the Corinthians.* Vol. 1, *Introduction and Commentary on II Corinthians I–VII.* ICC. Edinburgh: T&T Clark, 1994.

Tõniste, Külli. *The Ending of the Canon: A Canonical and Intertextual Reading of Revelation 21–22.* LNTS 526. London: Bloomsbury T&T Clark, 2016.

Tov, Emanuel. *The Greek Minor Prophets Scroll from Naḥal Ḥever (8ḤevXIIgr) (The Seiyâl Collection I).* DJD 8. Oxford: Clarendon, 1990.

———. *Textual Criticism of the Hebrew Bible.* Minneapolis: Fortress, 1992.

Trebolle-Barrera, Julio. "Qumran Evidence for a Biblical Standard Text and for Non-standard and Parabiblical Texts." In *The Dead Sea Scrolls in Their Historical Context,* edited by Timothy H. Lim with Graeme Auld, Larry W. Hurtado, and Alison Jack, 89–106. Edinburgh: T&T Clark, 2000.

Trobisch, David. *Die Entstehung der Paulusbriefsammlung: Studien zu den Anfängen christlicher Publizistik.* NTOA 10. Freiburg: Universitätsverlag, 1989.

———. *The First Edition of the New Testament.* Oxford: Oxford University Press, 2000.

———. *Paul's Letter Collection: Tracing the Origins.* Minneapolis: Augsburg Fortress, 1994.

Troxel, Ronald L. *Joel: Scope, Genre(s), and Meaning.* CSHB 6. Winona Lake, IN: Eisenbrauns, 2015.

Van Leeuwen, Raymond C. "Scribal Wisdom and Theodicy in the Book of the Twelve." In *In Search of Wisdom: Essays in Memory of John G. Gammie,* edited by Leo G. Perdue, Bernard Brandon Scott, and William Johnston Wiseman, 31–49. Louisville: Westminster John Knox, 1993.

Vanhoye, Albert. *La structure littéraire de l'Épitre aux Hébreux.* Paris: Desclée de Brouwer, 1963.

Vernoff, Charles Elliott. "The Contemporary Study of Religion and the Academic Teaching of Judaism." In *Methodology in the Academic Teaching of Judaism,* edited by Zev Garber, 15–40. Studies in Judaism. Lanham, MD: University Press of America, 1986.

Vogels, Walter. "La Structure symétrique de la Bible chrétienne." In *The Biblical Canons,* edited by J.-M. Auwers and H. J. de Jonge, 295–304. BETL 163. Leuven: Peeters, 2003.

Wal, A. van der. "The Structure of Amos." *JSOT* 26 (1983): 107–13.

Wall, Robert W. "The Acts of the Apostles." *NIB* 10:1–368.

———. "The Acts of the Apostles in Canonical Context." *BTB* 18 (1988): 16–24.

———. "The Apocalypse of the New Testament in Canonical Context." In *The New Testament as Canon: A Reader in Canonical Criticism*, ed. Robert W. Wall and Eugene E. Lemcio, 274–98. JSNTSup 76. Sheffield: JSOT, 1992.

———. "The Canonical View." In *Biblical Hermeneutics: Five Views*, edited by Stanley E. Porter and Beth M. Stovell, 111–30. Downers Grove, IL: InterVarsity, 2012.

———. "The Problem of the Multiple Letter Canon of the New Testament." *HBT* 8 (1986): 1–31.

———. "The Significance of a Canonical Perspective of the Church's Scripture." In *The Canon Debate*, edited by L. M. McDonald and J. A. Sanders, 528–40. Peabody, MA: Hendrickson, 2002.

———. "A Unifying Theology of the Catholic Epistles: A Canonical Approach." In *The Catholic Epistles and the Tradition*, edited by Jacques Schlosser, 43–71. BETL 176. Leuven: Peeters, 2004.

Wall, Robert W., and Eugene E. Lemcio. *The New Testament as Canon: A Reader in Canonical Criticism*. JSNTSup 76. Sheffield: JSOT, 1992.

Wallraff, Martin, and Patrick Andrist. "Paratexts of the Bible: A New Research Project on Greek Textual Transmission." *EC* 6 (2015): 237–43.

Walters, Stanley D. "Reading Samuel to Hear God." *CTJ* 37 (2002): 62–81.

Walton, Steve. "Where Does the Beginning of Acts End?" In *The Unity of Luke-Acts*, edited by J. Verheyden, 447–67. BETL 142. Leuven: Peeters, 1999.

Watson, Duane F. "A Rhetorical Analysis of Philippians and Its Implications for the Unity Question." *NovT* 30 (1988): 57–88.

Watson, Francis. *Paul and the Hermeneutics of Faith*. London: T&T Clark International, 2004.

Wegner, Paul D. *The Journey from Texts to Translations: The Origin and Development of the Bible*. Grand Rapids: Baker, 1999.

Wenham, Gordon J. "The Coherence of the Flood Narrative." *VT* 28 (1978): 336–48.

———. *Story as Torah: Reading the Old Testament Ethically*. Edinburgh: T&T Clark, 2000.

Whybray, R. N. "Qoheleth, Preacher of Joy." *JSOT* 23 (1982): 87–98.

Williams, Ronald J. *Hebrew Syntax: An Outline*. 2nd ed. Toronto: University of Toronto Press, 1976.

Williams, Sam K. "The 'Righteousness of God' in Romans." *JBL* 99 (1980): 241–90.

Williamson, H. G. M. *Israel in the Books of Chronicles.* Cambridge: Cambridge University Press, 1977.

Wilson, Gerald H. "Shaping the Psalter: A Consideration of Editorial Linkage in the Book of Psalms." In *The Shape and Shaping of the Psalter*, edited by J. Clinton McCann Jr., 72–82. JSOTSup 159. Sheffield: JSOT, 1993.

———. "'The Words of the Wise': The Intent and Significance of Qohelet 12:9–14." *JBL* 103 (1984): 175–92.

Wilson, Walter I. *The Hope of Glory: Education and Exhortation in the Epistle to the Colossians.* NovTSup 88. Leiden: Brill, 1997.

Wolfenson, L. B. "Implications of the Place of the Book of Ruth in Editions, Manuscripts, and Canon of the Old Testament." *HUCA* 1 (1924): 151–78.

Woolf, Virginia. *The Common Reader: Second Series.* Edited by Andrew McNeille. London: Hogarth, 1986.

Yarchin, William. "Is There an Authoritative Shape for the Book of Psalms? Profiling the Manuscripts of the Hebrew Psalter." *RB* 122 (2015): 355–70.

Yee, Gale A. "I Have Perfumed My Bed with Myrrh: The Foreign Woman in Proverbs 1–9." *JSOT* 43 (1989): 53–68.

Yeivin, Israel. *Introduction to the Tiberian Masorah.* Edited and translated by E. J. Revell. MasS 5. Missoula, MT: Scholars Press, 1980.

SUBJECT INDEX

Abraham, 38, 106, 126
Acts, 121, 181
  apostles, 110–12
  book title, 110–12, 122
  canon placement, 60–64
  Catholic Epistles and, 62–63
  Gospels and, 61, 62–63
  Luke, Gospel of and, 59, 60–61, 74, 110, 111–12
  Paul in, 61–63, 110–11, 122
  Pauline Epistles and, 61, 113–14, 121
  Peter in, 61–63
  text divisions, 158–59
Adath Deborim, 98, 100
Aleppo codex, 3, 25, 27n54, 29, 137n35
Alexandrinus (A) codex
  New Testament divisions, 150–52, 153–58, 166–67, 203
  New Testament ordering, 62, 70n74, 72n81
  New Testament titles, 118, 151
  Old Testament ordering, 33, 41–44, 45, 49n50, 50–51, 90
  Old Testament titles, 82–85, 92, 94, 97n60, 99, 100n70, 101
Allen, Garrick V., 104n2
Allen, Leslie, 139
Allison, Dale, 106, 155n24
Amos, book of, 22–23, 91, 138–39
ancient readers, 3–4, 6, 18, 24, 46, 52, 73, 121, 157, 163, 175, 179
apocalyptic, 73, 117n55, 118–19, 122, 138, 170n70, 176
apocryphal books, 34, 36–37, 43, 50n53, 111. See also individual books
apostles, 110–12

Athanasius, 67n62, 68
Augustine of Hippo, 4, 55n7, 92
Aune, David E., 118n56, 119n60
authors, 2, 91–92
  canon ordering by, 69–71, 74, 173–74
  Gospels, 105, 107–9
  Paul, of Hebrews, 67–68, 69–70, 114–15

Babylonian Talmud, 17, 26, 92, 129
  Baba Batra, 17–18, 19–21, 26, 27n52, 46, 99
Barton, John, 86
Bassler, Jouette, 160
Bauckham, Richard, 63, 109, 117, 119n61, 168n64, 181n5
Bayard, Pierre, 54n1
Beale, G. K., 119n59
Beckwith, Roger T., 17n14, 17n17, 20n24, 27n52
Ben Asher family, 129
Berlin, Adele, 178n2
Bomberg Rabbinical Bibles, 89, 99, 128
Book of the Twelve. See Minor Prophets, the Twelve
Boring, Eugene, 106–7, 155n25
Brownlee, W. H., 135

Campbell, A. F., 88, 90n38
canonical ordering, 3, 5–6, 11–12, 173–75, 181
  author groupings, 69–71, 74, 173–74
  geographical, 22–23
  historical, chronological, 13–15, 21–23, 26–27, 29, 75, 173–74
  by length, 17, 20, 27, 64, 66, 68, 70, 173
  liturgical, 27–28, 48–49

thematic, 20–21, 23–25, 26–27, 45, 46–48, 52, 70–71, 174
Zionist motivation, 33–34
Catholic Epistles, 57, 62, 71, 167
  Acts and, 62–63
  book titles, 112–13, 117–18
  canon order, 70–71
  Hebrews, book of and, 68–69, 114–15
chapter divisions, 127–28
  Hebrew Bible, 126, 128–29, 143, 144–45
  Vulgate, 127–28, 141
  See also text divisions
Childs, Brevard, 15, 64n50, 65n53, 68n69
Christian Bible, 35
  Hebrew Bible and, 32–34
  Christianson, Eric S., 97n59
1–2 Chronicles, 3–4, 27, 33, 37, 147
  book title, 100–101
  Ezra-Nehemiah and, 25–26, 29, 31, 40–42
  Hebrew Bible, end of, 25–26, 27, 29, 31, 33, 35
  as history, 27, 100
  Kings and, 27, 40–41, 52, 101–2
  as wisdom book, 14–15
Clarke, Kent D., 73n87
Clement of Alexandria, 110, 112n35
Colossians, 113–14, 163
commentary, commentaries, 4, 127, 171
  paratext as, 6–7, 63
  text divisions as, 127, 143, 156, 162, 165, 171, 178
  titles as, 104, 121, 175–76
  context, canon, 11–12, 41, 51–54, 63
  interpretation and, 24, 31, 46, 51–53, 174–75, 180–82
Cooper, Alan, 24
1–2 Corinthians, 115, 160–61
Craigie, Peter C., 85n21
Cranfield, C. E. B., 156
critical theories, 4–5, 46, 85, 109, 118n57
  biblical, 178–79
Cyril of Jerusalem, 110

Dahl, N. A., 66n58, 114n40
Daniel, book of, 24, 99, 119, 146–47
  canonical placement, 27, 30, 33, 43, 49–51, 52
  Esther and, 15, 26–27, 30
  Daniel as prophet, 49–50
Darnton, Robert, 6
David, 19, 29–30, 40, 88–89, 134
  dynasty, 41, 48, 143
  Psalms and, 88, 93, 140
  Ruth and, 46–47, 51–52
Davies, W. D., 106, 155n24
Dead Sea Scrolls, 21–22, 128–29, 134, 135, 137n35
Deuteronomy, 16, 38–39, 82, 85, 132
Dibelius, Martin, 112n32

early church, 34, 49–50, 60, 61–62, 67
early readers, 3–4, 6, 18, 24, 46, 52, 73, 121, 157, 163, 175, 179
Ecclesiastes, 26, 28, 30, 44, 49, 95–96, 144
Ecco, Umberto, 182
Edelman, Diana, 88
Edwards, James R., 152n15
Elliot, J. K., 67n62
English Bibles, 34
  book titles, 85–86, 92, 94–97
  canon order, 39n20, 42–43, 44–45, 60, 68–69
  early, 68–69
  text divisions, 129, 131–32, 139–40, 144–45, 153, 162
Ephesians, 113, 162
Ephraemi, Codex, 72n81, 114
Epiphanius, 92
eschatology, 23, 26, 32–33, 44–45, 70, 135
1–2 Esdras, 41–42
Eskenazi, Tamara, 41–42
Esther, book of, 27–28, 35, 39–40, 98, 145
  Ahasuerus, 42, 98, 145, 177
  Daniel and, 15, 26–27, 30
  wisdom and, 42–43
Eusebius, 48n45, 63n45, 67n62, 70n73
Exodus, 15, 83, 131

Ezra-Nehemiah, 24–25, 30, 39–40, 147
  book title, 99–100
  canon placement, 25–26, 27, 29, 31, 35,
    41–43, 46
  Chronicles and, 25–26, 29, 31, 40–42
Ezekiel, book of, 18, 20, 21, 91, 136

Farkasfalvy, Denis, 106n9
Fee, Gordon D., 160n40, 165
final form, 4–5
Fokkelman, J. P., 134
Former Prophets, 12, 14, 16–19, 21, 30,
    39, 86
  book titles, 86–90
Freedman, David Noel, 29

Galatians, 115, 161
Genesis, book of, 15, 81, 82, 106, 126–23
  Revelation and, 73, 74–75
  text divisions, 130–31
Genette, Gérard, 1n1, 80, 83–84, 95, 101,
    104, 111, 113, 175
Geneva Bible, 153
genres, 42, 174–75
  apocalyptic, 118–19
  Gospel, 60–61
  interpretation and, 75, 80, 103, 122,
    174, 179
  letters, 71–72, 112–13, 169
  narratives, 50, 72, 86, 89–91, 107, 110–11,
    126–27
  title and, 104–5, 175–76
  wisdom literature, 14–15, 26, 43–44,
    94–95, 95–97
Ginsburg, Christian D., 98n65
gospel, 104–5
Gospels, 57, 60–61
  authors, 105, 107–9
  book titles, 104–110
  canon ordering, 54–60
  chapter titles, 151–52
  text divisions, 149–50, 154–58
  witnesses, 57, 70, 71, 105, 108, 117–18
Greek New Testaments

canon order, 63–64, 67–68
critical editions, modern, 152–53
text divisions, 149–54

Greek Old Testament, 34
  book titles, 82, 85, 89–90, 93–94, 101
  Hebrew Bible and, 33, 37, 51
  historical books, 35, 37, 39–43
  historical ordering, 30, 32, 35, 37, 39, 41,
    51–52, 97
  Pentateuch, 33, 34–35, 36, 37–39
  poetic books, 33, 35, 43–44
  prophetic books, 35, 36, 44–45
  See also Septuagint
Greenberg, Moshe, 81
Green, Douglas, 139n40

Habakkuk, book of, 22, 24
Haggai, book of, 140
Haggai-Zechariah-Malachi, 16, 17, 20,
    22, 24–25
Hansen, Walter, 161
Hatch, W. H. P., 68n68
Hebrew Bible, 3, 34, 126
  book titles, 82, 84, 86–92, 93–97,
    100–101
  chapter divisions, 126, 128–29, 143,
    144–45
  Chronicles and, 25–26, 27, 29, 31, 33, 35
  Former Prophets, 12, 14, 16–17, 18–19, 21,
    30, 86–90
  Latter Prophets, 12, 14, 16–17, 19–25, 30,
    45, 90–92
  Mishnah, 84, 94n51
  Psalms, 140–41
  Tanak, 14, 25–26, 32, 35, 92–93
  Torah, 12, 14, 15–16
  tripartite structure, 11–15
  verse divisions, 129–30
  Writings, 3, 13, 25–30, 48, 52, 92–93
Hebrews, book of, 67–70, 112–13, 166–67
  Catholic Epistles and, 68–69, 114–15
  Paul as author, 67–68, 69–70, 114–15
Hengel, Martin, 105

Hill, Charles E.,
historical books, 35, 86
histories, biblical, 14
    canon order, 13–15, 21–23, 26–27, 29, 75, 173–74
    salvation, 32–33, 44–45, 72, 157, 181
Holy Spirit, 61, 73, 112
Hosea, book of, 22–23, 91, 137
Hurtado, Larry W., 149n1

interpretation, biblical, 4–5, 179–80
    book titles, 79–81, 100–101, 104–5, 176, 180
    canonical context, 24, 31, 46, 51–53, 174–75, 180–82
    comparing texts, 60, 65
    genres and, 75, 80, 103, 122, 174, 179
    Minor Prophets, 23–24
    Old Testament, 13–14, 18
    text divisions, 126–27, 137–38, 143, 146, 148–49, 163, 171, 177–78
Irenaeus, 55, 110
Isaac, 38
Isaiah, book of, 18, 20, 91, 135

Jackson, Kevin, 79
James, book of, 70–71, 112, 117
    Paul and, 68–69, 167, 168
    text divisions, 167-68
James, brother of Jesus, 57, 62, 70–71
Jashar, Book of, 87
Jeremiah, book of, 18, 20–21, 26, 91, 136
    Lamentations and, 49, 52, 97
Jerome, 3n11, 48n45, 99n68, 101n72
Jerusalem Council, 62, 110
Jesus Christ, as Son of God, 57, 58–59
Job, book of, 27, 44, 94, 141–42
Joel, book of, 23, 137–38
John, apostle, 57, 74, 118
1–3 John, epistles, 58, 73, 112–13, 117, 169–70
    canon placement, 57, 70–71
John, Gospel of, 73

book title, 107–9
canon placement, 55, 56
signs, 57–58
Son of God, 58–59
Synoptics and, 55, 57, 58–59, 105
text divisions, 157–58
Jonah, book of, 23–24, 91–92, 139
Jones, Bruce W., 119n58
Joseph of Constantinople, 98
Josephus, 48n45, 93
    prophets, 16n12, 37, 50, 99n68
Joshua, 18, 86–87
Joshua, book of, 18–19, 86–87, 133
Judaism, 50, 85
    Mishnah, 84, 94n51
    seder readings, 129, 130–34, 135, 136–40, 142–43, 144–48
    See also Talmud
Jude, book of, 70–71, 117, 170
Jude, brother of Jesus, 57, 70–71
Judges, 18–19, 48, 87–88, 133
judgment, 24–25
Judith, book of, 42–43

Kalimi, Isaac, 33–34
Keil, C. F., 22
Kidner, Derek, 126n7, 141n48
kindness, 46–47, 95
1–2 Kings, 19, 89–90
    Chronicles and, 27, 40–41, 52, 101–2
    Isaiah and, 19–20
    Jeremiah and, 20–21
    Samuel and, 18, 86, 89–90
    text divisions, 134–35
kings, kingship, 18–19, 20, 21, 85, 88–89
Koorevaar, Hendrik, 3
Korpel, Marjo C. A., 125n1, 143n52, 143n55
Kümmel, W. G., 110

Labuschagne, C. J., 132n23
Lambrecht, Jan, 164n52

Lamentations, book of, 26–28, 30, 48–49, 97, 144–45
Langton, Stephen
  New Testament divisions, 153, 156–57, 159–62, 164–65, 167–69, 203–4
  Old Testament divisions, 127–28, 130–34, 138, 140, 143
Latin Bible, 34, 63–64
  book titles, 89, 95, 97, 101
  See also Vulgate
Latter Prophets, 12, 14, 16–17, 19–25, 30, 90–92
law, 82, 85
leadership, 21, 87
Leningrad Codex, 3, 25, 27, 29, 47, 141
Leviticus, 15, 83–84, 131–32
Lewis, C. S., 121
Lockett, Darian, 182n7
Longenecker, Richard, 159
Luke, Gospel of, 56–57, 62, 156–57
  Acts and, 59, 60–61, 74, 110, 111–12
  book title, 105, 107, 108
  preface, 55–56, 110
Luther, Martin, 69

1–2 Maccabees, 34
Maimonides, 50
Malachi, book of, 33, 91–92, 140
Marcion, Marcionite, 60n28, 67, 110
Mark, Gospel of, 57, 59n23, 61n35, 62
  book title, 106–7, 108
  Matthew and, 55, 56, 60, 105
  text divisions, 155–56
Masoretes, 127, 143
Masoretic Text (MT), 16, 21, 100, 134, 142
  Kings and Isaiah, 19–20
  Minor Prophets, 21–22, 23, 45
  proto-, 35
Matthew, Gospel of, 56,
  book title, 104, 108
  Mark and, 55, 56, 60, 105
  priority, 55–56
  text divisions, 154–55
medieval manuscripts, 27, 99–100

Megillot, 13, 27–29, 30, 47–48, 52
Melito of Sardis, 16n12, 48n45, 50, 93, 95n52, 99n68
Menken, M. J. J., 164
Metzger, Bruce, 55n5, 116n48, 118n57, 153
Micah, book of, 24, 139
Miles, Jack, 34
Minor Prophets, the Twelve, 12, 16–17, 18, 92, 137n36
  canon ordering of, 21–25, 45
  interpretation, 23–24
  text divisions, 137–40
Moabite stone, 125–26
Moses, 16, 38–39, 85, 131
Muilenburg, James, 127n9
Muratorian Fragment, 63n45, 66n57, 67, 110

Nahum, book of, 22, 24, 139
narrative, 50, 72, 86, 89–91, 107, 110–11, 126–27
  frameworks, 19, 39, 181–82
nations, the, 23–24, 38–39, 39–40
Nehemiah, book of. See Ezra-Nehemiah, book of
New Testament, 120–21
  canon order, 62–64, 67–69, 72, 74–75
  Old Testament and, 32–34, 35, 39, 119–20
Noth, Martin, 40
Numbers, book of, 15–16, 84, 132

Obadiah, book of, 23, 138–39
O'Brien, Peter, 163
Oesch, Josef, 128
Old Testament, title, 119–21. See also Greek Old Testament; Hebrew Bible; Septuagint (LXX)
Olley, John W., 128n14, 154n19
Olsen, Dennis, 84
order, canon. See canonical ordering
Origen of Alexandria, 48n45, 50, 99, 108n19
Orthodox churches, 63

paratext, 63, 180-82
  definition, 1-3, 7
  as educational, 182-83
  titles as, 79-81
Parkes, M. B., 149n2
Paul, apostle, 57, 108
  in Acts, 61-63, 110-11, 122
  Hebrews, book of, 67-68, 69-70, 114-15
  Peter and, 61-62, 118
Pauline Epistles, 167
  𝔓46, 64n49, 65-66n57, 68, 113n39
  Acts and, 61, 113-14, 121
  book titles, 113-16
  canon order, 64-67
  canon placement, 61-63
  corpus writing, 115-16
  James and, 68-69, 167, 168
  Pastoral, 66, 114
  Revelation and, 66-67, 71
  superscriptions, 115-16
  text divisions, 150, 159-66
  theological primacy, 63-64, 68-69
Pentateuch, 15, 30, 81-83, 84-85, 102,
    129, 181
  Greek Bible and, 33, 34-35, 36, 37-39
  Megillot and, 28-29
  text divisions, 130-32, 141
Pervo, Richard, 61
Pesch, Rudolf, 139n41
Peshitta Syriac, 101
Peter, apostle, 57, 107, 108
  in Acts, 61-63
  Paul and, 61-62, 118
1-2 Peter, 70-71, 113, 117, 168-69
Philemon, letter to, 66, 114, 166
Philippians, 65-66, 162-63
Philo, 83n16, 93
poetic books, 35, 36, 44-45
Prior, Michael, 65n55
prophetic books, 35, 36, 90
Prophets, division, 12, 14, 16-18, 32-33
  pairing of, 17-18
  text divisions, 133-40
  See also Former Prophets; Latter
    Prophets

prophets, 21, 91-92, 119
Protestants, 34, 64
Proverbs, 27, 28, 44, 47
  Solomon and, 94-95, 142
Psalms, 27, 29
  book title, 93-94
  canon placement, 43-44
  David and, 88, 93, 140
  Ruth and, 46-47
  titles, 140-41
  as wisdom book, 43-44, 52, 93-94

Qoheleth, Ecclesiastes, 26, 28, 30, 44, 49,
    144
  Solomon and, 95-96
Quinn, Jerome D., 65n57
Qumran, 21-22, 128-29, 134, 135, 137n35

Rashi, 4, 85
readers, 63, 117, 169-70, 178-79
  authority, 2, 6-7
  early, ancient, 3-4, 6, 18, 24, 46, 52, 73,
    121, 157, 163, 175, 179
  knowledge, 57-58, 114, 180-83
  modern, 5, 7, 131, 179-81
Reformation, Reformers, 34
Rendtorff, Rolf, 81
restoration, 24-25,
  postexilic, 25-30
Revelation, 109, 118-19, 170
  canon order, 71-75
  Genesis and, 73, 74-75
  as letter, 71-73
  Pauline Epistles and, 66-67, 71
Richards, E. Randolph, 114n51
Robinson, John A. T., 57n14, 58
Rodenbiker, Kelsie G., 104n2
Romans, 64-65, 74, 115-16, 159-60
Rost, Leonhard, 89-90
Ruth, book of, 28, 29-30, 49, 95, 143
  canon placement, 26, 33, 46-48
  David and, 46-47, 51-52
  Psalms and, 46-47

Sailhamer, John H., 25, 143n54
Samuel, books of, 19, 88-89
  Kings and, 18, 86, 89-90
  text divisions, 133-34
Samuel, prophet, 88
Saul, 88, 89, 134
Schmid, Hansjörg, 117n55
Schnackenburg, Rudolf, 107
seder readings, 129, 130-34, 135, 136-40,
  142-43, 144-48
Sephardic Codices, 27
Septuagint (LXX), 49, 52, 92, 146, 173
  Former Prophets, 48, 86-88, 90
  Minor Prophets, 21n29, 23
  New Testament, 106, 119
  Pentateuch titles, 82-83, 84-85
  Psalms, 93-94, 141
  Writings, 93-95, 97, 100-101
Siker, Jeffrey S., 180n3
Sinaiticus (א) Codex, 141
  New Testament divisions, 150-51, 153,
    158-59, 166-67
  New Testament ordering, 62, 70n74
  New Testament titles, 113n39, 118,
    151-52
  Old Testament ordering, 39n20, 41-43,
    45, 49, 50n53, 51, 137n36
  Old Testament titles, 93, 94n50, 96
Smith, David E., 60
Smith, D. Moody, 55
Solomon, 41, 134-35
  Ecclesiastes and, 95-96
  Proverbs and, 94-95, 142
  writings, 26-27, 29-30, 44
Song of Songs, 27-28, 30, 47
  of Solomon, 44, 95-96
Steinmann, Andrew, 142
Spellman, Ched, 2n6, 182n7, 183n10
Stephanus, Robert Estienne, 153-54
Stevens, Chris, 115
Stone, Timothy, 27-28
superscriptions, 94-96, 97n60, 115-16
  New Testament books, 106, 111n29, 118
  prophetic books, 18-19, 22, 45, 90-91,
    92

Sweeney, Marvin A., 27n52, 39
  Greek Old Testament, 32, 35, 37, 38n17
  Tanak, 25, 32
Swete, H. B., 100, 119n61

Talmud, 3, 17, 26, 30, 92, 129
  Baba Batra, 17-18, 19-21, 26, 27n52, 46,
    99
Tanak, 14, 25-26, 32, 35, 92-93
Tannehill, Robert, 158
Tatian, 60n28
testaments, 66, 114, 119-121
text and paratext, 2-4
text divisions, 6, 125-26, 177-78
  as commentaries, 127, 143, 156, 162, 165,
    171, 178
  interpretation and, 126-27, 148, 171-72,
    177-78
  verses, 129-30, 153-54, 162
  See also chapter divisions
1-2 Thessalonians, 66-68, 150n4, 163-64
Thrall, Margaret, 160
1-2 Timothy, 66, 114, 164-65
titles, book, 1-2, 6, 101-3, 121-22, 179-80,
    182
  as commentary, 104, 121, 175-76
  functions of, 80-84, 95, 101-4, 111, 113,
    122, 175-76
  interpretation and, 79-81, 100-101,
    104-5, 176, 180
  See also superscriptions
Titus, book of, 66m 114, 165
Tobit, book of, 42-43
Torah, 12, 14, 15-16
  book titles, 81-85
Tov, Emanuel, 128, 134
Trobisch, David, 56n9, 62, 68, 111, 115
Troxel, Ronald, 137
Twelve, Book of the. See Minor
    Prophets, the Twelve

Vanhoye, Albert, 166n59, 167
Vaticanus (B) Codex, 33, 93
  1-2 Esdras, 41

Gospels divisions, 155, 156n26, 157n29–30, 203
Minor Prophets, 92, 137n36
New Testament ordering, 62, 68, 70n74, 150
New Testament text divisions, 149–50, 159–64, 166–67, 169–70, 204
New Testament titles, 113n39, 152
Old Testament ordering, 35–37, 42–45, 49n50, 50n53, 51, 174
Pentateuch titles, 83, 84, 85
Writings titles, 93, 94, 96, 97n60
Vernoff, Charles Elliott, 14
verses, versification, 129–30, 153–54, 162
Von Soden, 105n3
Vulgate, 3n11, 34, 43, 92, 114, 120
book titles, 84–85, 88–89, 92–93, 97, 100–101, 116
canon order, 63, 68, 90, 127
chapter divisions, 127–28, 141

Wall, Robert, 54, 59n25, 60n30, 111n29, 150
Walters, Stanley D., 88n28
Watson, Duane F., 162n49
Watson, Francis, 21n28
Wenham, Gordon, 130
Williamson, H. G. M., 29
Wilson, Gerald H., 43
wisdom literature, 14–15, 26, 43–44, 94–95, 95–97
Chronicles as, 14–15
feminine imagery, 42–43
Psalms as, 43–44, 52, 93–94
Writings, 3, 13
book titles, 92–93
ordering of, 25–30, 50–51
text divisions, 140–47
wisdom texts, 14–15, 26

Zechariah, book of, 16, 48, 140, 147
Zephaniah, book of, 24–25, 140
Zerubbabel, 41, 140
Zvi, Ehud Ben, 23

SCRIPTURE INDEX

Old Testament

Genesis

1	37
1–12	131
2	130
2:1	130
2:1–3	130
2:3	130
2:4	81, 82, 130
5:1	81, 129
5:1 LXX	106
6:1	126
6:1–4	126
6:3	126
6:9	81, 126, 130, 131
8:1	126, 129
11:1	129
11:1–9	**37**
11:27	81, 130, 131
12–25	126
12:1	129, 131
12:1–3	38, 131
12:7	44
12:10–20	38
12:16	44
13:2–13	44
14–23	148
15:1	148
16:16	148
17:1	148
18:22–33	44
20:1–18	38
22:1	148
25:7	44

25:19	130
26:6–16	38
27	38
34:30	38
37:2	130
38	38
49	133

Exodus

1:6	81
1:7	15, 83
1:9	83
3:12	83
7:6–7	131
7:8	131
8:19	131
10:1	131
10:1–2	131
14	83
15–18	15
18	83
19–24	83
19–40	84
19:1	83
19:1 LXX	83
19:4	83
20–23	82
24:7	120
24:8	120
25–40	83
32–34	38
34:6–7	39

Leviticus

1:1	131
4:1	131
6:1	131
6:19	131
8:1	131
12:1	131
13:1	131
13:33	129
14:1	131
16:1	131
20:1	131
22:1	131
23:1	131
25:32–33	84

Numbers

1	84
1–9	82
1–10	84
1:1	132
1:2 LXX	84
1:18	84
1:20	84
1:22	84
1:24	84
2:1	132
4:1	132
4:17	132
4:21	132
5:11	132
8:1	132

9:1 132
10–21 15
11–21...................... 84, 175
13–14 38
14:18–19 39
18:1 132
21:14 87
22–36 84
24:17.............................38
26...............................84

Deuteronomy

1:1 16
1:5 82
2:2.............................132
2:3 132
2:31–3:22.......................132
3:23–29.........................132
3:23–4:24.......................132
4...............................132
4:5–8 38
4:10 85
4:21–22 132
4:25 132
5:2–3............................16
5:26 [29]........................85
6:2...............................85
6:7–9 85
9 38
9:6..............................38
9:26–28 38
11:18–21.........................85
12–26...........................132
12:32 128
13:1 Heb........................128
14:23 85
15:6.............................38
16:18–18:22 132
17:18 85
29...............................38
29:14–15 16
30:1–10 39
31–32 38
32:15 87

33 133
33:26–27 87

Joshua

1...............................86
1–6 .... 86, 133
1:1.............................86
1:1–9 86
1:5 133
1:8 ....14, 82
1:9 87
1:15 87
1:17 87
3:7 .... 133, 148
6 133
6:27 .... 86, 133
7–12 .... 86, 133
8:31–34 14
10:13 87
13–21 86
13–22 133
13:1 133
23–24.................... 40, 86
23:1 133
24:29–30 87
24:29–31 18

Judges

1:1.....................18, 86, 87
2–3 40
2:6–10 .... 18, 87
2:10 18
2:11 133
2:16 87
3–16 87
3:7 133
3:12 133
3:31–5:30......................133
4:1.............................133
4:1–3 133
4:3 133
4:4...............................86
4:4–12 133
4:12...........................133

4:13–24 133
4:24 133
5..............................133
6:1 133
8:22–23........................ 19
10:6 133
13:1 133
17:6 ....19, 48
17:8–9.........................48
18:1 ....19, 48
19–21 87
19:1 ....19, 48
19:1–2.........................48
21 48
21:25......................19, 48

Ruth

1....................... 143, 177
1:1..............26, 48, 49, 173
1:3 95
1:3–5 95
1:5 49
1:5–6 95
1:20–21 49
1:21 95
2....................... 143, 177
2:1 .... 95, 143, 177
2:12 .... 46, 47, 143
2:21 143
3....................... 143, 177
3:1 143
3:7 143
3:8–13 143
3:11 ....47, 143
3:12 143
3:13 47
3:18 .... 143, 177
4.............................. 47
4:1 143
4:17 ....95, 143
4:18–22 ....30, 51, 143

1 Samuel

1–16 80

2:1 133
2:1–10 133
2:10 133
3:20................................86
8 ....19, 40
9–31................................88
10:27..............................134
11:1 134
12 ....14, 40, 88
12:23..............................88
13 88
15–16 88
16:13................................88
19:18–24 88
25:1.................................88
28.....................................88
31 ....41, 88

2 Samuel

1.......................................134
1:1......................... 86, 134
1:18.................................87
2:1 134
2:6....................................134
5...88
7:2......................................86
8 39
11–20 40
11:27b 134
12–20............................. 19
12:1 .... 86, 134
12:10–12.........................134
21–24...............................89
24:11 86

1 Kings

1–2 89
1:1.....................................89
2:10–12 89
2:46.................................134
3:1 134
3:3 19
3:3–14 95
4:1–20.............................134

4:20 135
4:21.................................134
4:21–5:18 134
5:1 Heb 134
5:1–32 Heb....................134
8:1 96
10:27b LXX 134
11:1–3 96
11:4 19
11:29 86
11:41................................90
14:19................................90
16:30 90
17:1 135

2 Kings

1......................................89
1:1......................... 86, 90
8:23 90
14:3.................................. 19
14:25 19
17 ....14, 39, 40
18–20 19
18:3 19
20:8.................................135
20:12–19 135
20:16–18 .... 20, 135
21 135
21–25.............................20
22:8 14
22:11 14
23–25..............................20
23:24–25 14
23:26–27 135
25 39
25:27–30 40

1 Chronicles

1:1................... 27, 41, 100
1–9 .... 29, 40–41
10.................................... 41
16:7–36 29
23–27..............................29
27:24 100
28:10 147

29:25 96
29:29 37

2 Chronicles

2:4....................................147
7:6.................................... 14
8:14 14
11:13–17 101
15:1 147
15:1–7 14
15:8–15...........................101
16:7–9 14
16:12 14
18:18 147
19:4 101
23:18 14
29:25–30 14
33:21–25.........................127
35–36............................. 41
35:15 29
35:25 97
36....................................29
36:20 100
36:22–23 .... 29, 33, 39,
                        40, 41, 100
36:23 25

Ezra

1.......................................29
1:1–3a 41
1:1–4 29
2.............................29, 100
4:6....................................42
5:1 147
6:1 147
6:14 147
7–10 100
8 29
9:1 100
9:1–2...............................42

Nehemiah

1.......................................99
1:11 147

2:1-8 147
3 ....29, 100
3:32 100
7 ....29, 100
8 ....41, 100
8:1 100
9 ....25, 40, 181
9:32 25
9:36 25
10 100
10:28-39 25
12:23 100
12:36 100
13:4-31 ....25, 40, 100
13:26 41

Esther

1:1 42
1:12 98
1:22 98
2:4 145
2:23 100
3:4 42
3:7 145
4:16 98
6:1 ....98, 100
6:10 145
6:11 145
6:13 30
8:15 145
9 ....28, 40
9:29-32 145
9:32 177
10 ....145, 177
10:1 145
10:2 ....98, 100

Job

1:1 ....94, 142
1:3 44
1:5 44
1:8 142
2:3 142
4-5 142

6-7 141
8 142
8:2 142
9-10 141
11 142
11:2-3 142
12-14 141
12:1 141
15:2 142
27:1 141
28 142
28:1 142
28:28 142
29:1 141
31:40 142
42:7-9 44
42:16 44

Psalms

1 ....42, 43, 50, 93
1-41 43
2:11 46
3 140
3-7 93
3:1 140
3:3 ....94, 174
7:1 46
7:11 ....94, 176
9 LXX 141
9-10 141
9:1-21 141
9:22-39 141
10 LXX 141
11:1 46
16:1 46
17:8 47
18:50 47
25 43
31 43
32 42
32:2 LXX 94
33:2 94
34 ....42, 168
36:7 47
37 ....42, 43

39-40 43
41:13 93
42-50 29
47-51 93
48:4 LXX 94
49 ....42, 43
49:4 94
51 140
56:8 LXX 94
57:1 47
57:8 94
61:4 47
62 ....29, 43
72:18-19 93
74 48
78 ....40, 43, 181
79 48
89:52 93
92 43
94 43
96 29
105-6 29
105-7 40
106:48 93
107-50 43
111 43
112 ....42, 43
113:9-26 141
114 LXX 141
115 LXX 141
116 141
116:1-9 141
116:10-19 141
119 43
127 43
128 42
145 93
146-50 ....93, 176
147 LXX 141
147:12-20 141
151 LXX 141

Proverbs

1-9 ....42, 94, 142

1:1...................... 94, 96
1:6 94
1:7 .... 94, 142
1:8 142
1:10...........................142
1:15...........................142
2:1 142
3:1 142
3:11...........................142
3:21...........................142
4:1..............................142
4:10 142
4:20 142
5:1 142
5:7..............................142
6:1 142
6:20...........................142
7:1 142
7:24 142
8:1 142
8:32...........................142
9:1 142
9:10...........................142
10–31 .... 94, 175
10:1............................142
16:1–2 44
16:9 44
19:14 44
19:21 44
20:24...........................44
21:30–31.....................44
25:1.............................142
30:1 142
31 .... 28, 43, 47, 143
31:1 142
31:10 47
31:10–31 174
31:23 47
31:31 47

Ecclesiastes

1:1......................... 30, 96
1:1–2 96
1:12 .... 30, 96
1:16............................96

2:4–11 96
2:7................................96
2:9................................96
3:1 144
4:1..............................144
5:1 144
6:1 144
7:1–13 96
7:27 96
9:1 144
12:8–10 96
12:9.............................96
12:9–14 44

Song of Songs

1:1............................95, 96
2:7..................44, 96, 144
3:5 ....44, 96, 144
3:11 30
3:11a 27
5:1 144
5:2 144
5:8 144
8:4...................44, 96, 144

Isaiah

1–33 135
1–39 18
1:1........................18, 90
1:10 14
2:2–4 18
6...................................64
9:7.............................135
11:1 135
13:1 135
15:1 135
16:5.............................135
17:1 135
19:1.............................135
21:1 135
22:1 135
23:1.............................135
26:1 135
27:1.............................135

28:1 135
29:1 135
30:1 135
31:1 135
33 135
33:1.............................135
34................................135
34–35 135
34–66 135
36–39 19
39:5–7........................20
40–66 ..... 18, 20, 21, 45, 135
40:3 106
52:7 106
66:23 18

Jeremiah

1.................................136
1:1–3 90
1:5 136
1:10.............................136
2:1 136
3:48 49
3:51.............................49
8:19 136
8:19b 136
8:22 136
8:23 Heb.....................136
9:1 ....97, 136
9:1 Heb.......................136
9:1–2 Heb. 136
9:2................................136
9:2b.............................136
9:2–3 136
12:15 136
17:7..............................136
20:7...............................97
20:14–18 49
23:6..............................136
24:2..............................136
25:1............................. 21
26–29 90
26:1 21
27:1 21

29............................ 112
30–33 21
30:9...........................136
31 120
31:33 ....120, 136
32–44 90
32:1............................. 21
33:16.........................136
39:18.........................136
42:12.........................136
52 .... 20, 49
52:29.........................146

Lamentations

1–2 144
1:1........................49, 97
1:5 49
1:17 49
1:20–21.......................49
2:1–2...........................49
3...............................145
3:1–20.........................49
3:14...........................97
3:20–33......................97
3:22–24.....................145
3:25–27.....................145
3:31–33.....................145
3:34 145
3:36 145
3:48 49
3:51 49
4........................ 144–45
4:1.............................97
5...............................145
5:3 49

Ezekiel

1.................................. 91
1:2 21
4–5 91
4:1.............................136
5:1.............................136
6:1.............................136
7:1.............................136

8:1 21
12 91
12:1...........................136
16 40
20 40
20:1 21
22:16.........................136
23 40
24:1 21
24:24 136
29:21.........................136
36–48 21
37:28 136
39:22 136
40–48 45

Daniel

1–6 ....15, 30, 50, 52
1:1...........................146
1:3–5 50
1:4 15
1:6 99
1:8 99
1:17 ....15, 99
1:20 15
2..................99, 119, 146
2:1 146
2:17...........................99
2:35 ....146, 148
2:36–45.....................146
2:38 146
2:48–49 50
3..................... 99, 146
3:1 146
3:32 146
3:33 146
4.................... 146, 147
4–6 99
4:1.............................146
4:1–3 146–47
4:3 146
4:33...........................146
4:34 146
6:25...........................146

6:27 146
7–12.................. 50, 52, 99
9 .... 26, 40, 181
9:2...............................26
9:24..............................26
11:33 .... 15, 50
11:35.................. 15, 50
12:3..............................50

Hosea

1–3........................ 23, 91
1:1........................22, 45
14:5...........................137
14:5–8.......................137

Joel

1–2 137
1–6 138
1:13–14 23
2................................138
2:1–11.......................138
2:15–16....................... 23
2:17...........................138
2:17/18 ....137, 138
2:18 138
2:18/19 137
2:18–26 137
2:27/28 ....137, 138
2:28–32..............137, 138
2:32/3:21 137
3................................138
3 Heb. 137
3:1 ....137, 138
3:1–8......................... 23
3:5/4:1 137
3:9–21 23
3:16a........................ 23
3:18a........................ 23
4................................138
4:1.............................138
4:1 Heb 137
5:1.............................138
5:18...........................138
6:1 138

6:4 138
7–9 138
7:1 138
7:4 138
7:7 138
8:1 138
9:1 138

Amos

1–2 23
1–6 138
1:1 ....19, 45, 90
1:2 .... 23, 138
1:2–3:8 138
2:12 91
3:1 138
3:3–8 138
3:4 91
3:8 ....91, 138
4:1 138
5:1 138
5:13 91
5:18 138
5:25–27 92
6:1 138
6:4 138
7–9 138
7:1 138
7:4 138
7:7 138
7:10–17 91
7:16 138
8–9 138
8:1 138
8:4 138
9 174
9:1 138
9:11–15 ....23, 45
9:12 ....23, 138, 139
9:12a 23
9:13b 23

Obadiah

15 23

19a 23
21 139

Jonah

1 139
1:4–5a 139
1:4–16 139
1:9–10a 139
1:15–16a 139
1:17 139
1:17b 139
2 139
2:1 Heb. 139
2:10 139
3 23
3:4 91

Micah

1:1 45
1:2 139
2:1 139
3:1 139
4:1–3 18
4:9–10 139
4:11–13 139
4:14–5:5 Heb. 139
5:1 139
5:1 Heb. 139
5:1–6 139
5:2 139
5:2–4 139
5:5–6 24
6:1 139
7:1 139
7:8–20 45
7:20 139

Nahum

1:1 22
1:1a 45
1:6 22
1:15 22
3:18–19 24

Habakkuk

1:6 ....22, 24

Zephaniah

1:2–3 24
2:11 23
3:9 23
3:9–20 25
3:14–20 25
3:20 ....25, 139–40

Haggai

1 140
1:1 140
1:14–15 140
1:15b–2:1 140
2:1 140
2:10–20 140
2:23 139–40

Zechariah

4:6–10 140
5:1 147
7:3 48
7:5 48
8:19 48
14:16 18
14:21 ....139, 140

Malachi

1 140
1:11 23–24
3:1 33
4:4 14
4:5–6 33

New Testament

Matthew

1	154
1–2	56
1:1	73, 106
1:2	106
1:2–17	106
1:6	106
1:16	106, 155, 171
1:17	106
1:18–25	154–55, 171
1:20	154
1:21–22	154
2:1	152, 154–55, 171
2:5–6	154
2:15	154
2:17–18	154
2:23	154
3	56
3:17	59
4:3	59
4:6	59
4:8	154
5–7	56
5:1–2	154
5:1–7:29	155
7:28	155
7:28–29	154
8:1	154
8:1–4	155
8:5–13	155
8:14–15	155
8:16–18	155
8:23–27	155
8:28–9:1	155
8:29	59
9:2–8	155
9:9–13	108
10	56
10:1–11:1	155
10:3	108
11:1	154, 155
11:27	58

13	56
13:34	155
13:52	120
13:53	154
14:13–21	60
14:33	59
16:16	59
16:21	178
17:1	154, 178
17:5	59
18	56
19:1	154, 155
19:18	106
21:1	154
23:1	154
24	73
24–25	56
24:3	154
24:15	50
25:1	155
26:1	154
26:63	59
27:40	59
27:43	59
27:54	59
28:16–20	61
28:20	55, 56

Mark

1:1	59, 106
1:1–15a	152
1:2–3	106
1:7–8	106
1:8	155
1:11	59, 155
1:13	155
1:15	155
1:15b–30a	152
1:23	151, 157
1:29–31	152
1:32–34	152
1:40–45	152

2:1–12	152
2:1–3:6	155
2:11	158
2:13	157
2:13–17	152
2:14	108
2:18	158
2:18–28	152
2:20	56
2:22	158
2:23–25	157
2:25	157
3:1	155
3:1–6	152
3:6	56, 155, 156
3:11	59
3:13–19	152
3:18	108
3:20–35	152
4:1	156
4:1–9	152
4:21–34	152
4:34	156
4:35	156
4:35–41	152
5:1–20	152
5:7	59
5:34	156
5:35–43	152
5:36	156
6:1	156
6:1–6a	156
6:3	117
6:6	156
6:6b	156
6:30–44	60
8:34	156
9:1	156, 171
9:2	156, 171
9:2a	156
9:2–8	156, 171
9:7	59

13:14 50
13:32 58
15:39 59
16:9–20 61

Luke

1 156
1–2 57
1:1...................105, 107, 110
1:1–4 ....55, 61, 105
1:2 55
1:5–23 57
1:35................................. 59
1:80 156
2:1 ....156, 157
2:40..............................157
2:52 157
3:1 157
3:4................................. 91
3:22 59
4:3 59
4:9 59
4:17............................... 91
4:20 .... 91, 115
4:41................................ 59
5:17................................157
5:17–26 61
5:27 108
5:39 120
6:1 157
6:12 157
6:15.............................. 108
7:1 157
7:37 157
7:37–50.........................157
7:39 157
8:1–3..............................157
8:2..................................157
8:28................................ 59
9:1...................................157
9:10–17 60
9:35 59
9:51................................157
9:51–19:46....................157
9:51–21:38 57

10:1...............................157
10:22 58
11:51.............................13
15 177
15:3–7 177
15:8–10 177
15:11–32.........................177
15:32 177
19:47–48 61
20:42.............................. 93
22:23–38........................ 61
22:53.............................. 57
22:70.............................. 59
24................................... 57
24:27 122
24:44..............................13
24:44–49...................... 61

John

1 157
1–2 158
1:1.................................. 109
1:4 109
1:14................................ 109
1:23.................................157
1:40 57
1:42.................................107
1:49 58
2.............................. 57, 58
2–11 57
2:1 157
2:11.................................158
2:13.................................157
2:18 158
2:22.................................158
2:23 158
2:23–25 ....157, 158
2:25 157
3:1 158
3:2..................................158
3:16 80
3:18 58
3:24 57
3:35 58

4:44 57
5...................................... 57
5:17................................. 59
5:25 58
6..................................... 58
6:1–14 60
6:67................................. 57
6:71................................. 57
7...................................... 57
10:15............................... 58
10:34 15
10:36 58
11:2................................. 57
11:4................................. 58
11:27 58
11:41............................... 59
12 57
12:34...............................15
13:21–30.........................70
15:25 15
16:32............................... 59
18:15–18 70
18:24............................... 57
18:28 57
19:7 58
20:1–10..........................70
20:31 58
21 61
21:2 107
21:15 107
21:15–24.........................70
21:16 107
21:17 107
21:24...............................107
21:25 ....56, 112

Acts

1–2 159
1–12 63
1:1...................61, 110, 112
1:1–2 111
1:12–14 117
1:15–26..........................110
1:20 93

2:42 158
2:42a 158
2:42b 158
2:42c 158
2:42d 158
2:42–47 158
2:43 158
2:43–47 158
2:44–45 158
2:46 158
2:47a 158
2:47b 158
3.......................................61
3–4 158–59
3:1 158
3:1–10 61
4:1.....................................159
4:32 159
4:32–37 159
4:32–5:11 159
5:1 159
5:1–11 159
6–8 110
6:7 ....111, 158, 178
7.......................................181
7:42 92
9:5 112
9:15...................................114
9:27 110
9:31.............. 111, 158, 178
9:32–35 61
10:1...................................171
11.......................................171
11:1 110
12:12 108
12:24.......... 111, 158, 178
12:25...............................108
13 181
13–28 .... 63, 111
13:5..................................56
13:15.................................112
13:23 112
13:24................................112
14:4 111
14:8–10 61

14:14 111
14:22................................69
15 ....110, 171
15:1–21 62
15:2..................................110
15:4..................................110
15:6–21 117
15:35 158
15:40................................151
16 ....65, 113
16:5...................................178
16:6–7 112
16:7 112
16:10–17 108
16:12 65
16:21.................................65
16:38.................................65
19:20 ....158, 178
20:17–38 169
20:23.................................111
21:1–18 108
21:11 111
21:28................................64
22:18................................112
22:21................................114
23:11 112
26:17.................................114
27:1–28:16 108
28......................................64
28:26–27..........................64
28:31................................64

Romans

1:3 64
1:7 113
1:8–15 64
1:15 113
1:17 159
1:18.......................159, 160
1:18–2:11...........................160
2:1 159
2:6 160
2:8–9 160
2:11.........................159–60

2:12 ....159, 160
3:1 159
3:19 15
4:1.....................................159
5:1 159
6:1 159
7:1 159
8:1 159
9–11 .... 64, 69
9:1 159
11:1 159
12:1 159
15:19 ....64, 65
15:22–29 64
15:24 64
15:28................................64
15:30................................159
15:33 159
16 159
16:17.................................159
16:22 116

1 Corinthians

1:1.....................................116
2:1 160
2:1–5.................................158
2:2....................................54
3:1 160
3:11 54
6:1 160
12–14 160
12:1–14:4 160
12:31a................................160
13 160
14:1 160
14:21.................................15
16:8 116
16:19 116
16:21 116

2 Corinthians

1:1..........................115, 116
2:1 160

2:1–4......................... 160
2:1–13......................... 160
2:4............................. 160
2:12 161
2:12–13....................... 161
2:14 161
2:14b.......................... 161
2:14–17....................... 161
3............................... 120
3:14........................... 120
5:16........................... 108
7:5 161
7:6............................. 161
8:18 108

Galatians

1:6–4:11....................... 161
1:13–2:21 161
2............................... 62
2:1–10 161
2:2–3 161
2:7–9 114
2:9....................... 62, 70
2:14 161
3:1 161
3:4............................. 161
3:10 115
4:11 161
4:12–6:10..................... 161
6:11........................... 116

Ephesians

1:1.............................. 113
1:3 162
1:3–14 162
1:4 162
1:5 162
2:1 162
2:6............................. 69
2:7............................. 162
2:8............................. 162

Philippians

1:1.............................. 116

1:12–26 162
1:27...........................162
1:27–30 162
2...............................162
2:1 162
2:1–11 162
2:12 162
2:12–18 162
2:19–24.......................162
2:25–30.......................162
3:1 162
3:2.............................162
3:12–16.......................162
3:20–4:3 162
4:1.............................163
4:1–3 162
4:2–3..........................65
4:4.............................162

Colossians

1:1.............................. 116
1:6 158
1:12 163
1:29 163
2:1 .... 61, 114, 163
2:6.............................163
2:6–7 163
2:7.............................163
3:1 69
3:15...........................163
3:15–17.......................163
4:2 163
4:10 108
4:14............................ 108
4:18............................ 116

1 Thessalonians

1:1.............................. 116
1:2–10 164
1:5 158
1:5–6.......................... 164
2:12–13.......................163
2:13............................163
2:13–16..................163, 164

3:9–10......................... 164
5:28 68

2 Thessalonians

1:1.............................. 116
1:12 164
2............................... 73
2:1 164
2:1–12 164
2:1–14 164
2:13–14........................ 164
2:14 164
3:1 164
3:17............................ 116

1 Timothy

1:1.............................. 114
1:18–20 164
2:1 164
2:1–7.......................... 164
2:1–3:16...................... 164
2:8–15......................... 164
3:1 164
3:1–7.......................... 164
3:8–13......................... 164
3:14–15........................66
3:15............................ 164
4:11 66

2 Timothy

1:1.............................. 114
1:15–17 165
2:1 165
2:7.............................165
2:13............................165
4:11 108
4:13 115

Titus

1:1–3 114
1:10–16.......................165
2...............................165
2:1 .... 66, 165

2:1–14 165
2:15 165
3 165
3:1 165
3:1–8 165
3:9–11 165
7:6 161

Philemon

1 116
1–2 66
2 114
4 166
7 166
8 166
10 166
12 166
13 166
15 166
17 166
18 166
19 ....116, 166
20 166
21 166
22 166
23 166
24 108
25 166

Hebrews

1–2 166
1:1–2 122
1:1–9:14 150
1:3 ....69, 166
1:5–14 166
1:5–2:4 166
2:1 166
2:1–4 166
2:2 166
2:5–18 166
2:5–4:13 166
3 166
3:1 ....166, 167
4:1 166

4:7 88
4:11 166
4:14 ....166, 167
5:1 166
6:1 166
7 166
8:1 167
8:8 120
9:11 167
9:14 ....150, 166
9:14a 68
9:19 115
10:32–4 114
10:39 69
11 69
11:1–2 69
13:22 .... 112, 166
13:22–24 69
13:23 112
13:24 112

James

1:1 ....112, 117
1:26 167
1:26–27 167
1:26–2:13 167
1:27 167
2:1 167
2:1–13 172
2:2–3 168
2:13–14 168
2:14–26 ....68, 167, 168
2:15 167
2:15–16 168
2:19 168
2:26 167
3:1–12 167

1 Peter

1:1 ....116, 118
1:1–2 113
1:18–25 168
1:22–2:3 168

2:9–10 168
2:12 168
3:1 ....113, 168
3:9 168
3:10–12 168
4 168
5:1–4 168
5:5a 168
5:12 116
5:12–14 113
5:13 108

2 Peter

1:1–2 113
1:4 169
1:13–14 169
1:15 169
1:16 169
1:16–21 169
2 169
2:1 169
2:1–3:3 69
3 73
3:1 ....70, 113, 169
3:4 169
3:15–16 .... 62, 116, 118

1 John

1:1 ....109, 118
1:5–2:6 169
2 169
2:1 ....113, 169
2:7 ....113, 169
2:12 113
2:18 117
2:19 117
2:21 113
2:26 113
2:28–3:10 169
3:1 169
3:2 169
3:8 58
3:11–24 169
4:1 ....117, 169

4:1–3 73
4:1–6........................... 169
4:7 169
4:15............................. 58
5:1 169
5:3 169
5:5 58
5:10 58
5:12............................. 58
5:13............... 58, 113, 169
5:20............................ 58

2 John

7................................. 117

Jude

1............................70, 117
4–18...........................69
5–16...........................170
12 170
17 ....169, 170
17–23 170
18 170

Revelation

1................................. 72

1:1.............72, 108, 118, 119
1:1–2 118
1:2 170
1:3 ....72, 119
1:4 .... 72, 108
1:4–5...........................71
1:4–20.........................170
1:9 .... 72, 108
1:10 .... 73, 119
1:11 170
1:17 109
2–3 .... 67, 71, 72, 113,
                              118, 170
2:23 109
4................................170
4:1..............................170
4:1–2 119
4:2 73
5................................170
5:1 170
6–7 170
6:1..............................170
6:3..............................170
6:5..............................170
6:7..............................170
6:9..............................170

6:12 170
7:15–17 170
8:1 170
15–16 72
17:3..........................73, 119
18:1............................170
19:10...................73, 119
20:1 170
21–22 73
21:1 170
21:6 109
21:10......................73, 119
22:6 73
22:7 ....72, 119
22:8 170
22:9 ....72, 119
22:10 ....72, 119
22:13 109
22:16........................... 109
22:18.....................72, 119
22:18–21.......................72
22:19....................72, 119
22:21...........................71
22:1–22:5...................... 72

Extrabiblical Texts

2 Baruch

78–86 112

1 Esdras

5:5 41

4 Ezra

14.45............................. 16

2 Maccabees

1–2 112
2:13–15................... 88, 90
15:35 98

Sirach or Ecclesiasticus

48:22–26...................... 21
49:1–10 21
49:10 ....16, 92

Tobit

1................................... 42
4................................... 42

Dead Sea Scrolls

4Q112 Daniel

3:1 146

4Q174 Florilegeum

2:3 .... 50, 99

Jewish Texts

BABYLONIAN TALMUD

Baba Batra (B. Bat)

14b 3, 16, 17, 20, 21, 22, 26, 30, 92

15a...............................98

57b 27

Sanhedrin (b. San.)

93b...............................50

JERUSALEM TALMUD

Megillah (y. Meg.)

74a 81

Qoheleth Rabbah

1:2 96

Sotah

36b...............................81

JOSEPHUS

Against Apion (Ag. Ap.)

1.8 .... 50, 99

1.38–41............... 16, 37, 93

Jewish Antiquities (Ant.)

5.318–337 48

10.11.7 50

10.26.7–8 50

11.8.5............................50

PHILO

On the Contemplative Life (Contempl.)

25 93

Early Christian Texts

AUGUSTINE

City of God

18.29.............................92

De Consensu Evangelistarum (Cons.)

1.2.4 55

4.10.11 55

EUSEBIUS

Historia ecclesiastica (Hist. eccl.)

2.23.25..........................70

3.3.4–5 67

3.25.1–2 63

4.26 .... 93, 99

4.26.13–14 ..... 16, 48, 50, 95

6.13.4–8 112

6.14.1–3........................112

6.25.2 48

6.25.6 108

6.25–26........................50

IRENAEUS

Adversus haereses (Haer.)

3.1.1 55

3.9–11............................ 55

3.11.7............................ 55

4.6.1............................. 55

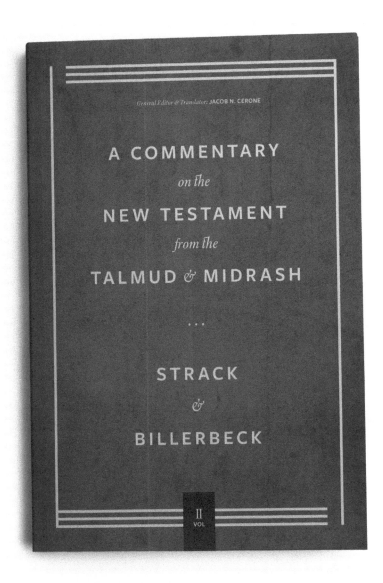

General Editor & Translator: JACOB N. CERONE

A COMMENTARY
on the
NEW TESTAMENT
from the
TALMUD *&* MIDRASH

· · ·

STRACK

&

BILLERBECK

II
VOL

ALSO AVAILABLE FROM LEXHAM PRESS

Translated in English for the first time

Visit lexhampress.com to learn more and order